REFERENDUMS

REFERENDUMS

A Comparative Study of Practice and Theory

Edited by
David Butler,
Nuffield College, Oxford
and
Austin Ranney,
American Enterprise Institute

American Enterprise Institute for Public Policy Research
Washington, D.C.

Library of Congress Cataloging in Publication Data
Main entry under title:

Referendums.

(AEI studies ; 216)
Bibliography: p. 247
1. Referendum. 2. Comparative government.
I. Butler, David E., 1924– II. Ranney, Austin.
III. Series: American Enterprise Institute for Public Policy Research. AEI studies ; 216.
JF491.R38 328'.2 78-22045
ISBN 0-8447-3318-0

AEI studies 216

Printed in the United States of America

For M.S.B. and N.B.R.
with love

CONTENTS

PREFACE

This book is intended to help renew the study of a long-neglected problem of comparative government. It originated in a discussion between the two coeditors at the American Enterprise Institute in the fall of 1977, stimulated by our impression that referendums are rapidly assuming significant roles in the politics of countries where they had previously been unimportant or nonexistent. We spoke, for example, of Britain's first referendum ever in 1975; of the Quebec separatists' intention to hold a referendum on secession from Canada; of Margaret Thatcher's statements that a Conservative government in Britain might well make increasing use of referendums; of the first congressional hearings in history on a constitutional amendment to establish a national initiative in the United States; and of the prospects for the passage of California's now famous Proposition 13 to limit the state's taxing powers. Where, we asked, could we find recent empirical and comparative studies of the frequency and consequences of referendums in various countries around the world? The answer was both surprising and frustrating: We were unable to discover in the literature even the extent to which the device has been used, let alone the policies and systemic consequences it has produced.

We therefore decided to ask experts on the countries in which referendums have been used most frequently to contribute short chapters to a general survey of the topic and to focus mainly on the politics rather than the law of referendums—that is, on the issues they deal with, on the groups that participate in their campaigns, on the conditions in which they produce outcomes that are pleasing to the left or the right, and, above all, on their impact on parliaments, political parties, and the other institutions of representative democracy. And we ourselves undertook the ambitious task of trying to recover the dates, subject matters, outcomes, and turnouts of all nationwide referendums held since their beginnings in the eighteenth century.

The present book is the result, and for its existence we have many debts to acknowledge. The American Enterprise Institute made the whole project possible. Our colleagues at AEI and at Nuffield College gave us much patient help and wise counsel as we pursued our new obsession. Our admirable assistants, Andrea Kozak and Paula Simmons in Washington and Audrey Skeats in Oxford, did the necessary chores cheerfully and efficiently. To find information about recherché referendums in distant lands we drew shamelessly on the expertise of many friends, librarians, and embassy officials. We should mention particularly how much we have benefited from the special knowledge of John M. Austen. And above all we must thank our six contributors for producing interesting and informative manuscripts so promptly.

In making the routine declaration that, except where it is shared with the authors of the signed chapters, responsibility for errors is ours alone, we are well aware that our information about referendums is necessarily incomplete. Our interest in the subject is a continuing one, and we should be most grateful for any guidance on errors or omissions in our listings of referendums as well as in our analysis of what they mean.

DAVID BUTLER
AUSTIN RANNEY
Oxford and Washington,
August 15, 1978

1 Practice

Referendums, as a means of making government decisions or giving legitimacy to them, have a history that is almost as old as democracy. But they have been invoked only sporadically. A few admirable democratic societies have never tried the device, while some authoritarian ones have grotesquely abused it. In the populist progressive upsurge at the beginning of this century referendums were welcomed by some as a liberating force, as a way of purifying government by enlisting the people against the politicians. But in the 1930s Hitler's plebiscites, with their 99 percent affirmatives, cast a cloud over the whole idea of referring specific questions to the voters. Referendums continued to flourish, of course; they have been used continually in Switzerland, as well as in California and other U.S. states, and intermittently in places where they had become a prerequisite of constitutional change.

Since the early 1970s interest in referendums has quickened. They were widely invoked in the enlargement of the European Economic Community (EEC). In Greece and Spain they played an essential role in the moves back from dictatorship to constitutional democracy. In Britain and in Canada they became very important in the debates over regional separatism. And they have been used increasingly by arbitrary regimes seeking legitimacy after coups or the establishment of one-party states.

In each polity referendums have operated under different rules and fitted into the political system in different ways. But they have raised some common problems which can be categorized and analyzed. Unfortunately, most writing about referendums has been either very abstract or linked to a particular national situation. The difficulty of finding any comprehensive or comparative work was the raison d'être for this book.

For the benefit of politicians arguing over proposed referendums and of students trying to understand this particular democratic phenomenon, we have tried to gather together the evidence from those countries that have had the most significant experience with it. We have focused less on the mechanics of election law or on constitutional niceties than on the political functions and consequences of such appeals to the people.

A distinction is often made between referendums and plebiscites. "Plebiscite" is much the older term; it goes back to the vote of the plebs in Rome in the fourth century B.C., and it was used for the popular consultations in France from 1793 onward. "Referendum" in its current sense appeared in English only in the 1880s, though Swiss cantons had decided issues *ad referendum* 200 years earlier. Eighty years ago "referendum" was the term used by reform movements throughout the English-speaking world to denote the idea of putting issues directly to the electorate. "Plebiscite" was the term used to describe the efforts by the League of Nations to settle boundary disputes on the principle of self-determination after World War I. "Plebiscite" was also used by the Nazis when they sought endorsement for their policies. The word "plebiscite" has tended to be applied to an ad hoc reference to the people of a specific question and in particular to one involving approval for a man or a regime. But there is no agreed usage. Since there does not seem to be any clear or generally acknowledged line that can be drawn to distinguish the subject matter, the intent, or the conduct of a referendum from that of a plebiscite, the word "referendum" will be used throughout this book.[1]

A second semantic point concerns our title. This book is called *Referendums* not *Referenda.* Both forms are legitimized by some dictionaries, but current authority seems to favor the Anglo-Saxon rather than the Latin form.[2]

---

[1] So as not to dismiss a weighty question too lightly, however, it should be noted that a French scholar has written a 350-page work on the difference between the two terms. But while Jean-Marie Denquin in *Référendum et Plébiscite* (Paris: Librairie générale de droit et de jurisprudence, 1976) makes many nice distinctions, he does not provide a generally acceptable separation of the two terms which matches actual usage. In what follows we have benefited from elements in his categorization, but we have not been persuaded to depart from an all-inclusive use of the word "referendum."

[2] The editor of the Oxford English Dictionary writes: "Usage varies, even in high places, and both *referendums* and *referenda* are found in print. My own view is that *referendums* is logically preferable as a plural form meaning ballots on one issue (as a Latin gerund, *referendum* has no plural). The Latin plural gerundive *referenda,* meaning 'things to be referred,' necessarily connotes a plurality of issues. A note to this effect is being added to our entry for the word

Three great instruments of direct democracy drew support at the turn of the century—the recall, the initiative, and the referendum. Of these, the recall, a vote to terminate the mandate of an elected person, has been the least used; as a negative variant of personal election, it does not belong in this discussion. But the initiative differs from a referendum only in that it originates with the electors rather than with the government or the legislature; it has not been much used at the national level—the German Weimar Republic, Italy, and Switzerland provide the main examples—but it has been widely employed by a number of states in the United States. It is plainly important as a subcategory of the species referendum.

For the purposes of this book there is little benefit in going back to the distant origins of referendums in the assemblies of Greek city-states and the *plebiscita* of Rome, or even in turning to the early instances in modern history in the cantons of fifteenth-century Switzerland and in France, which legitimized its annexation of Metz by a vote in 1552. The developing ideology of democracy by the end of the eighteenth century had opened the way to the modern referendum. The first examples are found in the popular votes by which after 1778 some American states adopted and altered their constitutions; they are also found in the efforts of the Girondins and subsequently of Napoleon Bonaparte to demonstrate support for successive annexations and constitutional revisions. In 1851 and 1852 Napoleon III, too, turned to referendums to establish his imperial authority, and during the Italian Risorgimento in 1848, and still more in the 1860s, Piedmontese sovereignty over the Italian peninsula was endorsed in a series of 99 percent affirmations. As the nineteenth century advanced, the development of the technology of mass voting, with electoral registers and secret ballots, made honest referendums far easier to conduct.

Before World War I, however, the most significant development of the referendum as a political institution undoubtedly came in Switzerland and in the United States. Since 1848 and still more since 1870 the Swiss have accepted the principle that almost every major national decision could become the subject of a popular vote. As Jean-François Aubert shows in Chapter 3, Switzerland developed the theory and practice of the referendum to a pitch which no other nation has begun to match. Only in a dozen individual American states (mostly in the West and notably in California, as Eugene Lee shows

---

in the forthcoming third volume of *A Supplement to the Oxford English Dictionary*. By preferring *Referendums* as your title you have the angels of Rome and of the O.E.D. on your side."

in Chapter 5) has direct legislation become a prominent part of the machinery for making political decisions.

Why are referendums widely used only in Switzerland and a dozen states of the American union? The most likely explanation is that only in these polities was there longstanding prereferendum experience with direct government by face-to-face assemblies of citizens. As Clifford Sharp points out, some small Swiss cantons have regularly made decisions by such assemblies, called *Landsgemeinden*, ever since the thirteenth century. Similarly, New England towns since the seventeenth century have conducted their affairs by town meetings, and the pioneer western territories and states in the nineteenth century continued the tradition. In both Switzerland and these American states, when population growth in the nineteenth and twentieth centuries made such assemblies impractical, referendums came into being as useful ways of adapting the principles of direct democracy to the limitations and necessities of large populations. The same experience, moreover, led these polities to establish the initiative. And since the initiative effectively strips the legislature of its exclusive power to prevent referendums from being held, and voters and pressure groups demand them, it leads to a considerable increase in their number.[3]

In Appendix A we attempt to list all referendums that have taken place at the nationwide level.[4] We have included the most blatantly propagandist attempts of dictatorial regimes to demonstrate popular support for their rule together with the most genuinely democratic references of problems to the voters.

Nationwide referendums up to September 1, 1978, totaled just over 500, but 297 of those were in Switzerland and 39 in Australia.[5]

---

[3] See Clifford D. Sharp, *The Case against the Referendum*, Fabian Tract no. 155 (London: The Fabian Society, 1911), p. 3.

[4] The catalogs in Appendix A and Appendix B, despite our own extensive efforts and the help of many friends, are almost certainly incomplete. They are also, necessarily, inaccurate because for many referendums official figures are unobtainable or nonexistent and because, where they do exist, they may be suspect.

[5] By limiting ourselves to nationwide referendums we are ignoring some major examples of referendums in states in federal countries where the electorate often exceeds that of most nation-states. For U.S. examples, see Chapters 4 and 5; for Canadian examples, see Chapter 4, footnote 7 and Table 4-3; for Australia, see Chapter 6; and for an example from Germany before World War II, see note 14 of this chapter. In postwar West Germany, before the Basic Law came into effect in 1949, there were three referendums on boundary questions in 1947 in Baden, Bremen, Rhine-Palatinate, Wurtemburg, and the Saarland. There was also a referendum on the nationalization clause in the Hesse constitution in 1946. Between 1949 and 1956 there were sixteen referendums on boundary matters under the Basic Law. The majority of Länder constitutions provide for

TABLE 1-1

NUMBER AND NATURE OF NATIONWIDE REFERENDUMS

		Subject (percent)				
Area	*Number*	Approve regime or new constitution	Amend constitution	Approve specific law or policy	Territorial issue	*Total*
Europe (excluding Switzerland)	101	28	27	29	16	100
Africa and Middle East	54	92	0	0	8	100
Asia	18	100	0	0	0	100
Americas	25	87	0	13	0	100
Australasia	45	0	82	18	0	100

SOURCE: Appendix A.

As the chapters on these two countries show, they are special cases in which the necessities of their federal systems have given a peculiar dynamic to the use of the referendum. In the rest of the world France, with twenty referendums, tops the list, while Denmark, with thirteen, is the only other country to have reached a double figure.[6] But a very large number of countries have experimented with referendums at the national level at least once—a majority of states in Europe and over a third of all members of the United Nations. In fact, the United States and the Netherlands are the only countries that have an uninterrupted democratic history reaching back to the nineteenth century but have never held a nationwide referendum. Table 1-1 and Table 1-2 show some remarkable features about the subject matter and the outcome of nationwide referendums.

The overwhelming bulk of referendums outside Europe and the old British Commonwealth have been attempts to seek endorsement for a new regime and its constitution or to demonstrate approval for

referendums or initiatives. They occurred in Bavaria in 1947 and in North Rhine Westphalia in 1978.

[6] This excludes New Zealand, which in addition to five ordinary referendums has, in twenty general elections since 1908, put a question on liquor control to the voters. Only the first of these is included in the subsequent analysis, since this routine question would distort the results.

TABLE 1-2

RESULTS OF NATIONWIDE REFERENDUMS
(percent)

	Affirmative Vote as Percentage of Total				
Area	Less than 50	50–90	90–99	More than 99	*Total*
Europe (excluding Switzerland)	19	41	23	17	100
Africa and Middle East	0	19	31	50	100
Asia	0	34	56	10	100
Americas	15	56	19	10	100
Australasia	61	37	2	0	100

SOURCE: Appendix A.

an established one. These attempts seem almost always to be successful. Australia stands out as the only country where referendums have been defeated more often than not. Even in Europe, Denmark, Estonia, France, Ireland, Luxembourg, Norway, and Sweden (and of course Switzerland) are the only places where there have been government-sponsored referendums that failed to secure a nationwide majority.[7]

It is tempting to dismiss all referendums which secure an affirmative vote of more than 99 percent—or even of more than 95 percent—as bogus, the manipulated demonstration of support by autocratic regimes. Although most of them plainly fall into this category, a few referendums that have unquestionably been conducted openly and counted honestly have produced similar majorities. In 1905 Norway voted 99.9 percent for separation from Sweden; in 1944 Iceland voted 99.5 percent for separation from Denmark; and in 1967 Gibraltar voted 99.6 percent to keep its ties with the United Kingdom. Some elections in French overseas territories have produced majorities almost as overwhelming, but these were all on territorial matters, raising strong national feelings. If such questions are left aside a look down the list of referendums in which there is a clear presumption of free voting and honest counting reveals hardly any examples

[7] Uruguay (1946 and 1971), Gambia (1965), and New Zealand (1967) provide the only examples outside Europe, apart from Australia.

where more than 90 percent voted yes.[8] Switzerland offers four cases in 29 votes. Elsewhere the approval of the Spanish reform program in 1976 (94 percent yes) and of Australian aboriginal rights in 1967 (91 percent yes) stand virtually alone.

It is interesting that absolutist regimes should think it worthwhile to turn to the ballot box and, by intimidation of voters or fraudulent counting, produce the implausible unanimity that has characterized so large a proportion of referendums. Perhaps it should be seen as a tribute to the power of democratic ideology that countries which lack the reality of open discussion and freely voted consent should embrace its forms. But dictators seem reluctant to accept the prima facie implausibility of any society recording a consensus of 999 to 1 (or even of any humanly fallible vote-recording system doing so).[9] The few cases where military regimes have held referendums which yielded less than 90 percent support are much the most challenging to the analyst of nondemocratic governments. Latin America, interestingly, has seldom produced instances of more than 90 percent yes, while in Africa 99 percent has been virtually the norm. Perhaps the most remarkable result was in Ghana in April 1978, where despite tight military control of the country the vote to establish a "no-party state" was reported as only 54 percent yes. In the list of African and Middle East referendums in Appendix A the Ghana vote stands out, together with one of the few others that carry conviction—the 65.9 percent yes in Gambia in 1965 where the government barely failed to secure the two-thirds majority required to make the country a republic. In general the controlled, hegemonic referendums used by Communist and fascist regimes and by many new states where competitive democratic processes have never taken root have little in common with the relatively open contests that are the primary concern of this book, except in their general purpose of giving a special legitimacy to a particular institution or course of action (see Chapter 2).

Western democratic states, however, have not been eager to exploit the referendum as a serious decision-making instrument. Switzerland stands out as the only country that has become addicted to the referendum. Apart from Switzerland there has been no ob-

[8] There were four cases where, despite a vote of 90 percent yes, the referendum was lost because there was a turnout condition which made abstention equivalent to voting no (Denmark, 1939; Germany, 1926 and 1929; Uruguay, 1971). The 98.5 percent Iceland vote (1944) for a republic was part of the package of separation from Denmark.

[9] Between 1956 and 1976 Egypt held nine referendums which never yielded less than 99.8 percent yes. In May 1978, however, a referendum was reported to have produced only 97.8 percent yes (see Appendix A).

servable tendency for countries that have solved one problem by referendum to use the device repeatedly. Vincent Wright shows in Chapter 7 how in France, one of the heaviest users of referendums, successive regimes have drawn back from the practice. In the world as a whole, referendums seem to be resorted to only because of constitutional necessity or short-term political expediency.

Let us see how referendums have been used in European democratic countries in this century. Tables 1-3 & 1-4 show that the subject matter has been overwhelmingly constitutional, although only Denmark, France, and Ireland have mandatory referendum provisions in their constitutions. Territorial issues come next. Remarkably few run-of-the-mill pragmatic problems have been put to the people. Sweden is quite exceptional in offering its people a choice of pension plan and a decision on the rule of the road, and, as Sten Sparre Nilson shows in Chapter 8, neither of those referendums was a great advertisement for the device. Except for the consumption of alcoholic drinks in the prohibition era, the great moral issues seem by general consent to have been avoided. Italy did vote on divorce, but no country in our list has put abortion, homosexual law, or capital punishment to a popular vote, though examples can, of course, be found in American states and in Switzerland.

One area where referendums have been most abused and yet most useful is in the settlement of territorial disputes. A list is provided in Appendix B. The 99 percent votes by which various territories opted to merge with France in the 1790s and with Italy in the 1860s were too overwhelming to carry full conviction, yet there is no doubt of the mood they reflected. After World War I the League of Nations implemented President Wilson's principle of self-determination in eight supervised plebiscites, while the United Nations gave legitimacy to the solution of some border disputes during the period of decolonization (Togo, 1958; Cameroons, 1959 and 1961). In most of these contests the national origins of the electors were known and the outcome was in little doubt, but the neutrally observed vote gave authority to the decision. The Upper Silesia plebiscite of 1921 (59.7 percent for Germany, 40.3 percent for Poland) certainly defused a delicate issue. One of the most interesting of internationally monitored referendums was in 1955 when a Franco-German agreement to Europeanize the Saar was rejected by the people of the Saar who chose, against the policy of the German government, to remerge with Germany.

In recent times, the issue of surrendering some sovereignty to an international body has provoked some of the most important refer-

TABLE 1-3

REFERENDUMS IN EUROPEAN DEMOCRACIES SINCE 1900

Country (No.)	*Date*	*Subject*	*Percent Voting Yes*	*Percent Turnout*
Belgium (1)	12 Mar. 1950	Return of Leopold III	57.6	92.4
Denmark (13)	14 Dec. 1916	Cession of Virgin Islands	64.2	38.0
	6 Sept. 1920	Incorporation of North Schleswig	96.9	50.1
	23 May 1939	Voting age lowered from 25 to 23; Landsthing abolished	91.9[a]	48.9
	28 May 1953	New constitution	78.4[a]	58.3
		Voting age 23 not 21	54.6	62.2
	30 May 1961	Voting age lowered from 23 to 21	55.0	37.2
	25 June 1963	Approve agricultural acquisition law	38.4	73.0
		Approve state smallholders law	38.6	73.0
		Approve municipal preemption law	39.6	73.0
		Approve nature conservancy law	42.6	73.0
	24 June 1969	Voting age lowered from 21 to 18	21.2	63.6
	21 Sept. 1971	Voting age lowered from 21 to 20	56.5	83.9
	2 Oct. 1972	Join European Economic Community	63.3	90.1
Finland (1)	29 Dec. 1931	Abolish prohibition of alcoholic beverages	70.5	44.4
France (10)	21 Oct. 1945	Assembly to draft constitution	96.3	79.9
		Interim power for assembly	66.8	79.9
	5 May 1946	Approve constitution	47.1	80.7
	13 Oct. 1946	Approve constitution	53.2	68.8
	28 Sept. 1958	Approve constitution	79.2	84.9

TABLE 1-3—Continued

Country (No.)	Date	Subject	Percent Voting Yes	Percent Turnout
	8 Jan. 1961	Algerian self-determination	75.3	76.5
	8 Apr. 1962	Agreement with Algiers	90.7	75.6
	28 Oct. 1962	Direct election of president	61.7	77.2
	27 Apr. 1969	Senate power and regional devolution	46.8	80.6
	23 Apr. 1972	Expand European Economic Community	67.7	60.7
Germany (2)	20 June 1926	Confiscation of royal property [c]	92.3 [b]	39.3
	22 Dec. 1929	Repudiation of war guilt (reparations) [c]	94.5 [b]	14.9
Greece (4)	14 Apr. 1924	Institute republic	70	—
	1 Sept. 1946	Return of George II	69	90
	29 July 1973	Institute republic	77.2	74.7
	8 Dec. 1974	End monarchy	69.2	75.6
Iceland (4)	19 Oct. 1918	Union with Denmark	92.6	43.8
	21 Oct. 1933	End prohibition of alcoholic beverages	57.7	45.3
	29 May 1944	Separate from Denmark	99.5	98.4
	29 May 1944	Institute republic	98.5	98.4
Ireland (7)	1 July 1937	Approve constitution	56.5	68.3
	17 June 1959	Abolish proportional representation	48.2	58.4
	16 Oct. 1968	Increase variation in electorates	39.2	62.9
	16 Oct. 1968	Abolish proportional representation	39.2	63.0
	10 May 1972	Join European Economic Community	83.1	70.9
	7 Dec. 1972	Lower voting age to 18	84.6	50.7
	7 Dec. 1972	Remove special constitutional position of church	84.4	50.7

TABLE 1-3—Continued

Country (No.)	*Date*	*Subject*	*Percent Voting Yes*	*Percent Turnout*
Italy (4)	2 June 1946	End monarchy	54.3	89.1
	12–13 May 1974	Repeal divorce law [c]	59.1	88.1
	11 June 1978	Repeal state financing of parties [c]	43.7	81.3
	11 June 1978	Repeal antiterrorist legislation [c]	23.3	81.4
Luxembourg (3)	28 Sept. 1919	Confirm grand duchess	77.8	68.0
	28 Sept. 1919	Economic union with France not Belgium	73.0	65.3
	6 Jan. 1937	Restrictions on extremist parties	49.3	—
Norway (5)	13 Aug. 1905	Separation from Sweden	99.9	84.8
	12–13 Nov. 1905	Approve monarch	78.9	75.3
	6 Oct. 1919	Retain prohibition of alcoholic beverages	61.6	66.5
	18 Oct. 1926	Repeal prohibition of alcoholic beverages	55.8	64.8
	24–25 Sept. 1972	Join European Economic Community	46.5	77.6
Spain (1)	15 Dec. 1976	Approve political reform program	94.2	77.7
Sweden (3)	6 Oct. 1922	Prohibition of alcoholic beverages	49.0	51.1
	16 Oct. 1955	Drive on right	15.2	53.2
	13 Oct. 1957	Three alternative pension plans	(1) 47.7 (2) 36.7 (3) 15.6	72.4
Turkey (1)	9 July 1961	Approve constitution	61.2	78.5
United Kingdom (1)	5 June 1975	Stay in European Economic Community	67.2	64.5

Dash (—): Data not available.

[a] Lost because this was less than 45 percent of the electorate.

[b] Lost because this was less than 50 percent of the electorate.

[c] Popular initiative.

SOURCE: Appendix A.

TABLE 1-4

Referendums in European Democracies since 1900

Issue	*Belgium*	*Denmark*	*Finland*	*France*	*Greece*	*Iceland*	*Ireland*	*Italy*	*Luxembourg*	*Norway*	*Spain*	*Sweden*	*Turkey*	*U.K.*	*Total*
Constitutional															
Approve new constitution		1		3			1						1		6
Approve or end monarch(y)	1				4	1		1	1	1					9
Change in constitutional machinery		1		4							1				6
Change in voting age		5					1								5
Change in electoral system							3								3
Ban on extreme parties									1						1
State financing of parties								1							1
Antiterrorist legislation								1							1
Subtotal															32
Moral															
Divorce								1							1
Prohibition of alcoholic beverages			1			1				2		1			5
Position of Church							1								1
Subtotal															7
Pragmatic															
Land law, pensions, rule of road		4										2			6
Territorial															
European Community membership		1		1			1			1				1	5
Other territorial		2		2		2			1	1					8
Subtotal															13
Total	1	14	1	10	4	4	7	4	3	5	1	3	1	1	58

Note: Switzerland is excluded because it would swamp the statistics (but see Chapter 3). Estonia and the German Weimar Republic are omitted as special interwar cases. Four of the eight Greek referendums are omitted as undemocratic. Outside Europe there are three British Commonwealth democracies of especial interest: For Australia, see Chapter 6; Canada has had one referendum on conscription and one on prohibition; New Zealand, in addition to twenty regular questions on liquor licensing has had two referendums on drinking hours, one on betting, one on conscription, and one on the life of parliament.

Source: Appendix A.

endums. The four applicants to join an enlarged European Community in the early 1970s all in due course put the issue direct to the people, and so did France. In almost every case, as is shown in later chapters, the result was of major political significance for the country's domestic politics.

There has been relatively little study of electoral behavior in nationwide referendums. On the whole, the countries where electoral research is most advanced have had few referendums. The most systematic work on the factors that sway votes has been confined to California, which Eugene Lee summarizes in Chapter 5, but the California experience can hardly be generalized to apply to the very different circumstances of recent European referendums. For every democratic referendum, however, two pieces of evidence about mass behavior are available: the turnout and the result. Democratic processes can be brought into disrepute by the refusal of the people to show any interest, and in a few referendums the low participation has been the most significant fact (for example, France in 1972 and Denmark in April 1953). But on the whole, referendum turnout has not been very far below each nation's normal level of involvement in elections.[10] One notable exception was in the Weimar Republic where a referendum could be carried only by 50 percent of all electors so that the simplest way of voting no was to stay at home; thus in two cases a vote of more than 90 percent yes meant defeat because once 39 percent and once a mere 15 percent of the electors had bothered to vote.

In a fair proportion of the referendums under consideration the outcome has not been in doubt, but this has had less effect on turnout than might be expected. In Britain in 1975, for example, when the opinion polls all forecast a two-to-one yes vote and there was none of the traditional door-to-door campaigning by the parties, the number going to the polls was only 8 percent less than in the general election eight months earlier. It was, of course, Britain's first referendum and had a curiosity value, but almost everywhere a referendum is an exceptional event. The only countries where the voter might have become blasé about referendums are Australia (where there is compulsory voting) and Switzerland where, as Chapter 3 shows, turnout has indeed fallen.

The bulk of referendum questions have been put to the public with the blessing of the government and often with the support of

[10] Referendums have usually been separated from general elections except in the United States. Other exceptions are provided by New Zealand's regular question on liquor control and Australia (1906, 1910, 1919, 1928, 1946, and 1974).

opposition parties. It is not surprising that so large a proportion have been successful. The notable defeats have been in Australia and Switzerland (repeatedly) and in Denmark (1963 and 1969), France (1946 and 1969), Ireland (1959 and 1968), Norway (1972), and Sweden (1955); they are all discussed later in the book. Each in its way represents a democratic contrariness, a rebuff for establishment authority. In most cases the defeat did not disturb the political scene, but there were two outstanding exceptions. The 1969 French vote was treated as a vote of no confidence by President de Gaulle and he resigned. The 1972 Norwegian vote, with its totally unexpected repudiation of the forces that had so long dominated the country's politics, led to a transformation of the party alignment.

Switzerland and Australia offer evidence for the proposition that referendums are essentially conservative in nature, though the lesson from the American states is less clear. Particularly in federal societies, the voters are cautious about giving new powers to the central authority. Almost all the negative votes have been repudiations of change. The 85 percent vote against right-hand driving in Sweden in 1955 is the most spectacular example of rejecting an innovation on which the establishment was agreed—and the way in which the establishment later circumvented that awkward vote is one of the most intriguing commentaries on the limitations of referendums.

The great bulk of referendums have taken the form of a single question put to the elector in an isolated contest. Occasionally more than one question has been put on the same issue (such as land reform in Denmark in 1963, constitutional change in France in 1945, electoral reform in Ireland in 1968). But Ireland (1972), New Zealand (1949 and 1967), and Italy (1978) offer the only examples of entirely separate issues being put on the same day, except of course for Switzerland and Australia, where a battery of questions has been common, though they never reached the California record of forty-seven different propositions on a single ballot. Several separate issues can be merged into one question as in France in 1969 (see Chapter 7 under "choice of question"), and occasionally the elector has been faced with a multiple choice question (Sweden, 1957; Finland, 1931; Newfoundland, 1948; Puerto Rico, 1948). Of course when a voter is asked to approve a constitution, his single yes or no applies to a whole host of propositions about the management of his country.

The wording of the referendum question can be a matter of controversy. Obviously, if a question is one of a large battery of issues, read perhaps for the first time by the voter in the polling booth, the phrasing can have a decisive influence on the result. But when the issue stands by itself and is well publicized and argued over by the politicians, the situation is different. People know what is at stake, and a loaded question may cause resentment and actually be counterproductive (as in France in 1969).

Most of the referendums we are concerned with have been consultative rather than mandatory. They have not enacted change but merely given authority to the legislature to bring it about. In a few cases the government has ignored or bypassed the verdict (Denmark, 1953; Sweden, 1955). But usually they have been conducted in the spirit exemplified by the British prime minister in 1975 when he said in advance that he would submit to a negative vote however small the majority. It is not easy to defy or ignore a popular verdict when it has been obtained with such formality. There are cases where the constitution lays down a condition for a yes vote to take effect:[11]

Weimar Republic	50 percent of electors
Denmark (until 1953)	45 percent of electors
Uruguay	35 percent of electors
Gambia	66.66 percent of voters
Australia	50 percent of voters and a majority of states
Switzerland	50 percent of voters and a majority of cantons
New Zealand (1908–1914)	60 percent of voters

A technical majority may not be enough. The Belgians voted in 1949 on whether Leopold III should resume his throne. On the strength of a 58 percent yes he came back to Brussels and then found it was not possible to function as king in a democratic society when 42 percent of the people had declared their opposition. If British membership in the Common Market had been confirmed by 51 percent and not 68 percent of the voters in 1975, its continuance would be much more uncertain today.

In Chapter 2 we deal with the theory of referendums, by which we mean relatively elaborate arguments that have been advanced,

[11] This was much discussed in Britain in 1978 when, against the government's advice, Parliament insisted that proposals for Scottish devolution should take effect only if supported in a referendum by 40 percent of the Scottish electors. In New Zealand in 1911 a 54 percent yes for prohibition had no effect because the enabling act laid down that 60 percent of the votes would be a prerequisite for change.

mainly in Switzerland and the United States, both for and against the proposition that direct legislation is, by universally valid principles, the most democratic, the most moral, the best way of making political decisions. In this chapter, however, we are concerned with empirically grounded explanations of why actual polities have chosen to hold referendums in some circumstances but not in others.

A look at the list of referendums offers a powerful deterrent to easy generalizations about why they have been held. Each seems to have a special history, rooted in an individual national tradition. The reasons for each referendum, its treatment by politicians and by voters, and its consequences fail to fit any clear universal pattern. But common elements can sometimes be detected.

First, there is constitutional necessity. Switzerland and Australia have constitutions which can be changed only by referendum; to a lesser extent, so have France, Ireland, and Denmark. Insofar as constitutional amendment is needed from time to time, some referendums in these countries are inevitable.

Second, there is a legitimating function. It is not only absolutist regimes that have felt the need to demonstrate the popular basis for their policies. Democratic governments have normally relied on ordinary elections for their authority, but since all parties have a multiplicity of policies an election victory cannot prove the popularity of a specific measure. A direct appeal to the people has sometimes been needed to show that the public is behind a policy. As one Labour member of Parliament, a convinced European federalist, said of the 1975 British referendum, "Britain had to have a referendum on EEC membership. It was a marriage service making it easier to live together."[12]

Third, there is the transfer of decision making. Governments have been reluctant to settle issues on which they were themselves divided; they have wanted to avoid responsibility for decisions which would be unpopular with a significant section of the public. Referendums have offered a way of passing the buck. The EEC referendums in Norway and Britain, the Leopold III referendum in Belgium, the divorce referendum in Italy, and the various prohibition referendums in Scandinavia and Australasia exemplified this. So, in a different way, did the military conscription referendums (Australia, 1916 and 1917; Canada, 1942; New Zealand, 1949).[13]

---

[12] David Butler and Uwe Kitzinger, *The 1975 Referendum* (New York: St. Martin's Press, 1976), p. 279.

[13] The following countries have constitutional provisions for submitting legislation before enactment: Austria (never used), France, Italy, Senegal, Switzerland, and Syria. A stipulated number of voters can demand a referendum only in

A pure democratic ideology such as that outlined in Chapter 2 has seldom lain behind the calling of referendums. Except in Switzerland and some American states, referendums have almost all been ad hoc affairs, called by governments as solutions to particular political difficulties. But, on the whole, politicians have been reluctant to call referendums. Referendums may go the wrong way. And referendums may undermine party solidarity.

These presumably are the reasons why there have been so few. If Switzerland and Australia are left out of the reckoning, the well-established democracies of the world have averaged a total of less than four apiece. It has been very rare for governments to seek this way out of their dilemmas, even on moral and personal issues that might most readily be thus taken out of the political arena.

Referendums must of course be fitted into each country's rules of the political game. Before the 1975 British referendum some constitutional purists argued that it was subverting the whole basis of representative and responsible government on which the Westminster model was based: It was an admission of failure by the party in power; it was a dangerous precedent that might encourage future governments to duck their responsibility to settle state policy in all matters and then to stand judgment for their performance as a whole; in the future awkward issues might regularly be passed over for the people to decide. These arguments ignored the fact that most of the well-established copies of the Westminster model had used referendums without any general departure from the principle of responsible government. They also ignored the fact, already noted, that there seldom seems to be anything addictive about calling referendums.

Referendums can, as we have seen, lead to government defeats, and even an affirmative majority that is narrow can damage a government's prestige. It is usually easier to manage a parliament than to manage the electorate; a defeat in the chamber can be more easily circumvented or reversed than a defeat at the polls.

Referendums, too, cut across normal routines. The question referred to the voters is not usually expressed as a party issue but is presented as a problem for each to judge independently. The politicians and the media may give the voters plenty of cues about

---

Italy (500,000) and Switzerland (50,000; but see Chapter 3). In other countries the decision to hold referendums rests with the president or legislature.

Hungary (never used), Yugoslavia (never used), and Sweden have provisions for consultative prelegislative referendums. Denmark and Switzerland have provisions for referendums during the legislative process. Bulgaria and the Soviet Union also have constitutional provisions for holding referendums: see V. Herman, *Parliaments of the World* (London: Macmillan, 1976).

the answer they should reach, but parties are at their peril if they invoke party loyalty too ostentatiously. Individuals can hardly be prevented from pursuing their own line, and cross-party alliances may spring up which can outlast the referendum and threaten party cohesion.

One area where generalization is hardest is that of referendum campaigns. In each country the roles of the state and the parties have differed in rules and in practices. The duration of the campaign and its costs, the intervention of organized or ad hoc interest groups, the efforts at public education, and the behavior of the media fall into no organized pattern. On the whole, the most significant efforts at voter manipulation seem to have been on the part of governments. At the national level there have been few grand-scale campaigns to defeat a referendum of the sort familiar in California. But the efforts of churchmen, farmers, fishermen, and some trade unionists to defeat the 1972 EEC referendum in Norway are worthy of note, as were the affirmative efforts of the socialists (1926) and the ultraright groups (1929) in the Weimar Republic.[14] The concept of umbrella organizations—ad hoc state-recognized, cross-party groups—set up to manage the campaign on each side was rapidly developed in Britain in 1975 and provides a model which is being copied in the 1978 Canadian and Québecois legislation for referendums.

One alternative to the referendum is the opinion poll. If a sample survey can tell what the people think, why go to the trouble and expense of a referendum? It is certain that opinion polls have warned governments of putting some subjects to a popular vote. Even if a sample survey provides a correct measurement of opinion, however, it lacks the credibility of a referendum. People will simply refuse to believe it; they could not repudiate an actual nationwide vote in the same way. And skepticism about an opinion poll finding may well be justified, however good the pollster. The answers a voter gives to an interviewer who unexpectedly raises some issue of public policy may be very different from what the voter would solemnly record in the polling booth at the end of a long campaign on the subject. During the fifteen years that Common Market membership was an issue in Britain, poll findings fluctuated wildly, varying from a 44 percent plurality for entry (1966) to a 42 percent plurality against (1970). What one says to a pollster involves none of the responsibility associ-

[14] The Prussian referendum of August 1931 is also worthy of note, since Prussia contained over half the population of Weimar Germany. The Nazis and the Communists joined forces in an attempt to dissolve the Prussian legislature by referendum. It was unsuccessful, but there was a 40 percent yes vote.

ated with deliberately putting a vote in a ballot box. France (1969), Norway (1972), and Britain (1975) offer notable examples of results well removed from the survey findings of a few months earlier.

If this chapter has a moral, it is that referendums have in fact been used—very sparingly in most countries—for a variety of reasons, mostly practical and circumstantial. What political theorists have said about how and why they *should* be used is our concern in Chapter 2.

2
Theory

This chapter is concerned with the main arguments people have advanced for and against the holding of referendums. Those arguments are best understood if we bear in mind throughout that there are several different species of the genus "referendum" and that they vary from one another mainly in the degree to which they remove control over the making of laws from elected representatives and transfer it to ordinary voters. In the order of increasing degrees of such transfer, the basic types of referendums are:

1. *Government-controlled referendums.* The government—which usually means a majority of the legislature acting in accordance with the wishes of the ruling party or coalition of parties—has the sole power to decide whether a referendum will be held, the subject matter and wording of the proposition to be voted on, the proportion of yes votes needed for the proposition to win, and whether the outcome will be binding on or merely advisory to the government.

2. *Constitutionally required referendums.* The constitution requires that certain kinds of measures adopted by the government—mainly but not exclusively constitutional amendments (see Chapters 3, 4, and 5)—be approved by the voters before they can take effect. The government has exclusive power to decide whether to propose each amendment and to determine its wording, but the mandatory referendum determines whether it becomes part of the constitution.

3. *Referendums by popular petitions.* Ordinary voters are authorized to file a petition demanding that a certain measure adopted by the government be referred to the voters. If their

petition contains the required number of valid signatures, a referendum must be held on the measure; and if a majority of the voters favor repeal, the law is voided regardless of whether the government wishes to retain it.

4. *Popular initiatives.* Ordinary voters are authorized to file a petition demanding that a certain measure which the government has not adopted be referred to the voters. If their petition contains the required number of valid signatures, a referendum must be held on the measure; and if the required majority of the voters vote in favor of it, it becomes law regardless of whether the government opposes it.

The discussion in Chapter 1 and the data in Appendixes A and B make clear that most countries have only the first type of referendum and that their governments have chosen to hold referendums only on a few occasions and mainly for reasons of political convenience rather than in response to overarching general theories about how laws should be made and unmade. Referendums of the third and fourth types (often jointly labeled "direct legislation") have been widely used only in Switzerland, at both the confederal and cantonal levels, and in about a dozen states of the American union. It should therefore come as no surprise that most of the proreferendum and many of the antireferendum arguments have been advanced by Swiss and American writers, in works published mainly between 1890 and 1920. Our task in this chapter is to review the main arguments on both sides.

The Case for Referendums

Legitimation. The first main argument for referendums consists of two basic propositions: (1) all political decisions should be as legitimate as possible, and (2) the highest degree of legitimacy is achieved by decisions made by the direct, unmediated vote of the people.

As political scientists use the term, legitimacy has two components. The first is the conviction by a polity's citizens that the institutions and processes by which its political decisions are made are, by law, custom, and moral principle, the right and proper ways to make such decisions. The second component is the popular conviction that the decisions themselves do not go beyond acceptable limits of fairness and decency in awarding privileges to or imposing burdens on any part of the people.

In this sense every government can use all the legitimacy it can muster, for it is a necessary condition for maximum voluntary compliance with governmental decisions. The long history of despotisms, ancient and modern, teaches that although the compliance of most subjects can be compelled most of the time by government force and intimidation, both methods are costly and their unit costs grow higher, not lower, the more they are used. Even repressive regimes therefore seek ways of persuading their subjects of the legitimacy of the rulers' decisions. The very existence of democracy rests upon the willing acceptance by minorities of decisions made by majorities—and upon the forbearance of majorities from imposing on minorities conditions they cannot bear.

It is not surprising, then, that perhaps the most widely accepted case for referendums concludes that decisions by referendums are the most legitimate of all. The argument goes something like this: People may or may not trust legislators, cabinets, and prime ministers, but they certainly trust themselves most of all. Hence a decision in which all have participated (or at least had a full opportunity to participate) is more legitimate in their eyes than one in which they have not participated. Moreover, decisions in which popular participation is direct and unmediated by others, as in referendums, produce more accurate expressions of their will than do decisions in which they participate only by electing others who make the decisions for them, as in acts of parliaments and cabinets.

Accordingly, even people who feel that most political decisions should be made by experts in public office rather than by uninformed ordinary citizens agree that the most important, the most fundamental decisions should at least be ratified by referendums. This explains why in some polities where ordinary laws are made exclusively by elected officials, amendments to the constitutions must be approved by referendums—although the distinction between constitutions and ordinary laws tends to blur and even disappear in polities where the initiative is available as well.[1] It also explains why governments sometimes find it prudent to hold referendums even when they are not required to. For example, although the proximate political cause of Great Britain's decision to hold a referendum was, as Chapter 10 shows, the Labour government's calculation of the party's self-interest, the most compelling argument set forth in debate preceding the decision was that accepting the Treaty of Rome would mean abridging the supremacy of Parliament and surrendering some portion of the nation's sovereign independence. It was thought that such a change would be legitimate only if approved by a direct vote of the people.

[1] See Chapter 3 on Switzerland and Chapter 4 on the United States.

The power of the legitimation argument also explains why plebiscites, as Chapter 1 describes, have been so widely used in decisions involving transfers of sovereignty over particular populations from one nation to another. And it explains why so many nondemocratic regimes hold referendums even when—or perhaps especially because—everyone knows in advance that the result will be reported as a 99 percent yes for the regime's policy on a 99 percent turnout. Other chapters of this book provide many examples of the legitimation argument's impact.

Direct Democracy. The legitimation argument is used to support the use of referendums only when it is thought necessary to endow a decision with maximum legitimacy. The second proreferendums argument, however, supports their use in *all* circumstances because they establish in modern mass societies the essentials of the most democratic of all forms of government—direct rule by face-to-face assemblies of all the citizens. Clifford Sharp pointed out in a 1911 Fabian Society pamphlet why this argument has been especially compelling in Switzerland and the United States:

> Historically the Referendum is the offspring by unbroken descent of the primitive mass meeting of self-governing citizens. Both in Switzerland and the United States, the only countries where it flourishes today, the whole body of citizens were from the earliest times (in the Swiss cantons from the thirteenth century, and in the American colonies from their foundation) accustomed to exercise all the functions of government for themselves in open assembly. This direct control over the affairs of State was never entirely surrendered, and when the assemblies of all the citizens became impracticable and more and more powers had to be delegated to representative councils, the Referendum came into being gradually and naturally, not as an accession of popular power, but as a mere retention by the sovereign people of certain important powers in their own hands.[2]

The most elaborate statements of the direct-democracy argument for referendums were made by some Swiss writers[3] and, in even greater

[2] Clifford D. Sharp, *The Case against the Referendum*, Fabian Tract no. 155 (London: The Fabian Society, 1911), p. 3.

[3] The writers on Switzerland include: Simon Deploige, *The Referendum in Switzerland* (London: King, 1898); Felix Bonjour, *Real Democracy in Operation* (New York: Frederick A. Stokes Co., 1920); and William E. Rappard, "The Initiative and Referendum in Switzerland," *American Political Science Review*, vol. 6 (August 1912), pp. 345-366.

volume, by the leaders of the Progressive movement in the United States. This is the label historians generally apply to the reform movement operating within both the Republican and Democratic parties in most American states (and, to a lesser degree, in national politics) from the 1890s to American entry into World War I.[4] Its principal leaders included Robert M. La Follette of Wisconsin, Hiram Johnson of California, Theodore Roosevelt of New York, and Woodrow Wilson of New Jersey. Much of its literature was written by muckraking journalists, especially Ida M. Tarbell and Lincoln Steffens, and by social scientists, especially John R. Commons and Edward A. Ross. Its central programmatic thrust was for a number of reforms in the nation's and states' law-making machinery, all intended to increase ordinary citizens' participation in and power over governmental decisions. The main Progressive reforms included the Australian (secret) ballot; nonpartisan elections, especially at the local level; legal regulation of the organization, membership requirements, finance, and campaign activities of political parties; the direct primary; the recall of elected officials; and the initiative and referendum. The argument for these reforms was set forth as described below.

The Premises.[5] The Progressives' case rested upon two beliefs. The first was their faith in the unorganized, free individual. As Richard Hofstadter points out:

> At the core of their conception of politics was a figure quite as old-fashioned as the figure of the little competitive entrepreneur who represented the most commonly accepted economic ideal. This old-fashioned character was the Man of Good Will, the same innocent, bewildered, bespectacled, and mustached figure we see in the cartoons today labeled John Q. Public. . . . In a great deal of Progressive thinking the Man of Good Will was abstracted from association with positive interests; his chief interests were negative. He

---

[4] Useful surveys of the Progressive movement include: Richard Hofstadter, *The Age of Reform* (New York: Random House, 1955); Lewis L. Gould, ed., *The Progressive Era* (Syracuse, N.Y.: Syracuse University Press, 1974); George Mowry, *Theodore Roosevelt and the Progressive Movement* (Madison, Wis.: University of Wisconsin Press, 1946); George Mowry, *The California Progressives* (Berkeley: University of California Press, 1951); and Arthur S. Link, *Woodrow Wilson and the Progressive Era* (New York: Harper and Row, 1954).

[5] The most complete expositions of the Progressives' general philosophy are: Walter E. Weyl, *The New Democracy* (New York: Macmillan, 1915); Benjamin Parke De Witt, *The Progressive Movement* (New York: Macmillan, 1915); Herbert Croly, *Progressive Democracy* (New York: Macmillan, 1914); and Ellen Torelle, ed., *The Political Philosophy of Robert M. La Follette as Revealed in His Speeches and Writings* (Madison, Wis.: Robert M. La Follette Co., 1926).

> needed to be protected from unjust taxation, spared the high cost of living, relieved of the exactions of the monopolies and the grafting of the bosses. . . . The problem was to devise such governmental machinery as would empower him to rule. Since he was dissociated from all special interests and biases and had nothing but the common weal at heart, he would rule well. He would act and think as a public-spirited individual, unlike all the groups of vested interests that were ready to prey on him.[6]

The Progressives' second premise was hostility to intermediary organizations. They believed that truly democratic government consists of all the John and Jane Q. Publics observing, discussing, pondering, deciding, and, finally, voting. The public interest is discovered by their discussions and ponderings, and it is served by the measures which majorities of them adopt when the deliberations have run their course. That being the case, any organization that seeks to interpose itself between the people and their government—that is, any intermediary organization—is bound to subvert democracy *and* the public interest to some degree. Left to themselves, to be sure, some citizens will often freely associate with other like-minded citizens in spontaneous ad hoc groups to advance their agreed views on particular issues. So long as such groups dissolve when their issue is settled, no harm is done. But when a group organizes itself permanently and seeks to influence government decisions on a wide range of issues, it will inevitably distort the popular will and promote its special interest over the public interest.[7]

Corporations and trusts were thought to be bad because they wreck the free market by forming monopolies to force their profits unnaturally high. Political parties are bad because, left unregulated by law, they are captured by bosses and become machines whose goal is to control nominations and win elections so as to ensure a steady supply of patronage jobs and favors for special interests. All pressure groups—a term used synonymously with special interest groups—are bad because they try, often successfully, to persuade or bribe public officials to give them franchises, monopolies, tax advantages, and

---

[6] Hofstadter, *Age of Reform*, pp. 260-261. See also Gordon E. Baker, "American Conceptions of Direct vis-à-vis Representative Governance," *Claremont Journal of Public Affairs*, vol. 1 (Spring 1977), pp. 5-18.

[7] A well-known non-American expression of this view was M. I. Ostrogorski's condemnation of political parties because they were "permanent"—that is, because they continued in existence long past the time when the issues which originally called them into being were settled. M. I. Ostrogorski, *Democracy and the American Party System*, trans. Frederick Clarke (London: Macmillan, 1902), vol. 1, chap. 8.

other special favors. Even popularly elected legislatures and municipal councils are bad because they are so easily purchased by special interests and dominated by party bosses.

Only when the power of all intermediary organizations is broken and all obstructions between John Q. and his government are removed can true democracy flourish and the public interest triumph. As Hofstadter sums it up:

> Bad people had pressure groups; the Man of Good Will had only his civic organizations. Far from joining organizations to advance his own interests, he would dissociate himself from such combinations and address himself directly and high-mindedly to the problems of government. His approach to politics was, in a sense, intellectualistic: he would study the issues and think them through, rather than learn about them through pursuing his needs. Furthermore, it was assumed that somehow he would really be capable of informing himself in ample detail about the many issues that he would have to pass on, and that he could master their intricacies sufficiently to pass intelligent judgment. Without such assumptions the entire movement for such reforms as the initiative, the referendum, and recall is unintelligible.[8]

The Anticipated Benefits. The Progressives' battlecry was "The cure for the ills of democracy is more democracy!" Given their faith in the free individual and their hostility to intermediary organizations, they were confident that the initiative and the referendum would give the citizens the best possible weapons for overpowering grasping corporations, greedy special interest groups, boss-ridden political machines, and weak and corrupt legislatures. If the fear of being bypassed by popular initiatives or overridden by popular referendums was enough to force public officials to behave honestly and responsively, well and good; if not, the people themselves would simply take over. In either event, the Progressives were confident that direct legislation would cleanse and enrich the political process in many ways.

All issues faced. In the nature of things, intermediary organizations, and especially political parties and legislatures, always try to ignore and suppress unusually hot and divisive issues simply because facing them might anger enough voters, contributors, special interest groups, and bosses to jeopardize the payoffs—indeed, even the jobs—of the intermediaries. But through the initiative and referendum, any issue, however novel or divisive or offensive to those in power, can

[8] Hofstadter, *Age of Reform*, p. 261.

be put on the law-making agenda by concerned citizens and brought to decision. In this way *all* the issues that concern the people are faced, not just the few that the special interests find unthreatening.[9]

Decisions brought close to the people. Decisions made in the capital city by governors and legislatures take place a long distance from most voters, both geographically and psychologically. Moreover, about the only way the people ever learn about such decisions is by reading the newspapers—which, after all, are just one more intermediary between the people and their government. Newspapers report only part of what is going on, edit their stories to promote whatever special interests their publishers are pushing, and thus give the voters an always incomplete and often badly distorted picture of what is going on. All this makes government remote and policy making incomprehensible to John Q. Public. But when the people set most of the political agenda by their petitions and make most of the decisions by their direct, unmediated votes, the government moves close to home and the mystery disappears.

Public decisions publicly arrived at. One of Woodrow Wilson's famous fourteen points for settling World War I was "open covenants, openly arrived at." It was an extension to international affairs of a principle he and his fellow Progressives had espoused domestically in New Jersey and national politics. The idea rests upon the conviction that all public decisions should be made in the full public gaze. The only reason for making them secretly is to conceal some part of the process that the decision makers know would be regarded as shameful. The clandestine, unethical, or illegal deal, venal bargain, or giving and taking of bribes, if disclosed, would discredit the whole policy. One of many evils characteristic of intermediary organizations is the fact that they make their decisions in secret whenever they can get away with it. Special interest groups choose strategies and lobby public officials in private; party bosses pick candidates and make deals privately in the legendary smoke-filled rooms; legislative committees write bills in executive sessions closed to the public; majority and minority leaders in legislatures privately decide what bills will be considered and when. Why all the secrecy? Because the intermediary organizations do not want John Q. Public to know what they are doing and why.

By contrast, decisions by initiative and referendum are always made in the clean open air of true democracy. The signatures on the

[9] See Bonjour, *Real Democracy*, p. 36.

petitions, the propositions on the ballots, the speeches on the issues, and the results of the votes are all matters of public record, freely available to all. They hide nothing and have nothing to hide. Therefore they cannot do anything underhanded or illegal or shameful. Open government guarantees honest government, and the initiative and referendum are the best possible guarantees that government will become and remain honest.

Popular will accurately expressed. In the Progressives' view, the popular will is the sum of the citizens' individual wills. When that will is expressed directly, without intermediation of any kind, it is bound to be expressed accurately. But when it is filtered through a political party or a legislature or any other intermediary organization, it is bound to be distorted to some degree. As Rousseau, the great prophet of direct democracy, put it:

> Sovereignty cannot be represented for the same reason that it cannot be alienated; its essence is the general will, and that will must speak for itself, or it does not exist; it is either itself or not itself; there is no intermediate possibility. The deputies of the people, therefore, are not and cannot be their representatives; they can only be their commissioners, and as such are not qualified to conclude anything definitively. No act of theirs can be a law, unless it has been ratified by the the people in person; and without that ratification nothing is a law.[10]

Accordingly, if the issue of, say, raising taxes were put before an assembly of legislators elected by party labels after a campaign in which taxes were only one of the many issues discussed, there is no way of telling whether its action on taxes would truly express the popular will. But if the question of raising taxes by $10 per capita were set before the voters in a referendum, the majority of their votes either for or against the proposition would constitute a clear and accurate expression of their will. What about other questions? Have referendums on them as well. Only when matters are settled by direct legislation can we be certain that government is acting in accordance with the popular will.

End of apathy and alienation. It is inevitable, said the Progressives, that governments dominated by special interest groups, boss-controlled parties, and corrupt legislatures should produce widespread apathy and alienation among the citizens. If the only choices offered

[10] Jean-Jacques Rousseau, *The Social Contract*, trans. Charles Frankel (New York: Hafner, 1947), Bk. III, chap. 15, p. 85. See also Bonjour, *Real Democracy*, p. 35.

in election after election are between Democratic tweedledees and Republican tweedledums served up by the two party machines, who can blame the people for not voting and for feeling cynical about the whole sorry business of politics? If legislatures constantly ignore the people's wishes and sacrifice the public interest to special interests, who can blame the people for ignoring public news and political discussions? And if the whole apparatus of government is nothing more than a flimsy façade, poorly masking the machinations of the special interests, who can blame the people for feeling powerless and alienated?

Direct legislation will end all that. It will enable people to control the law-making process and to *know* that they control it. When popular votes become the true coin of political power, people will know that their votes count, and they will make it a point to cast them at every opportunity. People will participate in their government because they believe in it, and they will believe in it because they participate in and control it.

The public interest served. To the Progressives the public interest is not merely the sum of all special interests. Rather it is whatever is best for the common life of the political community and all the people who compose it. It is giving all citizens their due, treating every citizen fairly, caring more for the next generation than for the next election. And it is discovered, not by raw competition among self-seeking special interests, but by consulting the best judgment of all the people about what is best for all. Intermediary organizations, no matter how pure their hearts and civic-minded their intentions, must by their very nature promote special interests. After all, they are established, organized, and operated by only some of the people, never all of them. No matter what other interests such an organization may pursue, its first interest—by definition a *special* interest—is to keep itself in business and its staff on the payroll. Where policy is made by competition, bargaining, and compromise among intermediary groups the result can only be a pastiche of benefits to special interests with no attention, let alone service, given to the public interest.

But where the people rule by direct legislation without intermediary organizations, there simply is no opportunity for logrolling or trading of payoffs or any other kind of special interest bargaining. All issues are judged by their expected impact on the public interest, and all judgments are made by majorities of ordinary citizens, not by coalitions of lobbyists or party bosses or legislative leaders. The people's interest *is* the public interest. Where the people rule, they will serve their own interest. Where special interests rule in their name, the public interest cannot and will not be served.

Citizens' human potentials maximized. The Progressives shared the classical conviction that political participation, quite aside from whether it makes for wiser and more legitimate government, makes for the full development of every citizen's human potential. Like Rousseau and his Athenian forebears, the Progressives believed that people are not naturally hermits. Rather they are political—that is, civic—animals, in that a high degree of participation in civic affairs is necessary for the full realization of all it means to be a human being. This realization is so important that even if it means sacrificing some measure of expertise, efficiency, and order in the public business—which the Progressives did not anticipate—it is well worth the price.

Some advocates of participatory democracy are not enthusiastic about direct legislation as the right path to human development. They do not agree that voting in initiative and referendum elections is the kind of participation that best elicits the human potential. After all, they argue, voting demands only the most minimal commitment and effort by the citizen. Voters need no qualification to participate other than legal proof of their presence on the roll of registered voters. Voting is conducted in secret and therefore irresponsibly. Voters need not engage in any confrontation between their preferences and opposing preferences. All in all, then, voting is a most passive, undemanding, uninspiring, and unimproving kind of civic participation, vastly inferior to taking an active part in the discussion of issues in town meetings, local caucuses, and other types of face-to-face assemblies.[11]

The Progressives strongly disagreed. Voting in direct legislation elections, they said, not only is a desirable activity in itself but also stimulates other forms of participation as well. The people know that their votes will make and break laws and thereby determine how government will impinge on their lives. Knowing this, in sheer self-interest they will inform themselves on the issues, defend their positions against those who feel otherwise, and seek to persuade others to vote with them. Thus, where voting truly controls government, as it does in initiative and referendum elections, it leads to the other forms of popular participation. Indeed, in a modern mass democracy voting may well be the only activity that can have this result for most citizens.

---

[11] See Carole Pateman, *Participation and Democratic Theory* (New York: Cambridge University Press, 1970); Terrence E. Cook and Patrick M. Morgan, eds., *Participatory Democracy* (San Francisco, Calif.: Canfield Press, 1971); and Wilson Carey McWilliams, "Down with Primaries," *Commonweal*, July 1, 1976, p. 429.

The Case against Referendums

As noted in Chapter 1, in most modern democratic nations referendums are held either infrequently and in unusual circumstances or not at all. This suggests that the case *against* any general use of referendums and initiatives as substitutes for representative assemblies, cabinets, and other elected agencies has had substantially more acceptance and influence than the direct-democracy proreferendum case just surveyed.[12] The most frequently encountered arguments against the general use of referendums are discussed below.

Weakened Power of Elected Authorities. One central argument against referendums, not always voiced explicitly, is that they threaten the control over the political system of the elected and other established authorities. In a free society the outcome of a referendum cannot be guaranteed. Moreover, a referendum on one subject may lead to demands for referendums on others—and on some subjects the verdict of the people will run counter to the consensus of those who hold public office.

Accordingly, the government-controlled referendum is the only acceptable type because only it poses no significant threat to the power and prestige of public officeholders. And governments are well advised to use it only in circumstances in which its short-run advantages clearly outweigh the long-run dangers it poses.

Inability of Ordinary Citizens to Make Wise Decisions. The problems facing modern governments are numerous, complex, and demanding. Only a person who spends full time thinking about them can hope to understand them well enough to cast intelligent votes. Ordinary people simply to do not have this time. Unlike the citizens of Periclean Athens, they do not have slaves to do all the work necessary to liberate them for full-time participation in civic affairs; they have to earn a living, and work leaves them only a little time and energy for studying questions of public policy. Hence elected representatives are better qualified to make such decisions, not because they are necessarily more intelligent or more public spirited, but because they are paid to spend full time on government affairs.

---

[12] The most comprehensive and sober cases against referendums are: Sharp, *Case against the Referendum;* and, at least by implication, A. D. Lindsay, *The Essentials of Democracy,* 2nd ed. (London: Oxford University Press, 1942). Among more polemical works are: Jane T. Stoddart, *Against the Referendum* (London: Hodder, 1910); and Martin W. Littleton, "Mob Rule and the Canonized Minority," *Constitutional Review,* vol. 2 (1923).

No Measurement of Intensity of Belief. In every referendum every recorded vote counts the same as every other. Even though most votes in favor of an issue may represent only unenthusiastic marginal preference, while most votes against represent passionate opposition, if there are more votes for than against the proposition wins. But elected representatives can and do—indeed, must—assess not only how many of their constituents approve or oppose a measure but also how intensely. If, say, 60 percent favor the measure but with little enthusiasm, while 40 percent oppose it as gross injustice, then the representatives not only can defeat the measure but are likely to do so if for no loftier reason than that an angry 40 percent is much more dangerous to their electoral future than an unenthusiastic 60 percent.

Forced Decisions, Not Consensus. The ultimate goal of democratic decision processes, say some commentators, is not a vote which identifies how many citizens support each of two irreconcilable alternatives. Rather it is consensus, a sense of the meeting, a general agreement that a particular course of action is the best way of promoting the interests of all the citizens. This ideal solution can be realized only by discussion among people who know and respect each other and who seek the truth, not forensic triumphs over their neighbors.[13] Moreover, true democratic discussion is not competitive; it is cooperative and heuristic. All who participate seek the best possible solution on which all can agree. Votes occasionally have to be taken to advance the business, but they take place only when all participants have gained a kind of knowledge and understanding of the problem in hand that they could not have had when the discussion began. As Ernest Barker put it:

> Discussion is not only like a war; it is also like love. It is not only a battle of ideas; it is also a marriage of minds. If a majority engages in discussion with a minority, and if that discussion is conducted in a spirit of giving and taking, the result will be that the ideas of the majority are widened to include some of the ideas of the minority which have established their truth in the give and take of debate. When this happens, the will of the majority will not be the abstract or isolated will of a mere majority, considered in itself and as standing by itself in opposition to the similar will of a mere minority. Some fusion will have taken place; some accommodation will have been attained.[14]

[13] Lindsay's illustration is the Quaker meeting (*Essentials of Democracy*, pp. 45-47); Sharp's is meetings of the Fabian Society's executive committee (*Case against the Referendum*, p. 14).

[14] Ernest Barker, *Reflections on Government* (London: Oxford University Press, 1942), p. 67.

This cannot happen in a referendum. The question in a referendum is never "What is the best way to deal with this problem?" It is always "Shall we or shall we not adopt proposition A?" The discussion is always adversary—pro-A arguments versus anti-A arguments. Since all the voters can never meet face to face, most of the discussion takes place in the mass media. Indeed, what the media choose to print or televise has a very great, perhaps too great, influence on how the choice is perceived. And media discussion provides no opportunity for the participants to discover that B is better than either A or not-A, that C is better still, and that in the ultimate judgment of most, D—which no one thought of at the beginning—is best of all.

Representative assemblies are far from perfect, but they have several crucial advantages over referendums: their members meet face to face regularly; they do not immediately or necessarily vote up or down every measure that comes before them; they discuss, refer, study, delay, amend, and give and take. Their decisions only occasionally approach unanimity, but their discussions approach the small-group ideal far more closely than the discussions preceding referendums. Even in national legislatures votes are mainly expedients to get decisions when the time available for discussion has run out. In referendums votes are the very essence of the decision process.

Danger to Minorities. Because they cannot measure intensities of belief or work things out through discussion and discovery, referendums are bound to be more dangerous than representative assemblies to minority rights. It is no accident, for example, that in many American states in recent years the legislatures have tended to adopt laws prohibiting discrimination against blacks and women, while referendums have tended to overturn them. Extensive use of initiatives and referendums in Western Europe might well result in such actions as the restoration and extension of the death penalty, the restriction of immigration by blacks and Asians, and limits on the level and redistributive quality of taxes.

Weakening of Representative Government. Many advocates of referendums portray them as no more than supplementary aids to representative democracy. So long as the legislature does what the people want, they say, there will be no need for referendums. But when the legislature ignores or flouts the popular will, the referendum will keep it from enacting bad measures and the initiative will allow good to be done despite the legislature's intransigence. Perhaps so, perhaps not, say some opponents of referendums. But in any case the price will be a grave weakening of representative government. As legislatures lose power they will lose popular respect, and outstanding citizens will be less inclined to seek public office. Even those who remain in office are likely to behave less responsibly, for their behavior is bound to be adversely affected by the knowledge that anything they do, good or bad, may be overriden by a referendum.

Conclusion

The arguments both for and against referendums share at least one important characteristic: Like all political arguments, they are compounds of preferences for certain values (such as responsiveness to the popular will, prudent government decisions, development of human potentials, protection of minority rights) and empirical causal statements (that referendums express the popular will more accurately than do representative assemblies, referendums tend to threaten minority rights while representative assemblies tend to protect them, people will vote in large numbers if they feel they are themselves making the laws rather than merely choosing the lawmakers).

Like all empirical propositions, these statements are amenable to verification by the systematic analysis of experience. From the 1880s to the 1920s, when the adoption, repeal, or extension of the referendum and the initiative were live questions in Great Britain, the United States, Australia, and other nations, many speeches were made and many books and articles published on these matters. Most were polemics but a few were efforts to analyze the actual experience with direct legislation, especially in Switzerland and the United States.

In the late 1970s, as we have seen, there has been a major revival of interest in referendums. Some nations that have never used the device (for example,the national government of the United States) are now considering adopting it, and some that have used it very rarely (such as Great Britain and Italy) are considering using it more frequently. The value choices and empirical questions that concerned scholars in the early 1900s may now be reconsidered in the light of nearly a century's additional experience. The chapters that follow are intended to contribute to that reconsideration.

3
Switzerland

Jean-François Aubert

In Switzerland referendums are popular votes on laws and constitutional decrees or issues which citizens are asked to approve or reject by a yes or a no. Referendums are clearly distinct from elections when citizens choose people to represent them. Issues submitted to referendum may come from the parliament in the form of constitutional reforms or laws, or from citizens in the form of a popular initiative. Referendums and initiatives are seen as institutions of direct democracy in contrast to elections, which are the basic instrument of representative democracy.

History

The referendum was used at the end of the Middle Ages in several Swiss cantons, notably in Bern. Then it was suppressed in the seventeenth and eighteenth centuries by the development of a form of oligarchic government. It reappeared in the nineteenth century, first in an isolated way at the time of a national vote on a constitution for the Swiss republic[1] and then more generally in the liberal "Regeneration" around 1830. At that period most cantons, including the conservative ones, accepted the custom of submitting their constitutions to the people—and some their laws as well. When Switzerland became a federation in 1848, imitating the United States,

[1] In June 1802 the Swiss people as a whole voted yes or no for the first time on the text of the Second Helvetic Constitution. It was clearly announced before the referendum that abstentions would be considered as affirmatives. The result is unique in Swiss history (though the same system had been used in some cantons): The constitution was accepted with 92,500 votes against and 72,500 votes in favor because there were 167,000 abstentions.

the new constitution was put to the people for ratification in the great majority of cantons.[2]

From the first, the compulsory referendum was provided for, but only for amendments to the federal constitution. In 1874 it was extended, on an optional basis, to cover any federal laws or decrees of general application adopted by the parliament. Later amendments in 1921 and 1977 made certain international treaties subject to referendum. Popular initiatives, which lead necessarily to a referendum, were originally envisaged only for the total revision of the federal constitution. A change in 1891 made it possible to use them for the partial amendment of the constitution, but federal law still does not allow for popular initiatives on ordinary laws.

The laws of different cantons make varied provisions for referendums and popular initiatives, usually more far-reaching than those on the federal level. Since the movement toward democratization in the 1860s, every canton has had, in addition to referendums on their own constitutions and laws, budgetary referendums (*référendum financier*) of a sort unknown in federal law. They have also had provisions for popular initiatives both on constitutional changes and on proposed laws. In this chapter attention will be confined to the federal situation.

The Current Federal Situation

Swiss referendums are always mandatory, never consultative. If the people vote no, the text submitted to them cannot be put into force, and, in the rare cases where it is already in force, it must cease to have effect. The citizens give strict orders to the authorities, not mere advice. Swiss referendums are sometimes compulsory, sometimes optional, depending on their subject. When they are optional they are usually demanded by a fixed number of citizens within a certain period. Optional referendums cannot be ordered by the parliament (in contrast to the rule in some cantons) nor by the government. This is in sharp distinction to many other countries; in Switzerland the referendum is not an instrument of central authority.

[2] The 1848 constitution was submitted to cantonal referendums, and each canton followed its own laws to determine the will of the people. Some cantons organized popular votes, some provided for a vote of the cantonal parliament. Fifteen and a half cantons accepted the constitution, five and a half rejected it, and one canton submitted a conditional vote (which was not valid and had to be considered as a rejection). No exact figures on the voting are available.

Swiss referendums are most often instruments of delay. The referendum procedure has to be completed before the law in question comes into force. It is only on matters of urgency that the referendum has a canceling effect. In such cases, the procedure is carried out after the text has gone into force, and the issue is whether it shall be sustained or abrogated.

All changes of the federal constitution, whether they be total revisions (which are rare) or amendments (which are common) must be submitted to a referendum. For an amendment to take effect it must secure a double majority—that is, it must win the support of a majority of the votes cast in the country as a whole and also a majority of votes in more than half the twenty-two cantons.

The Federal Assembly (the Swiss parliament, which, like the U.S. Congress, is bicameral) legislates by passing laws and decrees of general application. There is no substantial difference between laws and decrees, at least since they were redefined by a 1962 law. They both lay down legally binding rules. The only distinction is that laws are timeless while decrees have a limited duration (for example, five years). All laws and decrees are liable to a referendum if, within ninety days of publication, 50,000 citizens sign a petition demanding one. If there is a referendum, the law or decree takes effect if it secures a majority of those who vote; a majority of cantons is not required, as it is for constitutional referendums.

The Federal Council, that is, the Swiss government, ratifies international treaties. But generally speaking it can ratify them only if they have been approved by the Federal Assembly. Under the 1977 rules, the decree of approval is subject to a referendum in the following cases: If the treaty involves joining a collective security organization such as the UN or a supranational community such as the European Economic Community (EEC), a referendum is compulsory, and a double majority of people and of cantons is required. If the treaty involves joining an international organization, such as the General Agreement on Tariffs and Trade or the European Free Trade Association, or subscribing to a multinational treaty standardizing law, or if the treaty is of long duration or of any sort that the Federal Assembly thinks suited to a popular vote, the decree of approval is subject to an optional referendum, in which only a majority of votes is required.

Decrees of general application which brook no delay can include an urgency clause on the vote of a majority of each of the two chambers. If the decree is for one year or less there can be no referendum. If it is for more than one year, a referendum can be demanded and, in the case of a negative vote, the decree will cease to have effect at the end of one year. The Federal Assembly can even, in case of urgency, adopt decrees which are not in conformity with the constitution (for example in areas outside federal competence). In such a case, if the decree is for more than one year, a referendum must take place and the decree lapses at the end of one year unless it has been confirmed by a double majority of people and cantons.

In federal law there are no provisions for referendums against estimates, against the budget, or against the ordinances of the Federal Council. Thus when parliament delegates legislative power to the government, there can be a referendum against the delegating law but not against the ordinances which are made under the authority of that law. On the other hand, in contrast to the case in most countries, laws on taxes and laws on the position of officials are subjects for referendum. Some tax rates are even laid down in the constitution, which means that they can be changed only by a compulsory referendum.

Popular Initiatives

A hundred thousand citizens can demand the revision of the constitution. The signatures, set out on a special form, must be collected within eighteen months (this rule was laid down only in 1978; previously there was no time limit). Generally speaking, initiatives are used for amendments to the constitution. The citizens put forward a full draft of the text of a new article or a new clause. The Federal Assembly cannot change anything in this draft but can put forward an alternative of its own. The initiative needs assent by the majority of the people and of the cantons—and the same applies to the counterproposal from the parliament.

Sometimes citizens decide to put forward a general proposition. If the Federal Assembly does not agree, there is a referendum based on a simple majority of people and not of cantons as well. If the Federal Assembly or the people agree to the proposition, the Assembly must prepare a bill which gives effect to it, and this bill is finally submitted to a referendum requiring a double majority.

If the initiative demands the total revision of the constitution there is always a preliminary vote of the people. If this vote is positive the Federal Assembly is dissolved, and a new Assembly is elected to draw up a constitution for submission to a vote of people and cantons. This cumbersome procedure has only been invoked once —in 1935 when the preliminary popular vote was negative.

Citizens cannot demand the adoption, the modification, or the abrogation of a law or a decree. This bar makes them turn to constitutional change. For example, if they want to increase the level of old-age pensions, they have to propose an amendment not to the law on social insurance (for that is forbidden) but to the article of the constitution which covers old-age pensions.[3]

Statistics

Between 1848 and August 31, 1978, the Swiss people have voted on 297 questions (see Table 3-1). There were 212 compulsory referendums. The laws, decrees, and treaties that could have been subject to an optional referendum number about 1,200 since 1874; 85 (7 percent) have in fact had referendums called on them.

Out of the 212 compulsory referendums there were 206 which required a double majority of the people as a whole and of the cantons: 199 where the two majorities were in the same direction (107 double yes; 92 double no); five where the people said yes and the cantons said no (1866, 1955, 1970, 1973, 1975); and two where the people said no and the cantons said yes (1910, 1957); the other six were preliminary votes on popular initiatives. In each of the five cases where the cantons prevented a reform to which the people said yes, the question involved giving new powers to the federal government. For example, in 1970 the issue concerned taxing powers; in 1973 authority over education; and in 1975 powers of economic management (on this occasion the votes were 540,000 yes and 490,000 no, but the cantons were eleven yes and eleven no, which blocked the change).

Between 1848 and April 30, 1978, there were about 125 popular initiatives. Seventy-four of these were put to a referendum and seven have been accepted, the last being in 1949. Of the remaining fifty-two, two were declared void (in 1955 because the proposal

[3] The system rests on the following rules:

(a) Constitution

Article 123: Referendum on constitutional revision (1874)
Article 89 II: Referendum on laws and decrees of general application (1874)
Article 89 III, IV, V: Referendum on international treaties (revised 1977)
Article 89 *bis*: Urgent decrees (revised in 1949, following a popular initiative)
Articles 120 and 121: Popular initiatives leading to constitutional revision (revised in 1891)

The number of signatures required to secure a referendum or a popular initiative was increased in 1977 to 50,000 and 100,000 respectively.

(b) Laws

The main provisions covering referendums and initiatives were consolidated in a law of December 17, 1976. The parliamentary procedure covering these matters falls under a law on the relations between the chambers of the Federal Assembly and the government of March 23, 1962.

TABLE 3-1

SWISS REFERENDUMS, 1848 TO MAY 31, 1978

Referendum	*Vote* No	Yes
Total revision of the constitution		
Parliamentary proposals	1 (1872)	1 (1874)
Popular initiative	1 (1935)	0
Amendment of the constitution[a]		
Parliamentary proposals	30	77
Popular initiatives		
Full texts	61	7
General proposals	5	0
Parliamentary counterproposals to initiatives	7	11
Urgency decrees in breach of constitution	0	11
Referendums on laws and decrees (optional)	49	33
Referendums on international treaties (optional)[b]	2	1
Total	156	141

[a] The entry in the League of Nations (1920) and approval for the free trade agreement with the EEC (1972) are treated as amendments to the constitution.

[b] The refusal of a contribution to the International Development Association is regarded as a referendum on a treaty. The new rules for referendums on international questions, established in 1977, have not yet taken effect.

SOURCE: *Feuille Fédérale.* The years from 1848 to 1974 are covered by *Lois et arrêtés fédéraux soumis au référendum, Arrêtés urgents, Initiatives populaires, Votations* (Bern: Chancellerie, 1974).

could not be put into force, and in 1977 because there was no coherence in the issues involved). Forty were withdrawn before the referendum, and a dozen were still pending in April 1978.

The federal parliament has put forward eighteen counterproposals. In seven cases the initiative was then withdrawn but in eleven cases it was pursued. In one of these eleven cases the initiative won against the counterproposal (in 1920 over gambling houses); in six cases the counterproposal was successful; in four cases both initiative and counterproposal were rejected (1955, 1974, 1976, and 1977).

Participation in Referendums. The record of turnout in Switzerland is low, much lower than in neighboring countries where, of course, they have to vote much less frequently. Moreover, the average percentage of those voting has declined over the years:

1880–1913	58 percent
1914–1944	61 percent
1945–1959	54 percent
1960–1969	43 percent
1970–1978	42 percent.

Turnout has exceeded 80 percent on only five occasions: in 1872 and 1874 (over total revisions of the 1848 constitution); 1922 (a wealth tax); 1933 (a cut in civil service salaries); and 1935 (a new economic policy proposed by the Socialists). Turnout has also been falling in elections to the lower chamber, however, dropping from 80 percent in 1919 to 52 percent in 1975.

A Short Political Analysis. It is not possible here to analyze 297 popular votes. But some general observations are worth making, and some examples can be explored in more detail. From the results already set out, one can draw three simple lessons.

1. Votes on proposals from the parliament have usually been positive. Obligatory referendums on parliamentary proposals, counter-proposals, and urgency decrees have produced 100 yes and 38 no votes (or 104 yes and 34 no votes in terms of a majority popular vote as distinct from a majority of cantons). This is easily explained. Parliament is dealing with bills which it knows will be subject to a popular vote, and it prepares them with appropriate prudence, seeking the good will of voters through compromises and by offering guarantees. Moreover, their anxiety to secure a favorable vote leads the federal parliament to redraft passages at length. To satisfy everyone, one must not be brief; one must go into detail. For example, when a constitutional amendment is intended to give more power to the federal government, rather than putting forward a general clause, parliament may prefer to list detailed areas for fear of upsetting the entrenched defenders of cantonal rights (known in Switzerland as "federalists"). This is what happened over hydroelectric power (article 24 *bis* of 1975). Sometimes parliament, as a constitutional tactic, arranges a complete legislative program in such a way that citizens know in advance what the federal legislators plan to do with their increased powers. This is what happened over old-age pensions (article 34 *quater* of 1972).

2. Votes which are demanded over parliamentary proposals, laws, decrees, or treaties under the optional referendum procedures

are more often negative than positive—51 no and only 34 yes. This, too, is easily understandable, but the figures need to be compared with the total number of laws and decrees—1,200—which could have been subject to a referendum. In other words, 1,100 of these 1,200 laws and decrees were so devised that it was not possible to find 50,000 people (formerly 30,000) to attack them—strong evidence of the prudence of parliament in not provoking opposition. When opposition does materialize into a demand for a referendum, it is a sign of ill temper in a section of the population. The referendum therefore has a strong chance of being negative, and three times out of five (51 times out of 85) the law in question has been rejected.

3. Votes which arise from popular initiatives are almost always negative. There have been 67 no and 7 yes votes (or 66 no and 8 yes, if allowance is made for the negative vote of the cantons over one popularly voted initiative in 1955). Such an outcome is predictable because the proposition comes from a minority. If the issue were a popular one, parliament would already have taken action without being pushed from outside. What is proposed lacks the agreement of the federal parliament. Of course the federal parliament is not an exact reflection of public opinion, and it is conceivable that it would oppose a popular proposal. But it is in fact a rare phenomenon—the last case of a successful initiative was in 1949. One reason is that usually initiatives are over progressive issues (reduction of the work week, lowering the age of retirement, taxes on wealth, rights of conscientious objectors, bans on the export of arms, ecological safeguards), and the majority of the people are even more conservative than the parliament. That is why so many initiatives put forward by minorities get only minority support in the final referendum. Although they sometimes get respectable support (40 to 45 percent) they are nevertheless almost always rejected. But that does not mean that they have no effect. Often they provoke counterproposals or legislative reforms which at least partially satisfy their authors.

Political Parties

To understand the way in which the Swiss have used referendums it is necessary to give a brief summary of the Swiss party system. In the nineteenth century there was one dominant party, the Radical party, and a Catholic Conservative opposition which defended the rights of cantons. The creation of the federal state in 1848 and the reinforcement of federal powers in 1874 was imposed by the Radicals on the Conservatives. The Socialist party developed around 1900 and became one of the big parties after World War I. At the same time an Agrarian party separated from the Radicals. In the 1920s, as in so many European countries, a Communist party was set up to the left of the Socialists. In 1935 the Independent Alliance was formed, primarily to defend the interests of consumers. Finally, around 1970, the presence of numerous foreigners, particularly Italians, on Swiss soil (more than a sixth of the population) led to the creation of small nationalist parties such as the Republican Movement and Action Nationale. Three big parties have regularly received 20 to 25 percent of the numerical vote in elections to the National Council since 1919 when proportional representation was introduced: the Radical party, the Christian Democratic party, and the Socialist party. The Democratic Center Union (the former Agrarian party) is a moderate party with 10 to 12 percent of the vote. The independents get between 5 and 8 percent of the vote. The Communist party is weaker than in France or Italy and, except in 1947, has never won more than 2.5 percent of the vote. The nationalist parties seem to have had only a short-lived success—5.5 percent in 1971 and 3 percent in 1975.

Political Parties and Direct Democracy. In the nineteenth century the referendum was of great use to the Catholic Conservative party, which used it extensively. The party systematically opposed constitutional amendments and regularly demanded votes on laws (more than twenty times between 1874 and 1900). The results were often negative, and the party became an increasingly large political force. In 1891 the Radicals allowed them one place in the seven-man government; in 1920 they secured a second federal councillor.

After World War I the Socialist party turned to referendums as well as to initiatives. It succeeded in getting several negative votes on laws. When it entered the government in 1944, however, it was through special circumstances (the climate of the "sacred union") rather than through the use of direct democracy.

Since the middle of the century there have been parties, especially the independents and later the nationalists, which have instigated popular votes. The independents have objected successfully to several protectionist measures; the nationalists have three times unsuccessfully demanded the repatriation of foreign workers. The Socialists and the Communists have also launched several initiatives on taxes, on social security, and on rents. But these initiatives have never won electoral endorsement.

Appeals to the people originate less often with the parties than used to be the case. The larger parties are united in government: since 1960 there have been two Radicals, two Christian Democrats, two Socialists, and one Center Democrat in the Federal Council. Switzerland no longer has a clear and solid opposition as it used to with the Catholic Conservatives and the Socialists. Demands for referendums and initiatives now have very diverse origins: trade unions, interest groups (tenants, craftsmen, traders, farmers, car owners), federalists determined to preserve cantonal autonomy against centralization (especially in French-speaking areas), ecological associations, feminist movements, students, sometimes even a firm that has the means to organize the collection of signatures and to mount a referendum campaign (such as the Migros Cooperative or Maison Denner).

Weakness of the Political Parties. Sometimes laws or decrees which have the support of the big parties and even of some of the small parties secure a majority only with the greatest difficulty or even actually get rejected. The establishment does not always win. That is understandable enough. In the whole electorate, perhaps 5 percent are militant supporters and 20 percent are "sympathizers" with one of the three big parties. At least half the electors who actually vote have no links with any party. They have little affection for constituted authority—even some scorn. When they feel that their personal interests are threatened (and plenty of laws impose taxes or restrictions on them), they do not hesitate to vote no, without bothering about the fact that the parties are recommending the law and without making any effort to fit it into a more general framework. It is particularly difficult to get tax laws accepted. The people have even on occasion voted the federal government new functions and then refused the financial means to carry them out.

Defects of the Referendum

A common criticism of the referendum is that it increases the influence of pressure groups and gives them a particularly effective weapon. In a representative democracy pressure groups have only limited means of giving weight to their demands—financial promises and threats about the next elections. With referendums it is different. The big economic power blocs, which are consulted in the preparation of laws, let it be known that if their wishes are not met they will campaign against the law. The legislators are well aware that if the group has a large number of members, their votes cannot be ignored.

In other words, the most successful referendums are those which do not take place. The circles which might have fought the law do not do so because it contains what they want. This is the explanation for the compromise character of a large part of federal legislation; parliament does not make laws in a sovereign way but always under the threat of a referendum.

The referendum in Switzerland has other snags. It is often accused of dealing with complicated matters. The questions put in Switzerland are seldom as simple as those posed by General de Gaulle: Are you for or against the independence of Algeria? Are you for or against the election of the president by the people? Switzerland has sometimes voted on such questions as women's suffrage (1959, 1971) and the liberalization of abortion (1977), but many laws and decrees are more complicated matters of economic policy, agricultural policy, taxation, or social security.

The interpretation of referendum results is not easy, particularly when they are negative. A law may be rejected for a number of very different and even contradictory reasons. In the case of the value-added tax, which the government tried to introduce in 1977 but which was defeated, some voted no because they wanted the federal government to cut down on expenditure; others because they thought it right in a period of slump to turn to borrowing; others because they regarded indirect taxes as unjust. When the causes of defeat are so varied it is difficult to know whether to try again and in what way.

Some Swiss think that they have to vote too often. For federal referendums alone there are votes every three months and almost always on three or four questions. Added to these are the (less frequent) votes in cantons and communes and, of course, ordinary elections.

Advantages of Direct Democracy

But direct democracy has great advantages. It allows all citizens who so desire to express their opinion on the laws that are going to apply to them and thus, in some measure, to guide their own destiny. They cannot, in fact, vote on everything. Unless they decide to change the economic regime, Swiss voters do not vote on their salaries nor on private investment policy nor on the exchange rate of the Swiss franc, undoubtedly matters which affect them greatly. They do not even vote on the whole of Swiss legislation; only a minority of laws provoke demands for a referendum. Nonetheless the list of questions voted upon is impressive (see Table 3-2), and the most interesting and fundamental issues have, on the whole, emerged from popular initiatives.

TABLE 3-2

SWISS REFERENDUMS FROM 1866 TO MAY 1978

				Yes Vote		
Type [a]	*Date*	*Subject*	*Success or Failure*	Percent of voters	Cantons	*Percent Turnout*
1A	14 Jan. 1866	Weights and measures	F	50.4	9½	—
2A	14 Jan. 1866	Equality for Jews	S	53.2	12½	—
3A	14 Jan. 1866	Suffrage in communal matters	F	43.0	8	—
4A	14 Jan. 1866	Taxation of established citizens	F	39.9	9	—
5A	14 Jan. 1866	Suffrage in cantonal matters	F	48.0	10	—
6A	14 Jan. 1866	Religious liberty	F	49.1	11	—
7A	14 Jan. 1866	Exclusion of certain punishments	F	34.2	6½	—
8A	14 Jan. 1866	Copyright	F	43.6	9½	—
9A	14 Jan. 1866	Prohibition of lotteries	F	44.0	9½	—
10A	12 May 1872	Total revision of the constitution	F	49.5	9	—
11A	19 Apr. 1874	Total revision of the constitution	S	63.2	14½	—
12D	23 May 1875	Civil status and marriage	S	51.0	—	—
13D	23 May 1875	Voting rights act	F	49.4	—	—
14D	23 Apr. 1876	Bank notes	F	38.3	—	—
15D	9 July 1876	Tax of compensation for military duty	F	45.8	—	—
16D	21 Oct. 1877	Labor in factories	S	51.5	—	—
17D	21 Oct. 1877	Tax of compensation for military duty	F	48.4	—	—

18D	21 Oct. 1877	Voting rights act	F	38.1	—	—
19D	19 Jan. 1879	Subvention to a private railway	S	72.9	—	61.9
20A	18 May 1879	Death penalty	S	52.5	14	60.4
21B	31 Oct. 1880	Monopoly of bank notes	F	31.8	4½	60.3
22A	30 July 1882	Protection of inventions	F	47.5	7½	51.6
23D	30 July 1882	Epidemics	F	21.1	—	51.6
24D	26 Nov. 1882	Primary school	F	35.1	—	76.3
25D	11 May 1884	Organization of the Department of Justice	F	41.1	—	60.1
26D	11 May 1884	Tax on commercial traveler's license	F	47.9	—	60.1
27D	11 May 1884	Criminal code	F	44.0	—	60.1
28D	11 May 1884	Subvention to the Swiss embassy in U.S.	F	38.5	—	60.1
29A	25 Oct. 1885	Inns and alcohol	S	59.4	15	60.4
30D	15 May 1887	Federal monopoly of liquor	S	65.8	—	62.5
31A	10 July 1887	Protection of inventions	S	77.9	20½	42.4
32D	17 Nov. 1889	Bankruptcy act	S	52.9	—	70.9
33A	26 Oct. 1890	Health and accident insurance	S	75.4	20½	59.8
34D	15 Mar. 1891	Law on pensions	F	20.8	—	68.7
35A	5 July 1891	Popular initiative	S	60.3	18	49.3
36A	18 Oct. 1891	Monopoly of bank notes	S	59.3	14	61.9
37D	18 Oct. 1891	Customs tariff	S	58.0	—	61.9
38D	6 Dec. 1891	Nationalization of a railway	F	31.1	—	64.3
39B	20 Aug. 1893	Slaughtering of cattle	S	60.1	11½	49.1
40A	4 Mar. 1894	Legislation on professions	F	46.1	7½	46.7
41 B	3 June 1894	Right to work	F	19.8	0	57.6

TABLE 3-2—Continued

				Yes Vote		
Type [a]	*Date*	*Subject*	*Success or Failure*	Percent of voters	Cantons	*Percent Turnout*
42B	4 Nov. 1894	Sharing of customs income	F	29.3	8½	72.9
43D	3 Feb. 1895	Diplomatic service	F	41.2	—	46.3
44A	29 Sept. 1895	Monopoly of matches	F	43.2	7½	48.6
45A	3 Nov. 1895	Total centralization of the army	F	42.0	4½	66.5
46D	4 Oct. 1896	Warranties in cattle trading	F	45.5	—	57.6
47D	4 Oct. 1896	Accountability of the railways	S	55.8	—	57.6
48D	4 Oct. 1896	Disciplinary punishments in the army	F	19.9	—	57.6
49D	28 Feb. 1897	Federal Bank	F	43.3	—	64.7
50A	11 July 1897	Streams and forests	S	63.5	16	38.5
51A	11 July 1897	Control of food products	S	65.1	18½	38.5
52D	20 Feb. 1898	National railways	S	67.9	—	78
53A	13 Nov. 1898	Unification of the civil law	S	72.2	16½	53.5
54A	13 Nov. 1898	Unification of the criminal law	S	72.3	16½	53.5
55D	20 May 1900	Health, accident, and military insurance	F	30.2	—	66.7
56B	4 Nov. 1900	Proportional election of the National Council	F	40.8	10½	59
57B	4 Nov. 1900	Election of the Federal Council	F	35.0	8	59
58A	23 Nov. 1902	Subventions for public primary schools	S	76.3	21½	46.6

59D	15 Mar. 1903	Customs tariff	S	59.6	—	73.2
60D	25 Oct. 1903	Military criminal law	F	30.8	—	53.2
61B	25 Oct. 1903	Seats on the National Council	F	24.4	4	53.3
62A	25 Oct. 1903	Sale of liquor	F	40.7	4	53.1
63A	19 Mar. 1905	Protection of inventions	S	70.4	21½	40
64D	10 June 1906	Food sales act	S	62.6	—	51.4
65D	3 Nov. 1907	Organization of the army	S	55.2	—	74.6
66A	5 July 1908	Legislation on professions	S	71.5	21½	48.7
67B	5 July 1908	Ban on absinthe	S	63.5	20	49.3
68C	25 Oct. 1908	Legislation on water powers	S	84.4	21½	48.2
69B	23 Oct. 1910	Proportional election of the National Council	F	47.5	12	62.3
70D	4 Feb. 1912	Health and accident insurance	S	54.4	—	64.3
71A	4 May 1913	Human and animal diseases	S	60.3	16½	36
72A	25 Oct. 1914	Administrative court	S	62.3	18	44
73A	6 June 1915	War tax	S	94.3	22	56
74A	13 May 1917	Stamp tax	S	53.2	14½	42.1
75B	2 June 1918	Federal income tax	F	45.9	7½	65.4
76B	13 Oct. 1918	Proportional election of the National Council	S	68.8	19½	49.6
77A	4 May 1919	Navigation	S	83.6	22	53.9
78A	4 May 1919	New war tax	S	65.1	20	53.7
79A	10 Aug. 1919	Dissolution of the National Council	S	71.6	21½	32.8
80D	21 Mar. 1920	Labor conditions	F	49.8	—	60.3

TABLE 3-2—Continued

Type [a]	*Date*	*Subject*	*Success or Failure*	*Yes Vote*		*Percent Turnout*
				Percent of voters	Cantons	
81B	21 Mar. 1920	Gambling houses	S	51.0	14	60.5
82C	21 Mar. 1920	Gambling houses	F	20.3	½	60.5
83A	16 May 1920	Entry to the League of Nations	S	56.3	11½	77.5
84D	31 Oct. 1920	Working time in public transports	S	57.1	—	68.1
85B	30 Jan. 1921	Referendum on treaties	S	71.4	20	63.1
86B	30 Jan. 1921	Abolition of military justice	F	33.6	3	63.1
87A	22 May 1921	Legislation on cars and cycles	S	59.8	15½	38.5
88A	22 May 1921	Aviation	S	62.2	20½	38.4
89B	11 June 1922	Naturalization	F	15.9	0	45.6
90B	11 June 1922	Expulsion of foreigners	F	38.1	0	45.6
91B	11 June 1922	Civil servants in the National Council	F	38.4	5	45.6
92D	24 Sept. 1922	Federal criminal law	F	44.6	—	70.3
93B	3 Dec. 1922	Capital tax	F	13.0	0	86.3
94B	18 Feb. 1923	Internal security act	F	11.0	0	53.2
95F	18 Feb. 1923	Free trade convention	F	18.5	—	53.4
96B	15 Apr. 1923	Customs system	F	26.8	½	65.8
97A	3 June 1923	Legislation on liquor	F	42.2	10	64.6
98D	17 Feb. 1924	Labor legislation (amendment)	F	42.4	—	77.0

99B	24 May 1925	Old-age and sickness insurance	F	42.0	6	68.3
100A	25 Oct. 1925	Status of foreigners	S	62.2	18½	68.0
101A	6 Dec. 1925	Old-age and sickness insurance	S	65.4	16½	63.1
102A	5 Dec. 1926	Supply of cereals	F	49.6	8	72.7
103A	15 May 1927	Subventions for alpine roads	S	62.6	21	55.3
104D	15 May 1927	Traffic law	F	40.1	—	57.8
105A	20 May 1928	Naturalization	S	70.6	19½	45.2
106B	2 Dec. 1928	Gambling houses	S	51.9	14½	55.5
107B	3 Mar. 1929	Supply of cereals	F	2.7	0	67.3
108C	3 Mar. 1929	Supply of cereals	S	66.3	21	67.3
109D	3 Mar. 1929	Customs tariff	S	66.4	—	67.3
110B	12 May 1929	Federal traffic law	F	37.2	3	65.0
111B	12 May 1929	Prohibition (liquor)	F	32.7	½	66.4
112A	6 Apr. 1930	Legislation on liquor	S	60.6	17	75.7
113C	8 Feb. 1931	Prohibition of decorations	S	70.2	17	41.8
114A	15 Mar. 1931	Seats on the National Council	S	53.9	13½	53.4
115A	15 Mar. 1931	Term of federal mandates	S	53.7	16	53.4
116D	6 Dec. 1931	Old-age pensions act	F	39.7	—	78.1
117D	6 Dec. 1931	Taxation of tobacco	F	49.9	—	78.1
118D	28 May 1933	Salary of federal employees (reduction)	F	44.9	—	80.5
119D	11 Mar. 1934	Protection of law and order	F	46.2	—	78.9
120D	24 Feb. 1935	Military instruction	S	54.2	—	79.9
121D	5 May 1935	Diversion of traffic	F	32.3	—	63.2
122BE	2 June 1935	Measures against economic crisis	F	42.8	4	84.4

TABLE 3-2—Continued

Type [a]	*Date*	*Subject*	*Success or Failure*	*Yes Vote*		*Percent Turnout*
				Percent of voters	Cantons	
123B	8 Sept. 1935	Total revision of the constitution	F	27.7	—	60.9
124B	28 Nov. 1937	Prohibition of Freemasonry	F	31.3	1	64.6
125A	20 Feb. 1938	Romansh as fourth national language	S	91.6	22	54.3
126B	20 Feb. 1938	Modification of the optional referendum	F	15.2	0	54.3
127B	20 Feb. 1938	Private armaments industry	F	11.5	0	54.3
128C	20 Feb. 1938	Private armaments industry	S	68.8	22	54.3
129D	3 July 1938	Swiss criminal code	S	53.5	—	57.0
130A	27 Nov. 1938	Federal finances	S	72.3	21	60.3
131B	22 Jan. 1939	Extension of constitutional jurisdiction	F	28.9	0	46.6
132C	22 Jan. 1939	Abuse of the emergency clause	S	69.1	21	46.6
133A	4 June 1939	National defense and prevention of unemployment	S	69.1	19	54.7
134D	3 Dec. 1939	Status of civil servants	F	37.6	—	63.4
135D	1 Dec. 1940	Premilitary instruction	F	44.3	—	62.2
136B	9 Mar. 1941	Legislation on liquor	F	40.2	—	60.1
137B	25 Jan. 1942	Election of the Federal Council	F	32.4	0	61.9
138B	3 May 1942	Reorganization of the National Council	F	34.9	½	51.4
139D	29 Oct. 1944	Unfair competition	S	52.9	—	50.9

140D	21 Jan. 1945	National railways act	S	56.7	—	52.8
141C	25 Nov. 1945	Protection of the family	S	76.3	21½	55.5
142C	10 Feb. 1946	Coordination of public transport	F	33.6	1	65.2
143B	8 Dec. 1946	Right to work	F	19.2	0	51.3
144B	18 May 1947	Economic reforms/labor legislation	F	31.2	0	59.4
145A	6 July 1947	Economic articles	S	53.0	13	79.7
146D	6 July 1947	Old-age pension act	S	80.0	—	79.7
147D	14 Mar. 1948	Monopoly of sugar	F	36.2	—	56.5
148A	22 May 1949	Emission of bank notes	F	38.5	1½	61.0
149D	22 May 1949	Prevention of tuberculosis	F	24.8	—	61.0
150B	11 Sept. 1949	Direct democracy (emergency clause)	S	50.7	12½	42.5
151D	11 Dec. 1949	Status of federal officials	S	55.3	—	72.0
152D	29 Jan. 1950	State aid for housing construction	F	46.3	—	52.8
153A	4 June 1950	Federal finances	F	35.5	6	55.3
154B	1 Oct. 1950	Speculation on real estate and labor	F	27.0	0	43.7
155A	3 Dec. 1950	Seats on the National Council	S	67.3	20	55.7
156A	3 Dec. 1950	Federal taxes from 1951 to 1954	S	69.5	20	55.7
157D	25 Feb. 1951	Transport by automobile	F	44.3	—	52.4
158B	15 Apr. 1951	Emission of bank notes	F	12.3	0	53.1
159C	15 Apr. 1951	Emission of bank notes	S	68.1	22	53.1
160B	8 July 1951	Taxation of public enterprises	F	32.6	—	37.6
161D	2 Mar. 1952	Construction of new hotels	F	46.1	—	40.1
162D	30 Mar. 1952	Agriculture act	S	54.0	—	64.1
163B	20 Apr. 1952	Federal sales tax	F	19.0	0	49.1

TABLE 3-2—Continued

Type [a]	*Date*	*Subject*	*Success or Failure*	*Yes Vote*		*Percent Turnout*
				Percent of voters	Cantons	
164B	18 May 1952	Financing of armaments	F	43.7	4	53.9
165A	6 July 1952	Financing of armaments	F	42.0	3	44.2
166D	5 Oct. 1952	Tax on tobacco products	S	68.0	—	52.6
167D	5 Oct. 1952	Antiaircraft shelters	F	15.5	—	52.6
168A	23 Nov. 1952	Control of prices	S	62.8	16	56.4
169A	23 Nov. 1952	Supply of cereals	S	75.6	21½	56.4
170D	19 Apr. 1953	Postal tariff	F	36.5	—	52.7
171A	6 Dec. 1953	Federal finances	F	42.0	3	60.3
172A	6 Dec. 1953	Prevention of water pollution	S	81.3	22	59.1
173D	20 June 1954	Federal certificates of professional capacity	F	33.0	—	40.9
174D	20 June 1954	Aid for Swiss war victims	F	44.0	—	40.7
175A	24 Oct. 1954	Federal taxes from 1955 to 1958	S	70.0	21	46.8
176B	5 Dec. 1954	Protection of sites	F	31.2	1	51.9
177B	13 Mar. 1955	Consumers' and lessees' protection	F	50.2	7	55.5
178C	13 Mar. 1955	Consumers' and lessees' protection	F	40.6	8½	55.5
179A	4 Mar. 1956	Control of prices	S	77.5	22	48.7
180B	13 May 1956	Utilization of hydraulic forces	F	36.9	2½	52.1
181D	13 May 1956	State aid for a private enterprise	F	42.5	—	52.6

182A	30 Sept. 1956	Supply of cereals (amendment)	F	38.7	5½	44.0
183C	30 Sept. 1956	Referendum on expenses	F	45.5	9	43.8
184A	3 Mar. 1957	Civil defense	F	48.1	14	53.1
185A	3 Mar. 1957	Radio/TV legislation	F	42.8	10½	53.0
186A	24 Nov. 1957	Nuclear energy	S	77.3	22	45.5
187A	24 Nov. 1957	Supply of cereals	S	66.7	21½	45.5
188B	26 Jan. 1958	Misuse of economic power	F	25.9	0	51.8
189A	11 May 1958	Federal finances	S	54.6	17½	53.2
190A	6 July 1958	Cinema	S	61.3	20½	42.3
191C	6 July 1958	Highway system	S	85.0	21	42.4
192B	26 Oct. 1958	Forty-four-hour workweek	F	35.0	½	61.4
193A	7 Dec. 1958	Gambling in kursaals	S	59.9	20½	46.2
194F	7 Dec. 1958	Utilization of the Spöl River	S	75.2	—	46.4
195A	1 Feb. 1959	Women's suffrage	F	33.1	3	66.7
196A	24 May 1959	Civil defense	S	66.3	22	42.9
197A	29 May 1960	Control of prices	S	77.5	22	39.0
198D	4 Dec. 1960	Legislation on milk production	S	56.3	—	49.8
199A	5 Mar. 1961	Legislation on pipelines	S	71.4	22	62.8
200D	5 Mar. 1961	Taxes on motor fuel	F	46.5	—	63.3
201B	22 Oct. 1961	Legislative initiative	F	29.4	0	40.1
202D	3 Dec. 1961	Watch-making industry	S	66.7	—	45.8
203B	1 Apr. 1962	Nuclear arms prohibition	F	34.8	4	55.6
204A	27 May 1962	Nature and landscape protection	S	79.1	22	38.7
205D	27 May 1962	Salary of parliament members	F	31.7	—	38.7

TABLE 3-2—Continued

Type [a]	*Date*	*Subject*	*Success or Failure*	Yes Vote: Percent of voters	Yes Vote: Cantons	*Percent Turnout*
206A	4 Nov. 1962	Seats on the National Council	S	63.7	16	36.3
207B	26 May 1963	Nuclear arms	F	37.8	4½	48.8
208A	8 Dec. 1963	Federal finances	S	77.6	22	41.8
209A	8 Dec. 1963	Scholarships	S	78.5	22	41.7
210A	2 Feb. 1964	Fiscal amnesty	F	42.0	3½	44.3
211D	24 May 1964	Professional education	S	68.6	—	37.0
212A	6 Dec. 1964	Control of prices	S	79.5	22	39.2
213G	28 Feb. 1965	Limitation of credits	S	57.7	18½	59.7
214G	28 Feb. 1965	Limitation of construction	S	55.5	17	59.7
215D	16 May 1965	Milk and milk products	S	62.0	—	37.4
216A	16 Oct. 1966	Swiss abroad	S	68.1	22	47.9
217B	16 Oct. 1966	Fight against alcoholism	F	23.4	—	48.0
218B	2 July 1967	Speculation on real estate	F	32.7	1	37.9
219A	18 Feb. 1968	Fiscal amnesty	S	61.9	22	41.8
220D	19 May 1968	Fixed prices on tobacco products	F	48.2	—	36.9
221D	1 June 1969	Federal technical high school	F	34.5	—	33.9
222A	14 Sept. 1969	Town and country planning	S	55.9	19½	32.9
223D	1 Feb. 1970	Control of sugar	S	54.2	—	43.8

224B	7 June 1970	Foreigners, reduction of number	F	46.0	7	74.1
225A	27 Sept. 1970	Sports education	S	74.5	22	43.8
226B	27 Sept. 1970	Housing and family	F	48.9	8	43.8
227A	15 Nov. 1970	Federal finances	F	55.4	9	40.9
228A	7 Feb. 1971	Women's suffrage	S	65.7	15½	57.7
229A	6 June 1971	Protection of the environment	S	92.7	22	37.9
230A	6 June 1971	Federal finances	S	72.7	22	37.8
231B	5 Mar. 1972	Construction of lodgings	F	28.9	0	35.7
232C	5 Mar. 1972	Construction of lodgings	S	58.5	21	35.7
233A	5 Mar. 1972	Protection of lessees	S	85.4	22	35.7
234G	4 June 1972	Control of construction market	S	83.3	22	26.7
235G	4 June 1972	Defense of the Swiss money	S	87.7	22	26.7
236B	24 Sept. 1972	Exportation of arms	F	49.6	7	33.1
237B	3 Dec. 1972	Old-age and sickness pension (amendment)	F	15.6	0	52.9
238C	3 Dec. 1972	Old-age and sickness pension (amendment)	S	74.0	22	52.9
239A	3 Dec. 1972	Free trade agreement with the EEC	S	72.5	22	52.9
240A	4 Mar. 1973	Education	F	52.8	10½	27.5
241A	4 Mar. 1973	Scientific research	S	64.5	19	27.5
242A	20 May 1973	Repeal of the confessional articles	S	54.9	16½	40.3
243G	2 Dec. 1973	Prices and salary control	S	59.8	20	35.0
244G	2 Dec. 1973	Credits control	S	65.1	18½	35.0
245G	2 Dec. 1973	Control of the construction market	S	70.4	20	35.0

TABLE 3-2—Continued

Type [a]	*Date*	*Subject*	*Success or Failure*	*Yes Vote*		*Percent Turnout*
				Percent of voters	Cantons	
246G	2 Dec. 1973	Limit to amortization allowance	S	68.0	19½	35.0
247A	2 Dec. 1973	Protection of animals	S	84.0	22	35.0
248B	20 Oct. 1974	Foreigners, reduction of number	F	34.2	0	70.3
249A	8 Dec. 1974	Federal finances	F	44.4	4	39.6
250A	8 Dec. 1974	Brake to federal expenses	F [b]	67.0	22	39.5
251B	8 Dec. 1974	Health insurance	F	26.7	0	39.7
252C	8 Dec. 1974	Health insurance	F	32.1	0	39.7
253A	2 Mar. 1975	Economic policy	F	52.7	11	28.4
254A	8 June 1975	Federal finances	S	56.0	17	36.8
255G	8 June 1975	Defense of the Swiss money	S	85.5	22	36.8
256A	8 June 1975	Brake to federal expenses	S	75.9	22	36.8
257D	8 June 1975	Customs tariff, fuel	F	48.2	—	36.8
258D	8 June 1975	Financing of the highway system	S	53.5	—	36.8
259A	7 Dec. 1975	Freedom of domicile/social assistance	S	75.6	22	30.9
260A	7 Dec. 1975	Legislation on water resources	S	77.5	21	30.9
261D	7 Dec. 1975	Import and export of agricultural products	S	52.0	—	31.1
262B	21 Mar. 1976	Workers participation	F	32.4	0	39.4
263C	21 Mar. 1976	Workers participation	F	29.6	0	39.4

264B	21 Mar. 1976	More equal taxes	F	42.2	—	39.3
265A	13 June 1976	Compulsory unemployment insurance	S	68.3	21	34.5
266D	13 June 1976	Town and country planning	F	48.9	—	34.6
267F	13 June 1976	Loan to International Development Association	F	43.6	—	34.5
268A	26 Sept. 1976	Radio/TV legislation	F	43.3	3½	33.5
269B	26 Sept. 1976	Federal liability insurance for cars	F	24.3	0	33.5
270G	5 Dec. 1976	Money and credit policy	S	70.3	22	44.8
271G	5 Dec. 1976	Control of prices	S	82.0	22	45.1
272B	5 Dec. 1976	Forty-hour workweek	F	22.0	0	45.2
273B	13 Mar. 1977	Foreigners, reduction of number	F	29.5	0	45.2
274B	13 Mar. 1977	Naturalization of foreigners	F	33.8	0	45.2
275B	13 Mar. 1977	Referendum on international treaties	F	21.9	0	45.0
276C	13 Mar. 1977	Referendum on international treaties	S	61.0	20½	45.0
277A	12 June 1977	Introduction of value-added tax	F	40.5	1	50.0
278A	12 June 1977	Harmonization of cantonal taxes	S	61.3	17½	49.9
279B	25 Sept. 1977	Protection of lessees	F	42.2	3½	51.6
280C	25 Sept. 1977	Protection of lessees	F	41.2	1½	51.6
281B	25 Sept. 1977	Air pollution from cars	F	39.0	1½	51.7
282A	25 Sept. 1977	Number of signatures for a referendum	S	57.8	18	51.6
283A	25 Sept. 1977	Number of signatures for an initiative	S	56.7	19	51.6
284B	25 Sept. 1977	Free abortion during the first twelve weeks	F	48.3	7	51.9
285B	4 Dec. 1977	Higher taxes on big incomes	F	44.4	2½	38.3
286A	4 Dec. 1977	Civil service	F	37.6	0	38.1

TABLE 3-2—Continued

Type [a]	*Date*	*Subject*	*Success or Failure*	*Yes Vote*		*Percent Turnout*
				Percent of voters	Cantons	
287D	4 Dec. 1977	Exercise of political rights	S	93.7	—	38.1
288D	4 Dec. 1977	Balanced federal finances	S	62.4	—	38.2
289B	26 Feb. 1978	Democracy in highway construction	F	38.7	0	48.2
290B	26 Feb. 1978	Age of retirement	F	20.6	0	48.3
291A	26 Feb. 1978	Economic policy	S	68.4	22	48.0
292D	26 Feb. 1978	Old-age pension act (ninth revision)	S	65.6	—	48.3
293D	28 May 1978	Summer time	F	47.9	—	48.8
294D	28 May 1978	Customs tariff	S	54.8	—	48.8
295D	28 May 1978	Abortion act	F	31.2	—	48.8
296D	28 May 1978	University and research act	F	43.4	—	48.8
297B	28 May 1978	Twelve Sundays a year without motor traffic	F	36.3	0	48.8

Dash (—): Data not available.

[a] Types of vote:
- A: Constitutional decree
- B: Popular initiative
- C: Counterproposal of parliament
- D: Law (optional referendum)
- E: Referendum whether to revise the constitution completely or not
- F: Treaty
- G: Urgent decree deviating from the constitution

[b] Must be considered as refused because it was linked with 249.

SOURCE: Compiled by Mathias Adank, Chur (Grisons), master of law of the University of Neuchâtel, Switzerland.

Referendums force citizens to learn about the business of the state. Admittedly few enough do so—perhaps only 5 to 10 percent make a serious attempt to inform themselves from the press, radio, and television. But that means that 200 or 300 thousand people do actually study public affairs instead of just glancing at election manifestos.

The referendum also provides a good way for cantons to defend themselves against federal legislation that is regarded as too centralizing. In 1874 referendums over laws were provided as compensation for the extension of federal competence. The federal legislator could make more laws, but the citizens of the cantons could block them.

Conclusion

The composition of the Federal Assembly has varied little since 1919. Three major parties share three-quarters of the seats in the National Council, and proportional representation minimizes change. It is normal for the three parties to gain or lose half a dozen seats at most. Moreover, since 1960 the political composition of the Federal Council has been proportionate to that of the National Council. Thus regular elections have hardly any effect on the composition of either the Federal Assembly or the Federal Council. The elector chooses not between two programs but among a dozen programs often very little different from each other. Basically elections are about people.

The government prepares constitutional amendments and laws. Parliament discusses them. But the last word rests with the electors through the referendum. It is in referendums that electors express their political choices, decide on their economic system and their taxes, and draw their own line between capitalism and socialism.

Of course, laws and decrees submitted to referendum have the support of government—which is, after all, their prime author. The government takes part in the public debate and recommends that electors accept the law or decree. Similarly, with the initiative, there is a clear government lead, though in this case it is normally asking electors to vote no.

If the electors do not follow the government's advice, ministerial responsibility is not involved. Only three times in 94 hostile votes (156, less the 67 initiatives rejected, plus 5 of the 7 initiatives accepted) has a federal councillor, who was particularly involved, resigned because of the snub: in 1891, 1934, and 1953. On every other occasion the government has bowed to the electorate, changed its line, and continued in power. The referendum therefore does not constitute a motion of censure.

Switzerland, then, is the home of the referendum. It is the country that has used referendums most. It has made referendums an integral part of its political life. It has shown that, at least in a small, sophisticated country, direct democracy can work with almost none of the ill consequences which have been ascribed to it in political argument elsewhere. Switzerland provided the model on which American and other evangelists for direct democracy based their cases in the 1890s and 1900s. And the Swiss can claim that the original continues to work better than its imitators.

Bibliography

Aubert, Jean-François. *Traité de droit constitutionnel.* 2 vols. Neuchâtel and Paris, 1967.

Neidhart, Leonhard. *Plebiszit und Pluralitäre Demokratie.* Bern: Franke, 1970.

Ruffieux, Roland, ed. *La démocratie référendaire en Suisse.* vol. 1. *Analyse de cas.* Fribourg, Switzerland, 1972. Analysis of nos. 83; 56, 69, 76; 102, 107, 108; 99, 101, 116, 146.

Saladin, Peter. "Le référendum populaire en Suisse." *Revue internationale de droit comparé.* Paris, 1976, pp. 331–347.

See also the annual bibliographies in *Revue de droit suisse* (Swiss law review in German and French), Basel.

For the results of referendums see *Feuille Fédérale.* The years 1848–1974 are covered by *Lois et arrêtés fédéraux soumis au référendum, Arrêtés urgents, Initiatives populaires, Votations* (Bern: Chancellerie, 1974), with a supplement up to 1975; in French and German.

4
The United States of America

Austin Ranney

The United States is one of the very few democratic countries that has never had a referendum at the national level. Nevertheless, it rivals Switzerland as the nation with the most experience of referendums. Its states were early in the field with referendums to approve their constitutions, and in the Progressive era and since, they have been the scene of much experimentation with direct democracy.

In America the terms "referendum" and "initiative" are usually thought of as the two forms of direct legislation—a process by which ordinary voters to some degree control law making directly by their own votes rather than indirectly through the votes of their elected representatives. In the United States, as in the other polities considered in this book, the referendum is an arrangement whereby a measure that has been passed by a legislature does not go into force until it has been approved by the voters (in some specified proportion) in an election. The initiative, on the other hand, is an arrangement whereby any person or group of persons may draft a proposed law or constitutional amendment and, after satisfying certain requirements of numbers and form, have it referred directly to the voters for final approval or rejection. Thus the referendum enables the voters to accept or reject the legislature's proposals, while the initiative allows the voters both to make their own proposals and to pass upon the proposals of other voters.[1]

---

[1] For similar definitions, see William B. Munro, *The Initiative, Referendum and Recall* (New York, N.Y.: D. Appleton, 1912); and V. O. Key, Jr., and Winston W. Crouch, *The Initiative and the Referendum in California* (Berkeley, Calif.: University of California Press, 1939).

Origins of Constitutional Referendums

Extensive use of both forms of direct legislation has been made by the states of the American union for many years. Popular referendums on constitutional amendments proposed by state legislatures or constitutional conventions are the oldest and most often used form. Some commentators believe that in 1778 the commonwealth of Massachusetts became the first polity in history to use the constitutional referendum as we use the term in this book.[2]

Soon after the Declaration of Independence in 1776 declared the thirteen British colonies to be free and independent states, four of them—Connecticut, Massachusetts, New Hampshire, and Rhode Island—decided to replace their old colonial charters with new constitutions *and* to require that those constitutions should take effect only after they had been considered, voted upon, and approved by the states' voters. Massachusetts was the first to take action. In 1777 its legislature drew up a new constitution, directed that copies of it be delivered to all the state's town meetings for the citizens to discuss and vote on, and stipulated that the constitution would take effect only if it was approved by two-thirds of those voting. In 1778 the discussions and votes took place throughout the state, and when the towns' voting totals were cumulated in Boston it was learned that the legislature's proposal had been defeated by a margin of five to one. It was believed people objected in large part because it lacked a bill of rights and because it had been drawn up by an ordinary legislature rather than by a special constitutional convention. Thus the first American state constitutional referendum, like so many since, rejected a legislative proposal.

The Massachusetts legislature got the message. In 1779 they established a separate constitutional convention whose specially elected members proposed a new constitution that met most of the objections raised against the 1778 document. The new proposal was referred to the town meetings in 1780 and won the necessary two-thirds approval. It went into force immediately thereafter. The basic document, though altered considerably by 104 amendments since 1780,

[2] Direct democracy in the town meetings of Periclean Athens, the *Landsgemeinden* of certain Swiss cantons, and the town meetings in the New England states antedated the Massachussetts referendum by centuries. However, these pre-1778 procedures were not referendums as we are using the term. Their decisions were made only by citizens physically present at the decision sites and meeting face to face. In a modern referendum all citizens, no matter where they may be on the day of voting, may participate, and they do not all meet face to face.

remains in force today and is the oldest of the state constitutions still in force.[3]

New Hampshire was not far behind Massachusetts. In 1779 its legislature submitted a new constitution to the voters in the towns, but they rejected it for many of the same reasons the 1778 Massachusetts proposal had lost. In 1783 the New Hampshire legislature tried again, and this time the proposed constitution received the necessary two-thirds majority and went into effect in 1784. Other early users of constitutional referendums were the states of Rhode Island (1788), Maine (1816), Mississippi (1817), Connecticut (1818), and Alabama (1819).[4]

Present Status of Direct Legislation

Most states have used constitutional referendums from the very beginning of their establishment as states of the union. The other forms of direct legislation have grown more slowly (see Table 4-1). South Dakota (1898), Utah (1900), and Oregon (1902) pioneered the use of the initiative for constitutional amendments or ordinary legislation. Nineteen more states followed suit between 1906 and 1918. There was a long pause from 1918 to 1959, but since 1959 four more states have added the initiative.

The incidence of the four main forms of direct legislation—constitutional referendum, constitutional initiative, statutory referendum, and statutory initiative—in the American states as of January 1, 1978, is shown in Table 4-2. By far the most widespread form of direct legislation is the constitutional referendum. Delaware is the only one of the fifty states that does not submit proposed amendments to its constitution to the voters in constitutional referendums. Among the other forty-nine states, forty-five require approval by simple majorities of the votes cast on the proposed amendments.[5] Minnesota, Tennessee, and Wyoming require approval by pluralities equal to or greater than a majority of all persons casting valid votes on any other issue or office in the election held simultaneously with the constitutional referendum.[6] And New Hampshire

[3] See *The Book of the States, 1967–77* (Lexington, Ky.: Council of State Governments, 1976), table 1, p. 174; and Stanley Alderson, *Yea or Nay: Referendums in the United Kingdom* (London: Cassell, 1975), pp. 10-13.

[4] *Book of the States*, table 1; Samuel Robinson Honey, *The Referendum among the English* (London: Macmillan, 1912), pp. 38-56; and Philip Goodhart, *Referendum* (London: Tom Stacey, 1971), chap. 2.

[5] Hawaii and Nebraska require majorities equal to at least 35 percent of all votes cast in the election on all issues and offices.

[6] Illinois allows the option of approval by three-fifths of those voting on the proposed amendment.

TABLE 4-1
ADOPTION OF LEGISLATIVE INITIATIVE AND REFERENDUM IN THE UNITED STATES, BY STATE

State	*Year*
South Dakota	1898
Utah	1900
Oregon	1902
Oklahoma	1907
Maine, Missouri	1908
Arkansas, Colorado	1910
Arizona, California, Montana, New Mexico	1911
Idaho, Nebraska, Nevada, Ohio, Washington	1912
Michigan	1913
North Dakota	1914
Kentucky, Maryland	1915
Massachusetts	1918
Alaska	1959
Wyoming	1968
Illinois	1970
Florida	1972

SOURCE: *Initiative and Referendum: Its Status in Wisconsin and Experiences in Selected States,* Informational Bulletin 76-Ib-4 (Madison, Wis.: Legislative Reference Bureau, State of Wisconsin, 1976).

requires approval by two-thirds of the votes cast on each proposed amendment.

The second most widespread institution is the statutory referendum. Thirty-nine states have it in some form, and twenty-four have the most liberal version, one which requires a referendum whenever a stipulated number of voters submit a petition requesting one.

Third comes the statutory initiative, which operates in twenty-two states. Of these, fifteen use the more "progressive" direct version, whereby a petition places the proposed measure on the ballot for submission to the electorate without any legislative action. The other seven use the indirect version, which requires the legislature to act upon an initiated measure within a reasonable time before it is voted upon by the electorate. If the legislature fails to act within the

TABLE 4-2

TYPES OF DIRECT LEGISLATION IN THE UNITED STATES, 1978

Region and State	*Constitutional Amendment Initiative*	*Statutory Initiative*[a]	*Statutory Referendum*[b]	*Constitutional Referendum*[c]	*Local Government Referendums*[d]
New England					
Connecticut				MA	
Maine		I	P, L, C	MA	*
Massachusetts		I	P	MA	*
New Hampshire			L	⅔MA	
Rhode Island			C	MA	*
Vermont			L	MA	*
Middle Atlantic					
New York			C	MA	
New Jersey			L, C	MA	*
Pennsylvania			C	MA	*
South Atlantic					
Delaware[e]					
Florida	X	I	C	MA	*
Georgia			L, C	MA	*
Maryland			P, L	MA	*
North Carolina			L, C	MA	*
South Carolina			L, C	MA	*
Virginia			L, C	MA	*
West Virginia				MA	*
East North Central					
Illinois	X		L	MA	*
Indiana				MA	
Michigan	X	I	P, L, C	MA	*
Ohio	X	I	P, C	MA	*
Wisconsin			L, C	MA	*
West North Central					
Iowa			C	MA	*
Kansas			C	MA	*
Minnesota				ME	*
Missouri	X	D	P, L	MA	*
Nebraska	X	D	P	MA	*
North Dakota	X	D	P	MA	*
South Dakota		I	P	MA	*

TABLE 4-2—Continued

Region and State	*Constitutional Amendment Initiative*	*Statutory Initiative* [a]	*Statutory Referendum* [b]	*Constitutional Referendum* [c]	*Local Government Referendums* [d]
East South Central					
Alabama				MA	
Kentucky			P, C	MA	*
Mississippi				MA	
Tennessee				ME	
West South Central					
Arkansas	X	D	P	MA	*
Louisiana				MA	
Oklahoma	X	D	P, L, C	MA	*
Texas				MA	*
Mountain					
Arizona	X	D	P, L	MA	*
Colorado	X	D	P, L	MA	*
Idaho		D	P	MA	*
Montana		D	P, L	MA	*
Nevada	X	I	P	MA	*
New Mexico			P, C	MA	
Utah		D	P	MA	*
Wyoming		D	P, C	ME	*
Pacific					
Alaska		D	P	MA	*
California	X	D	P, C	MA	*
Hawaii				MA	
Oregon	X	D	P, L	MA	*
Washington		D	P, L, C	MA	*

[a] I = indirect, D = direct.

[b] P = by petition of the people, L = submitted by the legislature, C = constitutional requirement for certain measures.

[c] MA = approval by majority voting on amendment, ME = approval by majority of all voters in election.

[d] An asterisk (*) indicates that referendums are available to local governments on certain measures.

[e] Delaware has never held a referendum.

SOURCES: *The Book of the States, 1976–77* (Lexington, Ky.: Council of State Governments, 1976), table 2, p. 175; table 3, p. 176; table 6, pp. 216-217; table 7, p. 218; and Charles M. Price, "The Initiative: A Comparable State Analysis and Reassessment of a Western Phenomenon," *Western Political Quarterly*, vol. 28 (June 1975), p. 246.

specified period, or if it rejects the proposed measure, the measure is then put on the ballot at the next election for final acceptance or rejection by the voters.

The least common form of direct legislation is the constitutional initiative, whereby a petition places a proposed constitutional amendment on the ballot without legislative action. Fourteen states use such a device.

A glance at Table 4-2 shows that direct legislation is far more widespread in the western states than in the eastern. Of the eight states with only the constitutional referendum, only one is entirely west of the Mississippi River (which runs through both Louisiana and Minnesota); all fifteen states with the direct legislative initiative are in the West; and all ten states with the complete set of direct legislation devices are in the West. Charles Price offers an explanation for this regional pattern:

> It may well be that the initiative was able to catch on in at least some western states because the political institutions and channels for doing things were not as firmly rooted in tradition as they were in the eastern, southern and midwestern states. After all, the Progressive Movement swept the western states only a few decades after most had attained statehood.[7]

In the Localities. Table 4-2 also shows that thirty-nine states require or allow various units of local government to hold referendums on proposed local ordinances. They make full use of their powers. After a comprehensive survey of the use of local direct legislation, Howard Hamilton estimated that "the national volume of [local] referenda may be ten to fifteen thousand annually."[8] The most frequent contests in recent years have been those approving or rejecting proposals to issue local bonds and raise local taxes to expand public school facilities. There have also been frequent—and often bitterly fought—local referendums on the fluoridation of municipal water supplies, the adoption of ordinances prohibiting racial discrimination in the sale

[7] Charles M. Price, "The Initiative: A Comparative State Analysis and Reassessment of a Western Phenomenon," *Western Political Quarterly*, vol. 28 (June 1975), pp. 243-262, at p. 248. In Canada the populist-Progressive enthusiasm for direct legislation has also been confined mainly to the western provinces. New Brunswick and Quebec have never held referendums, and the number and subjects of those held in the other provinces are shown in Table 4-3.

[8] Howard D. Hamilton, "Direct Legislation: Some Implications of Open Housing Referenda," *American Political Science Review*, vol. 64 (March 1970), pp. 124-137, at p. 125. See also Howard D. Hamilton and Sylvan H. Cohen, *Policymaking by Plebiscite: School Referenda* (Lexington, Mass.: D.C. Heath, 1974).

TABLE 4-3

REFERENDUMS IN SEVEN CANADIAN PROVINCES

Country (No.)	Date	Subject
Alberta (7)	15 July 1915	Prohibition of liquor
	25 Oct. 1920	Prohibition of liquor
	5 Nov. 1923	Temperance act
	17 Aug. 1948	Ownership of power companies
	30 Oct. 1957	Additional outlet for sale of liquor
	23 May 1967	Daylight saving time
	30 Aug. 1971	Daylight saving time
British Columbia (2)	12 June 1952	Daylight saving time
	12 June 1952	Regulating sale of liquor
Manitoba (7)	23 July 1892	Prohibition of liquor
	2 Apr. 1902	Prohibition of liquor
	13 Mar. 1916	Temperance act
	22 June 1923	Government control of liquor sales
	11 July 1923	Amendments to temperance act
	28 June 1927	Three questions on sale of beer
	24 Nov. 1952	Marketing of coarse grains
Nova Scotia (2)	25 Oct. 1920	Regulation of liquor sales
	1929	Temperance act
Ontario (2)	1902	Prohibition of liquor
	1919	Temperance referendum act
Prince Edward Island (1)	28 June 1948	New temperance act
Saskatchewan (4)	11 Dec. 1916	Abolish liquor store situation
	21 Oct. 1920	Importation of liquor by export houses
	16 July 1924	Government liquor control
	19 June 1934	Sale of beer by the glass

of property, and the adoption of ordinances guaranteeing equal rights in employment and other matters to homosexuals. Social scientists have paid relatively little heed to these referendums, and they remain a rich and largely untapped source of data for studying the operation of direct legislation in America.[9]

In the National Government. Although the United States has never had a nationwide referendum or instituted any form of direct legislation, in 1977 a proposal to establish a national statutory initiative began to receive considerable attention. Senator James Abourezk (Democrat, South Dakota) introduced the first bill in the Senate, and Representatives Guy Vander Jagt (Republican, Michigan) and James Jones (Democrat, Oklahoma) introduced similar bills in the House of Representatives. The Abourezk bill proposed an amendment to the U.S. Constitution under which legislation on most subjects could be set before the voters by a popular petition. The petition would have to be signed by a number of voters equal to 3 percent of the ballots cast in the most recent presidential election (in 1978 the number would be 2,446,677), and it would also have to be signed by 3 percent of the voters in at least ten different states. The bill specifically exempted from action by initiative constitutional amendments, declarations of war, and calling up the militia. Any petition certified as valid by the secretary of state would be put on the ballot at the first congressional election after certification, and any proposal approved by a majority voting on it would become law thirty days after the election. For two years thereafter such a law could be repealed only by a two-thirds vote of the full membership of both houses of Congress, though after that it could be repealed by an ordinary congressional majority.

The Abourezk bill was pressed mainly by a small pressure group called Initiative America, founded in 1977 by Roger Telschow and John Forster, two young veterans of state initiative campaigns. Its prospects of immediate adoption by Congress were very slight, but a Gallup poll showed that 57 percent of the nation's adults favored it and only 21 percent opposed it, with the rest undecided. Some observers felt the proposal might eventually gain support from the same forces that were supporting such other extensions of the principles of direct democracy as the abolition of the electoral college and

[9] A sample of the few studies available in addition to Hamilton's include: William Gamson, "The Fluoridation Dialogue," *Public Opinion Quarterly*, vol. 25 (1961), pp. 526-537; Clarence Stone, "Local Referendums: An Alternative to the Alienated Voter Model," *Public Opinion Quarterly*, vol. 29 (1965), pp. 213-222; A. F. Carter and W. E. Savage, *Influence of Voter Turnout on School Board and Tax Elections* (Washington, D.C.: U.S. Office of Education, 1961); and John E. Mueller, "The Politics of Fluoridation in Seven California Cities," *Western Political Quarterly*, vol. 19 (March 1966), pp. 54-67.

the institution of a national direct primary.[10] Until that moment arrives, however, American experience with direct legislation will continue to take place entirely in the states and localities.

Usage and Electoral Success of Direct Legislation

Initiatives. Table 4-4 shows the number and electoral success of all referendums on statutory and constitutional measures initiated by popular petitions in each of the initiative states up to 1 January 1977. The data suggest several interesting patterns: The heaviest users of the initiative have been the states of Oregon (with a total of 207 measures voted on), California (159), North Dakota (137), Colorado (119), and Arizona (117). All are western states, as would be expected from the earlier discussion of the spread of direct legislation.

Many legal theorists hold that constitutions should be reserved for the basic authorizations of, procedures for, and limits on the exercise of governmental power, and that all other matters should be left to ordinary statutes. Whatever may be the merits of this position, it is clear that the citizens in the fourteen states using both statutory and constitutional initiatives have not agreed: they voted on almost as many constitutional initiatives (538) as statutory initiatives (553). Moreover, eight states (Arkansas, California, Colorado, Michigan, Missouri, Nebraska, Ohio, and Oklahoma) voted on *more* constitutional than statutory initiatives—often because the legal requirements for getting proposed constitutional amendments on the ballot were as easy or easier than those for proposed statutes.

Many theorists also hold that because constitutions deal (or should deal) only with the basic structures of government, they should change more slowly than ordinary laws. Similarly, proposals for constitutional amendments should be viewed with more caution than proposals for ordinary laws, and substantial doubt about their desirability should weigh more heavily against them than against ordinary laws. The states appear to have lived up to these ideals reasonably well: Only 34.5 percent of the constitutional initiatives were approved by the voters, as compared with 38.1 percent of the statutory initiatives. But even here the record is mixed: In four of the states (Massachusetts, Nebraska, Nevada, and North Dakota) constitutional proposals have fared much better than proposed statutes, and in four more (Arizona, California, Oklahoma, and Oregon) the two types of

[10] *Congressional Quarterly Weekly Report,* December 24, 1977, pp. 2653-2656. The Gallup poll is reported in the *Washington Post,* May 14, 1978, p. A17.

TABLE 4-4

INITIATIVE PROPOSITIONS SUBMITTED TO THE VOTERS, 1898–1976

	Statutes			*Constitutional Amendments*		
State	Number proposed	Number approved	Percent approved	Number proposed	Number approved	Percent approved
Alaska	6	3	50	0	0	0
Arizona	71	28	39	46	19	41
Arkansas	17	8	47	47	30	64
California	69	19	27	90	24	27
Colorado	48	21	44	71	20	28
Florida	0	0	0	1	1	100
Idaho	11	5	45	0	0	0
Illinois [a]	—	—	—	0	0	0
Maine	12	4	33	0	0	0
Massachusetts	26	11	42	2	2	100
Michigan	4	3	75	34	8	23
Missouri	14	5	36	30	7	23
Montana	26	15	58	2	1	50
Nebraska	9	1	11	15	7	47
Nevada	11	5	45	3	2	67
North Dakota	107	45	42	30	19	63
Ohio	6	2	33	38	8	21
Oklahoma	26	6	23	42	10	24
Oregon	119	39	33	88	28	32
South Dakota	19	2	11	0	0	0
Utah	6	2	33	0	0	0
Washington	78	37	47	0	0	0
Wyoming	0	0	0	0	0	0
Total	685	261	38	539	186	35

[a] Illinois has the constitutional initiative only.

SOURCE: Virginia Graham, *A Compilation of Statewide Initiative Proposals Appearing on Ballots through 1976* (Washington, D.C.: Congressional Research Service, Library of Congress, 1978).

proposals have enjoyed about the same rate of success. In a majority of the states using both types of initiatives, then, there is no reason to suppose that measures to change the constitution are approached more gravely or more suspiciously than measures to change the laws.

Table 4-5 classifies the two types of initiative proposals according to their subject. Both constitutional and statutory initiatives dealt most frequently with the nature of government and the political process. Some typical examples of such proposals are:

- Arizona, 1912, constitutional initiative to permit women's suffrage (succeeded, with 68 percent yes)
- Colorado, 1932, statutory initiative to reapportion the state legislature (succeeded, with 53 percent yes)
- Michigan, 1938, constitutional initiative to establish nonpartisan nominations and appointment of supreme court justices for eight-year terms (failed, with 40 percent yes).

TABLE 4-5

INITIATIVE MEASURES CLASSIFIED BY SUBJECT, 1898–1976

	Statutes		*Constitutional Amendments*		*Both*	
Subject	Number	Percent	Number	Percent	Number	Percent
Governmental and political processes	148	22	177	33	325	26
Public morality	102	15	69	13	171	14
Revenue, taxation, bonds	106	15	148	28	254	21
Regulation of business and labor	129	19	41	7	170	14
Health, welfare, and housing	72	10	35	6	107	9
Civil liberties and civil rights	23	3	15	3	37	3
Environmental protection and land use	68	10	16	3	84	7
Education	38	6	38	7	76	6
Total	685	100	539	100	1,224	100

SOURCE: Author's classification from descriptions given in Graham, *A Compilation of Statewide Initiative Proposals.*

Other topics included in this category were proposals to establish civil service merit systems, allow the use of voting machines, place or remove limits on the number of terms governors could serve, and so on. Proposals to alter governmental structures and political processes accounted for one-third of all constitutional initiatives and over one-fifth of all statutory initiatives.

In both types of initiatives together, measures on revenue, taxation, and bond issues were the second most frequent subject, accounting for 21 percent of all measures voted on. Some examples:

- Michigan, 1976, a constitutional initiative to remove the constitutional prohibition against a graduated income tax (failed, with 28 percent yes)
- Montana, 1926, statutory initiative to impose a gasoline tax of three cents per gallon for a fund to improve public roads (succeeded, with 61 percent yes)
- Oregon, 1972, constitutional initiative to prohibit the financing of public schools by real property taxes (failed, with 38 percent yes).

There have been some differences between the content of constitutional and statutory initiatives. For example, measures affecting revenue, taxation, and bonds account for 28 percent of constitutional initiatives but only 15.5 percent of statutory initiatives. On the other hand, measures regulating business and labor constitute 19 percent of statutory initiatives but only 7.5 percent of constitutional initiatives. Some samples from this category are:

- Arkansas, 1944, constitutional initiative to prohibit union membership as a precondition for employment (a right-to-work measure; it succeeded, with 55 percent yes)
- Massachusetts, 1976, statutory initiative to regulate electric utility charges and permit peak-load pricing (failed, with 25 percent yes)
- Montana, 1918, statutory initiative to authorize and regulate the practice of chiropractic (succeeded, with 54 percent yes).

The third most frequent subject for initiatives has been measures regulating public morals, which constitute 15 percent of statutory initiatives and 13 percent of constitutional initiatives. Some examples:

- Arizona, 1914, constitutional initiative to prohibit the sale of alcoholic beverages (succeeded, with 53 percent yes)

- California, 1964, constitutional initiative to establish a state lottery (failed, with 31 percent yes)
- North Dakota, 1972, statutory initiative to allow physicians to terminate pregnancies if they deem it desirable (failed, with 23 percent yes).

Since the early 1950s there has been a marked increase in initiative measures affecting civil liberties and civil rights. Some of the more notable examples include:

- Washington, 1975, statutory initiative to make the death penalty mandatory in cases of aggravated murder in the first degree (succeeded, with 68 percent yes)
- Colorado, 1976, constitutional initiative to repeal the constitutional guarantee of equal rights under law for women (failed, with 29 percent yes)
- Colorado, 1974, constitutional initiative to prohibit busing of pupils to achieve racial balance in public schools (succeeded, with 69 percent yes).

The most recent development has been an increase in initiatives on environmental protection, such as proposals to regulate or prohibit the development of nuclear power plants, to regulate the use of no-return food and beverage containers, and, perhaps best known of all, Colorado's 1972 constitutional initiative "to prohibit the State from levying taxes and appropriating or loaning funds for the purpose of aiding or furthering the 1976 Winter Olympic Games." The initiative succeeded, with 59 percent yes, and the games had to be transferred from Colorado to Innsbruck, Austria.

Referendums. The foregoing analysis of initiatives rests mainly on a comprehensive set of data collected by Virginia Graham of the Congressional Research Service of the Library of Congress.[11] No comparable collection has yet been made of data on referendums initiated by legislatures, and the disarray of some states' records makes such a compilation both costly and time-consuming. However, the secre-

[11] Virginia Graham, *A Compilation of Statewide Initiative Proposals Appearing on Ballots through 1976* (Washington, D.C.: Congressional Research Service, Library of Congress, 1978). For an analysis of the states' experience with the popular initiative that differs somewhat from that presented in the text, see Larry L. Berg, "The Initiative Process and Public Policy-Making in the States: 1904-1976," paper prepared for the annual meeting of the American Political Science Association, New York, 1978.

taries of state of some eighteen states have provided usable data. Their information on referendums, compared with that on initiatives summarized in Table 4-3, shows that voters have generally approved measures initiated by legislatures and constitutional conventions far more often than those initiated by popular petitions. The difference is 60.1 percent to 38.1 percent for statutory proposals, and 60.6 percent to 34.5 percent for constitutional proposals.

We have exactly comparable data for only those states that use both the initiative and the referendum, and these data are set out in Table 4-6. Once again it is plain that measures proposed by legis-

TABLE 4-6

RELATIVE SUCCESS OF STATE INITIATIVES AND REFERENDUMS

	Proposed by Legislatures			*Proposed by Popular Petitions*		
State	Number proposed	Number approved	Percent approved	Number proposed	Number approved	Percent approved
Statutory Proposals						
Alaska	4	2	50	6	3	50
Arizona	14	6	43	71	28	39
Idaho	4	3	75	11	5	45
Maine	124	89	72	12	4	33
Michigan	7	3	43	4	3	75
Montana	43	25	58	26	15	58
Nebraska	11	5	45	9	1	11
Ohio	16	3	19	6	2	33
Oklahoma	11	9	82	26	6	23
Oregon	35	18	51	119	39	33
Subtotal	269	163	61	290	106	37
Constitutional Proposals						
Arizona	105	67	64	46	19	41
Arkansas	79	37	47	56	27	48
California	476	294	62	90	24	27
Michigan	93	59	63	34	8	23
Nebraska	243	167	69	15	7	47
Ohio	113	74	65	38	8	21
Oklahoma	159	73	46	42	10	24
Oregon	238	138	58	88	28	32
Subtotal	1,506	909	60	409	131	32
Total, all proposals	1,775	1,072	60	699	237	34

SOURCE: Data on referendums supplied by secretaries of state; data on initiatives taken from Graham, *A Compilation of Statewide Initiative Proposals.*

latures or constitutional conventions are approved by the voters at a rate almost double that for measures proposed by initiative petitions. The only exceptions are the states of Michigan (statutes only), Ohio (statutes only), and Arkansas (constitutional amendments). Evidently, then, the voters in most states are far more likely to think well of a proposed new law or constitutional amendment if it has previously been considered and approved by their elected representatives than if it is solely the creature of an unofficial pressure group, whether it be regarded as a "special interest" or "public interest" group. This is entirely consonant with the view that direct legislation is not an alternative to representative democracy but, at most, a useful supplement to and check on its basic machinery.

Liberal or Conservative Outcomes? Much of the debate about the desirability of direct legislation in the United States continues to turn on the question of whether it is likely to produce mainly liberal or mainly conservative laws and constitutional amendments. A number of American conservatives believe that most ordinary Americans are basically conservative, but their policy preferences are systematically flouted by legislators, executives, and bureaucrats who are guided solely by the liberal-dominated mass media. Some of these conservatives despair of ever reforming the media or breaking its grip on public officials, and they hail direct legislation as a promising way for the people to bypass the irredeemably liberal officials and institute the conservative legislation the people long for. Some liberals agree with this diagnosis, though they recommend the opposite prescription: They believe that the people are indeed conservative and that direct legislation should be opposed for precisely that reason.[12]

On the other hand, the Abourezk proposal for a national initiative has been pressed mainly by liberals and environmentalists, such as Ralph Nader, Representative Michael J. Harrington, Senator Mark Hatfield, and Senator Abourezk himself. As we have seen, the main organized group pushing for the initiative is Initiative America, and

[12] Conservative writers who take this general view of the frustrated conservatism of ordinary voters in the 1970s include William Rusher, *The Making of the New Majority Party* (New York: Green Hill, 1975); Kevin Phillips, *Mediacracy: American Parties and Politics in the Communications Age* (New York: Doubleday, 1975); and Patrick J. Buchanan, *Conservative Votes, Liberal Victories* (Chicago: Quadrangle, 1975). A left-liberal commentator who opposes a national initiative because the people are too conservative is Peter Bachrach, who argues that such a device would promote conservative values through the manipulation of voters' minds by capitalist power groups (U.S. Congress, Senate, Subcommittee on the Constitution of the Committee on the Judiciary, *Hearings on S.J. Res. 67*, December 13–14, 1977 [Washington, D.C., 1978], pp. 59-65).

most of its chief organizers have previously been associated with such liberal pressure groups as Common Cause and the Consumers Federation of America. Initiative America's national director, John Forster, offered the following measures, all dear to liberals, as examples of what has actually been achieved by direct legislation in the states:

> Florida and California have strict political honesty laws on the books; Missouri law now protects customers from unfair utility charges; North Dakota has outlawed huge corporation farming in their state; Michigan and Maine are saving energy and stopping litter with returnable bottles and cans; in 1976, a California initiative enabled the Legislature to pass a nuclear waste disposal law against what had previously been strong lobbying efforts by power companies.[13]

Who is right? Has direct legislation in the states generally produced liberal or conservative outcomes? In the early years the record was mixed: in 1932 William B. Munro summed it up as follows:

> The adoption of the initiative and referendum was urged a quarter of a century ago by the progressive elements, who took for granted that if the people were allowed to legislate directly they would give their assent to progressive measures. On this basis the conservatives fought the movement in its early stages, while liberals welcomed the initiative and referendum as weapons with which to curtail the political power of the vested interests. But direct legislation has not proved to be revolutionary; on the contrary, it has been at least of equal value as a bulwark of conservatism. Voters in American cities and states have not hesitated to reject proposals for adopting the single tax or undertaking municipal ownership of public utilities, for giving pensions to city employees or imposing progressive income taxes.

And he added that in Switzerland "as in the United States, the effect of direct legislation has been slightly conservative."[14]

But what about the recent record? What has direct legislation produced in, say, the years since the end of World War II? These questions cannot be answered definitively with the limited data at hand. But some preliminary estimates of the answers can be drawn from the outcomes of all state referendums on popular initiatives from

13 Milwaukee *West Post*, October 26, 1977, p. A-3.

14 William B. Munro, "Initiative and Referendum," in *Encyclopaedia of the Social Sciences*, E. R. A. Seligman and Alvin Johnson, eds. (New York, N.Y.: Macmillan, 1932), vol. 8, p. 52.

1945 to 1976 on six issues that involved clear liberal-conservative choices. The results are mixed.

- Of the twelve referendums on right-to-work laws, six supported the conservative position by approving such laws and six supported the liberal position by defeating them.
- Of the thirteen referendums on proposals to limit the level of taxation or abolish the graduated income tax or both, only three won and ten lost—a clear victory for liberals.
- There were five referendums on measures to prohibit racial discrimination in the sale of housing, assignment of school pupils, and the like. All five lost—a clear victory for conservative values.
- Six referendums were held in 1974 and 1976 on measures to restrict or prohibit development of nuclear power-generating plants. Three won and three lost—another standoff.
- Four measures for restoring the death penalty for major crimes were voted on, and all four won—more victories for the conservatives.
- Three proposals to allow abortion on demand were voted on, and all three lost as most conservatives believed they should.

We could add together these apples and oranges and declare a score of twenty-four victories for conservatives to nineteen for liberals. But it seems more appropriate to conclude that, at least from 1945 to 1976, liberal positions on economic questions (right to work and taxation laws) generally won, conservative positions on social issues (death penalty, abortion, and racial discrimination) won, while the environmentalists broke even with the advocates of economic growth on nuclear power issues. This pattern is consistent with the widely held view that American voters are predominantly liberal on economic questions and conservative on social issues.[15]

In mid-1978 some American commentators argued that the June 6, 1978, California vote on Proposition 13 proved that direct legislation is clearly a conservative device, at least in America. They pointed out that the 1978 measure, which succeeded with a vote of 64 percent yes, limited the state's tax powers far more severely than did a comparable proposal sponsored by California's Governor Ronald Reagan in 1973, which failed with only 46 percent yes. And they called attention to the tax-limitation measures adopted by refer-

[15] For a recent discussion, see Jeane J. Kirkpatrick, "Why the New Right Lost," *Commentary*, February 1977, pp. 34-39.

endums in several other states and many localities in recent years as further evidence that the referendum produces conservative policy outcomes.

Perhaps so, but the evidence presented in this and other chapters of this book—admittedly incomplete, yet more comprehensive than that presented in any other recent study—suggests that the referendum is neither an unfailing friend nor an implacable enemy of either left or right. As is the case with most electoral arrangements, the policies that referendums produce depend on the state of public opinion at the time the vote is taken, and in a democratic polity the voters observably lean right on some occasions and left on others. The question, then, is not whether the referendum always, or even almost always, produces conservative outcomes, but *under what circumstances* it produces such outcomes. Surely the institution should be evaluated according to whether it is a good way of making political decisions, not according to the predicted content of those decisions.

Conclusion

Experience with direct legislation in the United States must be taken into account in the kind of cross-national comparative study undertaken in this book. That experience has exhibited several noteworthy patterns. Citizens have used the initiative to try to amend their state constitutions almost as often as to change ordinary state laws, and the constitutional proposals fared almost as well as the statutory measures. Altering various aspects of governmental machinery and political processes has been the most frequent subject for popular initiatives, followed by measures on revenue and taxation, regulation of public morals, and regulation of business and labor. Since the 1950s there has been a substantial increase in measures dealing with civil rights and civil liberties, and in the 1970s measures dealing with environmental issues have increased. Generally speaking, measures proposed by state legislatures and constitutional conventions have been approved twice as frequently as measures proposed by popular initiatives. There is some reason to believe that voters have tended to favor liberal economic measures and conservative social measures.

Whether this experience will ever induce the national government to adopt some form of direct legislation remains to be seen. But however that question may ultimately be resolved, it is clear that direct legislation will continue to play a significant role in the political life of many American states—as it has ever since 1778 when Massachusetts became the modern world's first polity to hold a referendum.

Bibliography

Gazey, Penelope J. "Direct Democracy: A Study of the U.S. Referendum." *Parliamentary Affairs* (Spring 1971), pp. 123–139.

Graham, Virginia. *A Compilation of Statewide Initiative Proposals Appearing on Ballots through 1976.* Washington, D.C.: Congressional Research Service, Library of Congress, 1978.

Hamilton, Howard D., and Sylvan H. Cohen. *Policymaking by Plebiscite: School Referenda.* Lexington, Mass.: D. C. Heath & Co., 1974.

LaPalombara, Joseph G. *The Initiative and Referendum in Oregon, 1938–1949.* Corvallis, Oreg.: Oregon State University Press, 1950.

Lewis, Mark F. "Direct Democracy in Theory and Practice," in *Democracy in Urban America,* York Wilbern, ed. Bloomington, Ind.: Indiana University Press, 1969.

Lobingier, Charles S. *The People's Law.* New York, N.Y.: Macmillan, 1909.

Munro, William Bennett. *The Initiative, Referendum and Recall.* New York, N.Y.: D. Appleton & Co., 1912.

Newfeld, John L. "Taxrate Referenda and the Property Taxpayer's Revolt." *National Tax Journal* 30 (December 1977): 441–452.

Oberholtzer, Ellis P. *The Referendum in America.* New York, N.Y.: Charles Scribner's Sons, 1911.

Pollock, James K. *The Initiative and Referendum in Michigan.* Ann Arbor, Mich.: University of Michigan Press, 1940.

Price, Charles M. "The Initiative: A Comparative State Analysis and Reassessment of a Western Phenomenon." *Western Political Quarterly* 28 (June 1975): 243–262.

Tallian, Laura. *Direct Democracy: An Historical Analysis of the Initiative, Referendum and Recall Process.* Los Angeles, People's Lobby Press, 1977.

U.S. Congress, Senate. Subcommittee on the Constitution of the Committee on the Judiciary. *Hearings on S.J. Res. 67,* December 13–14, 1977. Washington, D.C., 1978.

Wisconsin, State of. *Initiative and Referendum: Its Status in Wisconsin and Experiences in Selected States.* Informational Bulletin 76-Ib-4. Madison, Wis.: Legislative Reference Bureau, State of Wisconsin, 1976.

5

California

Eugene C. Lee

California contains more people than all but twenty-five countries; its area is larger than nearly two-thirds of the nations; and its output of goods and services is exceeded by only five or six nations. Comparisons with nations are appropriate for other than quantitative reasons, for California manages to retain many of the psychological and emotional overtones which enter into the state of mind called nationalism. A distinct culture or way of life, a style of government and politics, a sense of identity with the past and involvement with the future make crossing the California border something more than a step across an artificial geographical boundary.

A critical part of the culture is a weak party system. The formal political structure is divided and diffuse. State and congressional candidates are nominated in primary elections, in which direct appeals to the electorate circumvent party machinery. Once nominated, candidates tend to develop personal campaigns rather than run as members of a party slate. Party leaders, when they can be identified at all, have little leverage over the rank and file, and a politician who attempts to exert influence is promptly labeled a "boss." Formal activity by the parties at the local level of government is discouraged, if not damned. Split-ticket voting is on the rise, and voters call themselves "independents" in increasing numbers.

Complementing and contributing to this state of affairs is the widespread use of direct legislation, particularly the initiative—the right of the people by petition to place constitutional amendments and

This research was conducted under the auspices of the Committee on the Study of Public Organization of the Institute of Governmental Studies, University of California, Berkeley. Prompt and helpful assistance was provided by Edward G. Arnold, elections assistant to the California secretary of state, the official responsible for the conduct of state elections.

statutes directly on the ballot without recourse to the legislature or the governor. The initiative and referendum came to California in 1911, when both were adopted by an overwhelming three-to-one majority in a special election involving 220,000 voters. In the late 1970s California stands alone among the large urban industrial states of the American union in employing both the constitutional amendment initiative and direct statutory initiative. The institution appears as firmly grounded in the political culture of the state as the legislature itself.[1] Indeed, the initiative may be more widely employed and by more people in the state than in any other democratic society in the world. It is most appropriate, therefore, to include the California initiative in a volume on the referendum in Western democracies.

The move to adopt direct legislation statewide "originated with a small group of business and professional men who were determinedly opposed to machine control of the political and economic institutions of the state by the Southern Pacific Railroad. It was a revolt against a monopoly-control situation."[2] These "Progressives," a faction of the California Republican party, conceived of the initiative as an instrument to neutralize the power of special interest groups (although they themselves could be so characterized), to curtail corrup-

---

[1] In adopting direct legislation, California moved into the vanguard of what Charles Price describes as largely a western phenomenon in the United States, reflecting the particular impact of the Progressive reforms of the early 1900s on this section of the nation. As of 1978, only five of the twenty-six states east of the Mississippi River had provided for the initiative, in sharp contrast to seventeen of the twenty-four states west of the river. None of the five eastern states had adopted the direct initiative for statutory changes, whereas fifteen of the western states had done so. Only ten states—all in the West, including California—had *both* the constitutional and direct statutory initiative. Among all the states in recent years, California was by far the most active. For example, from 1962 to 1972 twenty initiatives qualified in California, compared with fifteen appearing on the ballot in Washington (including three indirect initiatives) and twelve each in Oregon and Colorado. (Charles M. Price, "The Initiative: A Comparative State Analysis and Reassessment of a Western Phenomenon," *Western Political Quarterly*, vol. 28 [June 1975], p. 246; modified by information from *The Book of the States, 1978–79* [Lexington, Ky.: Council of State Governments, 1978], pp. 129, 187.)

Over the entire history of the initiative, California ranks second in the number of measures appearing on the ballot. In Oregon, the first to use the initiative in 1904, 206 propositions had appeared on the ballot as of 1976. For all states employing the initiative, Larry Berg reports that 1,211 measures had qualified for the ballot as of 1976, of which 442 received voter approval, a somewhat higher ratio—36.5 percent—than California's 26.9 percent. (Larry L. Berg, "The Initiative Process and Public Policy-Making in the States: 1904–1976," paper presented at the annual meeting of the American Political Science Association, New York, August 31, 1978.)

[2] V. O. Key, Jr., and Winston W. Crouch, *The Initiative and Referendum in California* (Berkeley: University of California Press, 1939), pp. 423-424.

tion on the part of political machines, to provide a vehicle for civic education on major policy issues, to create pressure on state representatives and governors to act on specific measures, and, when they failed to act, to bypass these representative institutions altogether, in short, to make "every man his own legislature."[3] Against this vision, how has California fared?

Types of Direct Legislation

The 1911 provisions for direct legislation involved four distinct concepts and procedures: (1) *the constitutional amendment initiative* proposed by popular petition and submitted to the voters; (2) *the direct statutory initiative*, statutes proposed by petition and submitted to the voters; (3) *the indirect statutory initiative*, statutes proposed by petition, submitted to the legislature and, failing of passage by that body, then submitted to the electorate (repealed in 1966); and (4) the *referendum*, the suspension of the enforcement of a law until it has been referred to the voters and approved by them. These four measures must be considered in a political and electoral context of other propositions directly submitted to the voters by the legislature: constitutional amendments, bond issues, and amendments to statutes originally adopted by the initiative and requiring voter approval. The frequency of use and the approval rate of these various kinds of propositions since 1911 are set forth in Table 5-1.

Constitutional amendments proposed by the legislature are by far the most numerous of the ballot measures, as indicated by the length and detailed nature of California's constitution. (As noted in Table 5-1, nearly 300 constitutional amendments were approved by the voters between 1912 and 1976.) Such proposals must receive a two-thirds vote of the full membership of each house of the state legislature. Thus, the measures must have widespread approval before submission to the electorate and tend to be less controversial than most initiatives. While having much in common with initiatives in terms of interest-group activity, campaigns, voter behavior, and the like, legislative amendments comprise a separate field of study and are not included in this analysis. Nevertheless, on average there have been three propositions proposed by the legislature on the ballot for every initiative measure, competing for voter attention with state and county candidates and local propositions—a critical factor in the

[3] Hugh A. Bone and Robert C. Benedict, "Perspectives on Direct Legislation: Washington State's Experience, 1914–73," *Western Political Quarterly*, vol. 12 (June 1975), p. 332.

TABLE 5-1

PROPOSITIONS SUBMITTED TO THE VOTERS OF CALIFORNIA, 1912–1976

Type of Proposal	*Number Proposed*	*Number Approved*	*Percent Approved*
Measures proposed by petition			
Constitutional amendments	90	24	27
Statutes, bypassing legislature	65	18	28
Statutes, submitted first to legislature, then to voters [a]	4	1	25
Referendums	35	21 [b]	60
Subtotal	194	64	33
Measures proposed by legislature			
Constitutional amendments	476	294	62
Bond referendums	52	41	79
Amendments to law originally adopted by initiative	15	13	87
Subtotal	543	348	64
Total	737	412	56

[a] This procedure was repealed in 1966.

[b] Action by the voters overruled the legislature and sustained the referendum.

SOURCE: California Secretary of State, *Statement of the Vote* (various years); California Legislature, Session Statutes, as presented in Winston W. Crouch et al., *California Government and Politics*, 6th ed. (Englewood Cliffs, N.J.: Prentice-Hall, 1977), p. 125, figures updated and revised for this volume.

overall process of direct legislation. "In total, a voter must make approximately fifty separate decisions in the average election, fifty marks he must place on the ballot." [4]

The difference between direct initiatives and constitutional amendments proposed by the legislature is also revealed in the relative success rates of the propositions. The proportion of legislative proposals approved by the voters (62 percent), is more than double that of the initiatives. The odds against adoption of a successful initiative are better than three to one. As seen in Table 5-2, this pattern has varied only slightly over the entire period of direct legislation. Legislative amendments to statutes originally adopted via the initiative

[4] John R. Owens et al., *California Politics and Parties* (New York: Macmillan, 1970), p. 105. In addition to voting for eight state executive officers every four years and one to four state and national legislators in any given election year, Californians also vote in state elections for municipal and superior court judges, and county supervisors and executive officers.

TABLE 5-2

CALIFORNIA INITIATIVES "TITLED," ON THE BALLOT, AND ADOPTED, BY DECADE, 1912–1976

		Qualified for Ballot		Adopted	
Decade	*Number Titled* [a]	Number	Percent of titled	Number	Percent of qualified
1912–19	45	30	67	8	27
1920–29	51	35	69	10	29
1930–39	66	35	53	9	26
1940–49	42	19	45	6	32
1950–58	17	10	59	2	20
1960–68	44	9	20	3	33
1970–76	104	17	16	4	24
Total	369	155	42	42	27

NOTE: Excluded from the table are four indirect initiatives: one each in 1938 and 1942 and two in 1952.

[a] Titled initiatives include all proposals officially submitted to the attorney general prior to circulation of petition, regardless of whether the proposal subsequently qualified for the ballot.

SOURCE: California Secretary of State.

process have fared best of all, for these have been largely of a technical and noncontroversial nature, for example, revisions to the act governing chiropractors. Initiated statutes may be amended by the legislature alone only if the original measure expressly authorizes such action. Otherwise, amendments to statutory initiatives and all constitutional amendments must be approved by the electorate.

The procedure for initiating constitutional amendments and statutes is identical, save for the number of signatures of registered voters required on the qualifying petition.[5] Prior to 1966 the required

[5] In both cases, sponsors of the measure submit it (via the secretary of state) to the attorney general. The latter prepares a title and summary description of the measures, 100 words or less, which must appear in readable type on each page of the petition on which signatures are to appear. Upon the return of the summary, the sponsors have 150 days to circulate and file their petitions. If the required number of signatures has been obtained and they are validated by the respective county clerks, the measure must be placed on the ballot at the next statewide election held at least 131 days after qualification. All in all, this procedural calendar runs nearly a year from the request for an official title until the election and does much to shape the politics of the initiative process.

number of signatures for both constitutional and statutory initiatives was 8 percent of the total vote cast for gubernatorial candidates in the previous election. Constitutional measures were obviously favored, however, as suggested by the fact that nearly half again as many constitutional amendments as statutes were initiated from 1912 to 1976. A constitutional amendment is in a stronger legal position in the event of a court test, and there is no bar to proposing detailed legislation—statutory in character—for inclusion in the constitution. In the face of the growing length and complexity of California's constitution an attempt was made to reverse this trend, and in 1966 the petition requirement for statutory measures was reduced to 5 percent.[6]

The 5 percent requirement had previously applied to the indirect initiative, that part of the original 1911 package which enabled voters to submit a measure to the legislature for adoption with the proviso that the measure would appear on the ballot if the legislature failed to enact the proposal. Nearly forty years elapsed before the indirect initiative was used at all, however. Employed only four times, most recently in 1952, it was removed from the constitution in 1966. In none of the four cases had the legislature adopted the proposal, and only one received voter approval.[7] A referendum may also be triggered by a 5 percent petition, but it, too, has fallen into virtual disuse. As discussed below, after rather active and successful use in its first three decades, this kind of referendum has been employed only twice since 1940. The ninety-day petition period has apparently proved too short a time in which to acquire more than 300,000 signatures.

The number of signatures of registered voters required to qualify a measure for the ballot has, of course, increased dramatically over the years, consistent with the growth of the state. In 1912 approximately 30,000 signatures were necessary for a constitutional initiative, and a referendum required less than 20,000. By 1978, however, these numbers had increased more than fifteenfold. A constitutional initia-

[6] At least in the short run, the requirement has worked. From 1950 through 1966, thirteen constitutional amendment initiatives qualified for the ballot, compared with only five statutory initiatives. From 1967 through 1976, however, eleven statutes qualified in contrast to seven constitutional amendments, and there has been a decided increase in efforts to qualify statutory initiatives.

[7] Crouch suggests that the demise of the indirect initiative resulted from the fear of proponents of ballot measures that publicity and popular support built up in the petition drive would be lost during the more than two years it would take for a measure eventually to reach the voter. They prefer the direct initiative with its shorter calendar and more immediate impact. (Winston W. Crouch, *The Initiative and Referendum in California* [Los Angeles: Haynes Foundation, 1950], p. 12.)

tive required nearly 500,000 valid signatures to qualify, while more than 300,000 were necessary for a statutory initiative or a referendum.

The number of initiatives titled by the attorney general (which includes proposals which failed to qualify as well as those which did), the number of qualified initiatives, and their success rate have varied over the decades, as indicated in Table 5-2. There was a decided decline in the use of the initiative during the 1940s and 1950s. In the 1960s it appeared that sponsors had difficulty in meeting the initial requirements, since only nine out of the forty-four submitted were titled by the attorney general. But from 1970 through 1976, 104 initiative measures were titled, a far greater number than in any preceding period.[8] Of these, seventeen qualified for the ballot, a much higher number than in recent decades: one in 1970, ten in 1972—a near record—and six from 1973 through 1976. (These measures are listed in Table 5-3.) In 1978 a ballot measure radically altering the state's tax system—the now famous Proposition 13—dominated the primary election, while an antismoking initiative, a measure designed to bar homosexuals from being employed in schools, and a proposal to change and expand categories of murder for which the death penalty could be applied qualified for the November general election ballot.

Attention once again focused on the political realities of direct legislation in the nation's largest state, on its uses and abuses, and on proposed "reforms." Could direct democracy work in an electorate of over 9 million registered voters?

The Uses of the Initiative

From local option over the sale of liquor to the regulation of nuclear power plants, from the eight-hour workday to agricultural labor relations, the critical issues of the moment have found their way onto the ballot via the initiative process. Lesser but equally controversial contests have ranged from antivivisection in an earlier day to greyhound racing in 1976.

Table 5-4 summarizes the subjects of all 155 direct initiative measures by decade from 1912 through 1976. As Winston Crouch

[8] The reasons for this record number of measures introduced and titled are not clear. In 1974 alone, the office of secretary of state reports that one couple introduced twenty-one initiatives—each titled and summarized by the attorney general and each requiring payment of a $200 fee. Not one of the measures was qualified for the ballot or even actively pursued. In 1977 another sixteen proposals were titled, of which three qualified, one on the 1978 primary ballot and two on the November general election ballot. As of June 30, 1978, another sixteen had been titled, but none had qualified. Any which did would not appear on the ballot until 1980.

TABLE 5-3

INITIATIVE MEASURES ON THE CALIFORNIA BALLOT, 1960–1976

Year	*Subject*	*Percent Voting Yes*	*Percent of Voters* [a]
1960	Senate reapportionment	35.5	81.2
1962	Senate reapportionment	46.6	79.9
	Control of subversive activities	40.3	83.8
1964	Repeal of fair housing act	65.3	96.1
	Prohibition of pay television	66.4	94.5
	Lottery	30.9	92.5
	Control of railroad train crews	61.0	92.5
1966	Obscenity regulation	43.6	88.2
1968	Property tax limitation	31.9	91.6
1970	Tax shift for schools and social welfare	28.5	93.2
1972	Air pollution control	35.3	93.0
	Property tax limitation	34.1	92.6
	State employee salaries	32.5	91.3
	Highway patrol salaries	39.1	91.2
	Death penalty	67.5	94.4
	Obscenity regulation	32.0	94.3
	Marijuana decriminalization	33.5	95.6
	Coastal zone conservation	55.1	92.5
	School busing limitation	63.0	92.5
	Agricultural labor relations	42.0	93.1
1973	Tax and expenditure limitations	46.0	98.5 [b]
1974	Political reform	69.8	90.0
	Protection of wild and scenic rivers	47.1	87.8
1976	Nuclear power plant restrictions	33.0	95.0
	Greyhound racing	24.6	94.2
	Agricultural labor relations	37.8	95.9

[a] Percent of those voting in the election who marked their ballots on this measure.
[b] Special election involving only this issue.
SOURCE: California Secretary of State.

TABLE 5-4

NUMBER OF INITIATIVE MEASURES ON THE CALIFORNIA BALLOT, BY SUBJECT AND DECADE, 1912–1976

Subject	*1912–19*	*1920–29*	*1930–39*	*1940–49*	*1950–59*	*1960–69*	*1970–76*	*Total*	*Percent of Total*
Governmental and political process [a]	7	7	11	1	1	2	3	32	21
Public morality [b]	9	6	7	3	1	1	2	29	19
Revenue, taxation, bonds	6	10	4	2	3	1	3	29	19
Regulation of business and labor	6	2	6	6	2	2	2	26	17
Health, welfare, public housing [c]	2	7	6	5	2	0	0	22	14
Civil liberties and civil rights	0	1	0	1	0	3	3	8	5
Environmental protection, land use	0	1	0	0	0	0	4	5	3
Education	0	1	1	1	1	0	0	4	2
Total	30	35	35	19	10	9	17	155	100
Percent of total by decade	19	23	23	12	6	6	11	100	—

[a] Includes voting, reapportionment, initiative process, executive organization, local government, judicial process.

[b] Includes liquor, gambling, boxing, racing.

[c] Includes veterans' benefits.

SOURCE: Laura Tallian, *Direct Democracy: An Historical Analysis of the Initiative, Referendum and Recall Process* (Los Angeles: People's Lobby, 1977), pp. 172-210.

explained in his 1950 study, early ballot propositions were often concerned with moral issues, such as prizefighting and the reading of the Bible in public schools, and with economic issues, such as taxation and the granting of franchises. In the 1920s initiatives began to deal with questions of state administrative organization, such as the requirement of an executive budget and the creation of licensing boards to supervise chiropractors and osteopaths. The 1930s featured economic issues such as income and gasoline taxes and various measures dealing with old-age pensions, which continued to be presented during the 1940s and 1950s.[9]

In the 1960s the issue of civil rights was presented in dramatic form in measures to repeal the state's fair housing law and to limit school busing as a means of promoting integration. Civil liberties was the issue in measures dealing with the death penalty, subversive activities, and obscenity. In 1972 a successful initiative to conserve California's coastal lands illustrated the importance in this decade of the environmental movement. And in 1978 the continuing force of social issues was reflected in proposals to bar public funds for abortions, outlaw affirmative action admissions systems in public higher education, and—once again—to limit school busing for the purpose of racial integration.

Of the forty-two measures approved by the voters from 1912 through 1976, those dealing with state and local governmental and political processes, public morality (liquor control through the 1930s), economic regulation, and health, welfare, and public housing have been most frequent. Supporters of direct legislation point to the passage of the state's civil service law and the more recent political reform act regulating lobbying and campaign expenditures. Critics note the adoption of measures ruled wholly or partially unconstitutional by the courts—the limitation on school busing, the anti–fair housing measure, the death penalty, the ban on pay television, and aspects of political reform. Indeed, measured by the number of successful initiatives, the recent impact of direct legislation has been modest. From 1960 to 1976 only seven measures were approved, including those later ruled unconstitutional.

Who employs the initiative? The groups do not differ significantly from those lobbying before the legislature. Brestoff notes that "Almost two-thirds of the 18 initiative measures submitted to the California electorate in the past decade (1964–74) have been drawn by pro-

[9] Crouch, *Initiative and Referendum*, pp. 8-9.

ponents with substantial economic means."[10] In this category he included realtors supporting an anti–open housing measure, movie theatres opposing pay television, a state lottery sponsored almost exclusively by the American Sweepstakes Corporation, the railroad industry in support of an antifeatherbedding proposal, land investment companies supporting a property tax shift, agricultural growers opposed to farm labor unionization, and public employee groups seeking higher salaries. Grass-roots organizations have also been active, however, as in the case of coastal zoning, marijuana decriminalization, nuclear safety, wild rivers, and political reform measures in 1972 and 1976, and an antismoking proposal in 1978.

Why do these groups promote direct legislation? "The reason most often assigned is that the legislature refuses to pass a measure that is dear to the group requesting its passage."[11] This was clear in the case of the successful coastal conservation act of 1972, which was placed on the ballot by environmental groups only after the legislature had repeatedly demonstrated its unwillingness to move on the issue. A second reason is that groups wish to have the measures adopted in a certain form rather than be "amended to death" in the legislature, the charge that led to the passage of the political reform act of 1974. The special status attached to an initiative constitutes a third motivating factor. Successful constitutional initiatives become part of the fundamental law of the state, and statutory initiatives, once adopted, can be amended only by a vote of the people, unless the measure expressly allows legislative revision.

But the reasons for the use of the initiative go beyond possible acceptance at the polls. The educational impact of a ballot campaign provides a fourth basis. Groups, like that proposing to decriminalize marijuana in 1972, may not anticipate victory at the polls. Instead, they hope that enlightened public opinion, stimulated by the campaign, will lead to subsequent legislative action, which in this instance did result in more liberal marijuana laws. Indeed, the organizational effort involved in the campaign—even in a losing cause—strengthened the effectiveness of the group in its subsequent lobbying activities. Thus, another reason for an initiative may be the hope of the sponsors that the campaign will provide a catalyst for organization and action which will extend beyond the election.

[10] Nick Brestoff, "The California Initiative Process: A Suggestion for Reform," *Southern California Law Review*, vol. 78 (March 1975), p. 944. For a description of the kinds of groups using the initiative prior to 1939, see Key and Crouch, *Initiative*, p. 487; and Crouch, *Initiative and Referendum*, p. 17.

[11] Crouch, *Initiative and Referendum*, p. 10.

In short, direct legislation—or the threat to circulate initiative petitions—has become an integral part of the strategy of law making. In 1976, for example, statutes to regulate nuclear power plants passed the legislature only because of the threat of a much more stringent initiative measure on the June ballot. Important political figures in California withheld their judgment on the initiative until the legislature had acted and only then suggested to voters that the ballot measure was not needed. In 1978 the threat of a radical initiative to limit property taxes forced the legislature to propose major adjustments in the state's tax structure; this duplicated an identical action in 1968, when the legislature successfully countered a tax initiative with a less drastic measure of its own. In 1978, however, the voters chose the initiative measure rather than the alternative proposed by the legislature.

The continuing controversy over the death penalty provides a different example of the close relation between the normal legislative process and the politics of the initiative. In this instance the overwhelming public support for the death penalty revealed in the 69 percent vote for the 1972 initiative created pressure on the legislature to adopt a measure that would meet the constitutional requirements imposed by both the state and national supreme courts. Proponents of capital punishment were able effectively to point to the vote as a mandate for legislative action. Subsequently, the threat of an even more stringent death penalty initiative was influential in persuading legislators first to adopt and then to override the governor's veto of a statute providing for capital punishment.

The defeat of an initiative can also have an impact, in this case often against the interests of the measure's sponsors. For example, pressures for strengthening California's laws governing collective bargaining of farm workers were weakened by the loss of Proposition 22 in 1976, a measure sponsored by Cesar Chavez and the United Farm Workers. Just as legislators could point to a mandate in the case of the death penalty, opponents of farm unionization cited a reluctant public opinion as a reason to slow down change in that policy area.

It is not always clear, of course, just what a negative vote on an initiative really means. People may favor a measure when being considered by the legislature as a statute, yet oppose it when placed before them via the initiative as a constitutional amendment. At least part of the reason initiatives have a poor record of success at the polls lies in this apparent reluctance of voters to freeze a measure into the constitution, immune from legislative amendment.

There is also a relation between initiative measures and candidate campaigns. In 1973 Governor Ronald Reagan's tax limitation proposal was regarded as an important part of his drive for the presidency. In 1974 Edmund "Jerry" Brown, Jr., centered his successful "Mr. Clean" campaign for governor around the political reform initiative of that year. In 1978 conservative Republican State Senator John Briggs announced that "I intend to make [a death penalty initiative] a very big part of my gubernatorial campaign," while Los Angeles' Democratic Senator Alan Robbin's sponsorship of an anti-busing amendment was seen as a "substantial political issue for the Senator, who is up for re-election this year after losing a bid to unseat Mayor Bradley in 1977."[12]

Candidates may also suffer from being associated with—or forced to take a stand on—an initiative measure. The ouster of John Tunney from his U.S. senatorial seat has been related to his position favoring the farm labor initiative in 1972. Similarly, Pierre Salinger's unsuccessful bid for the Senate in 1964 can be partially explained by his support of fair housing legislation, which was overturned by the voters that year.

What emerges from this review is that while a few groups outside the main political stream occasionally try to employ the initiative process, the main actors are those who regularly do battle in legislative corridors or in campaigns for elective office. For these groups, the initiative is mainly another weapon—or hurdle—in the contest for political power and influence.

The Referendum

The referendum—the suspension of enforcement of a law until it has been sustained by the voters (which requires that the referendum be *rejected*)—involves an extraordinary effort. Petitions equal to 5 percent of the previous gubernatorial vote must be submitted within ninety days following adjournment of the legislature. This requirement has limited its use primarily to those groups able to mount a quick, substantial, and costly circulation drive. As Key and Crouch noted in 1939,

> Legislative acts are suspended and brought to the electorate obviously by those groups which have not been fortunate enough to control the legislature on particular matters. . . . It would be expected that highly conscious and well-organized groups, equipped with funds and machinery for action would

[12] *Los Angeles Times*, November 10, 1977, and January 20, 1978.

> be most likely to employ the referendum when directly threatened by specific legislation. And this has been the situation in California.[13]

Thus, for example, referendums have involved the successful popular overthrow of proposed taxes on oleomargarine on two occasions and a special tax on chain stores. Five measures were brought to the voters during the 1930s relating to the production of oil and the use of state-owned tidelands for drilling, and the voters overruled the legislature on four of these.[14] On the other hand, the voters have sustained legislation that threatened special interests, as in the case of a 1914 referendum promoted by San Francisco real estate interests to overthrow an act to curtail houses of prostitution, or another sponsored by osteopaths in 1920 attempting to negate a bill which denied them the right to prescribe narcotics.

As noted in Table 5-1, 60 percent of all referendums have been approved by the voters and the affected legislation suspended, a higher success rate than for initiatives. Nevertheless, the practice has fallen into virtual disuse, having been last employed in 1952. The short ninety-day petition period has proved too difficult a hurdle in the context of the need to acquire more than 300,000 signatures. Then too, since 1966 the legislature meets almost continuously, in contrast to the previous limited biannual sessions, and groups have more opportunity to seek amendments to statutes within the regular legislative process, rather than oppose them in costly and uncertain referendums. Furthermore, the referendum cannot be used to enjoin "urgency statutes"—those declared by a two-thirds vote of the legislature as necessary for the "immediate preservation of the public peace, health, or safety." This power to declare a statute urgent is liberally utilized and has reduced the potential of referendums as an instrument of direct legislation.[15]

Several recent attempts to refer legislation have failed for lack of sufficient signatures, and it is doubtful that the referendum will ever again resume the importance that it had in its early years. Instead, it appears likely that opponents of particular legislation will turn to the direct initiative as an alternative, as in the case of the highly controversial 1964 initiative statute which repealed the state's fair housing act.[16]

---

[13] Key and Crouch, *Initiative*, pp. 504-505.

[14] Crouch, *Initiative and Referendum*, pp. 28-29.

[15] The California experience is in marked contrast to that in Washington, where eight indirect initiatives and ten referendums appeared on the ballot from 1943 to 1973. (Bone and Benedict, "Perspectives on Direct Legislation," p. 337.)

[16] This statute was subsequently ruled unconstitutional by the state supreme court.

Campaigns and Campaign Expenditures

There is far more than a quantitative difference between the 30,000 signatures initially needed to qualify a proposed constitutional amendment for the ballot and the 500,000 needed in 1978. Writing in 1939, Key and Crouch observed that "The tremendous task of manipulating the attitudes of an electorate of over 2,000,000 [the 1940 registration exceeded 4 million] . . . has led to the development of campaign organization and expenditures on a scale rarely seen in states where the only issues voted on are constitutional amendments proposed by the legislature."[17] Forty years later and with several million more voters, the "tremendous task" has led to a direct legislation "industry," which dominates the initiative process.

Because petitions must be circulated and filed within a 150–day period and many extra signatures must be obtained to compensate for those that may be declared invalid, only a few mass-membership or grass-roots organizations have the capability to conduct a successful petition drive within the alloted time. For most groups there is no alternative but to seek the services of a professional organization, several of which exist in California solely to serve this function. In 1978 the going rate for such a campaign was 50 cents per signature, with perhaps a minimum fee of $225,000.[18] Circulators were drawn from the ranks of students, housewives, and retired persons and were paid 20 cents per signature.

Volunteer organizations are still able to circulate petitions without relying on professional circulators. In 1972, for example, the People's Lobby spent only $9,000 in obtaining sufficient signatures to qualify the Clean Air Act. In 1978 the property tax limitation initiative was qualified with an expenditure of only $28,000. But the California State Employees' Association, with a membership of 115,000, reported an expenditure in 1972 of $400,000 in its drive to qualify a state employees' salary measure, and in 1973 proponents of Governor Reagan's tax limitation initiative spent $436,000 to obtain a place on the ballot.

Do people know what they are signing? Perhaps most of the time they do. But with respect to a complicated oil conservation measure in 1956, an experienced California pollster tested the matter. "Mrs. Corey's poll of signers showed that most of them couldn't remember signing the petitions, and of those who did the majority

---

[17] Key and Crouch, *Initiative*, p. 507.

[18] Laura Tallian, *Direct Democracy: An Historical Analysis of the Initiative, Referendum and Recall Process* (Los Angeles: People's Lobby, 1977), p. 102.

didn't in any way connect signing that petition with the oil controversy then raging through the state. And among the signers of the petition, about half were for the measure they qualified for the ballot and half against it!"[19] (Some persons may sign a petition because they favor a popular vote on the measure, whether or not they actually support the proposal.) In addition, it is evident that "Because proponents must gather so many signatures in a short period of time, they have often resorted to collection methods that seriously tarnish the integrity of the process." Some examples are the use of "dodger cards" to cover up the official statement of the attorney general with one more favorable to the proponents, misleading summaries in campaign literature, or forgery of signatures on petitions.[20]

Proposals to reform the petition process have included the abolition of professional petition circulators and a ceiling on the amount that could be expended for this purpose. An outright ban would not be acceptable to many California interest groups, however, and is of doubtful constitutionality. A ceiling of 25 cents per name for petition circulation, included in the 1974 political reform act, was ruled unconstitutional as an impermissible infringement of free speech.[21]

Once an initiative measure has qualified for the ballot, "The methods used . . . do not differ fundamentally from those employed in campaigns for public office."[22] In California—even more for initiatives than for candidates—this has meant the professionalization of campaigns and the dominance of public relations firms with their media consultants, public opinion pollsters, and direct-mail specialists.[23]

To be sure, grass-roots organizations, still alive and well, originated two of the four initiatives adopted in the past decade. Yet even these groups succeeded because they were able to "out-professionalize" their opponents. The Coastal Alliance, for example, with its "broad-based organization, led by experienced people, could mobilize a small army of volunteers to blunt the overwhelming financial

[19] Herbert M. Baus and William B. Ross, *Politics Battle Plan* (New York: Macmillan, 1968), p. 61.

[20] Brestoff, "The California Initiative Process," pp. 928-929.

[21] *Hardie* v. *Eu*, 18 Cal. 3rd 1971 (1976).

[22] Key and Crouch, *Initiative*, p. 507.

[23] A listing of the most active California political campaign firms would include Winner/Wagner, Braun and Company, Spencer-Roberts-Woodward and McDowell, Weiner and Company, and—the founders of the movement, as discussed below—Whitaker and Baxter. Each of these firms plans and manages campaigns for both candidates and ballot propositions.

superiority of Proposition 20's opponents."[24] And for all groups, the weak political party organizations in California only occasionally offer leadership in the initiative process and more often are totally indifferent to it.[25]

Baus and Ross, successful California political consultants to both candidates and interest groups, describe an initiative campaign as follows:

> The basic strategy approach to an issue is set by whether a "yes" or "no" vote is sought. Those managing the "yes" side are attempting to change the status quo by selling something new to the voters. Their general approach therefore must be one of persuasion and affirmative interpretation. The "yes" strategy will be soft and smooth—a technique doctors call the "sugar-coated pill" approach.
>
> Ballot propositions, being written by lawyers, have a degree of complexity, and some are Gordian knots of language. This very intricacy interposes a barrier to success. What the voter does not understand he may reject. The confused voter votes "no." Thus a campaign of enlightenment with affirmative psychology is imperative to pass the "yes" side of a proposition.[26]
>
> In campaigning on the "no" side, the situation is reversed. Here a rougher, negative approach is strategically indicated.

---

[24] Carl E. Lutrin and Allen K. Settle, "The Public and Ecology: The Role of Initiatives in California's Environmental Politics," *Western Political Quarterly*, vol. 28 (June 1975), p. 370. The authors concluded that the coastal initiative provided a classic example of a successful grass-roots campaign, which involved a "good, well-staffed organization, a broad-based coalition, the support of many of the state's important legislators, and a superior public relations effort. . . . At the outset of the campaign for Proposition 20, the Alliance had 34 member organizations. This number grew to 1,500. . . . These organizations provided thousands of enthusiastic workers, raised money, and kept their members and the general public informed about the issue. . . . Tens of thousands of volunteers got the Alliance's message to the public. In conservative Orange County, volunteers formed a telephone tree, which was able to phone every voter in the county twice on behalf of Proposition 20."

[25] "Parties can be extremely important in shaping opinion on the propositions. However, this influence is limited (and made difficult to examine fully) by the fact that the parties take positions on only a few ballot measures. This is sensible from their point of view, of course, since they do not wish their position on the propositions to harm them in the partisan races—after all, every stand alienates somebody." (John E. Mueller, "Voting on the Propositions: Ballot Patterns and Historical Trends in California," *American Political Science Review*, vol. 63 [December 1969], pp. 1206-1207.)

[26] The tactics of initiative drafting often involve attempts to co-opt various groups into active support. For example, the greyhound racing measure of 1976 provided that a share of the revenue would be devoted to heart research, blind relief, senior citizen nutrition, day care centers, and high school athletics!

> The campaign strives to point out the pitfalls of the contested measure, and sometimes just one is enough to do the job.[27]

Charles Winner of Winner/Wagner and Associates, who managed the campaign against the 1978 property tax limitation initiative—unsuccessfully as it turned out—put it this way: "If you just look at that thing on the ballot, you're going to vote for it. It's too simple. Maybe what we've got to do is complicate it a little. Show the voters it's not all that simple."[28]

Whether seeking a yes or a no vote, the successful campaign almost always requires money. "Increased complexity of measures leads quite naturally to simplification by sponsors and opponents seeking to persuade an amorphous public. The result . . . is the need for massive financial resources for public relations firms and television, billboard, and newspaper advertising that usually rely more on simplistic propaganda than on reasoned discourse."[29]

Proponents and opponents of the sixteen propositions on the ballot from 1972 through 1976 spent a grand total of $22,518,000 on campaigning.[30] The funds involved in the individual campaigns varied tremendously, from under $60,000 spent on both sides of the school busing initiative in 1972 to the $3.8 million spent on the nuclear power measure in 1976. There was also generally a big difference between the amounts spent by proponents and opponents. In some cases, advocates of a measure were the heavy spenders; in other instances, opponents were forced into massive expenditures to defeat a proposal not of their choosing.[31]

The expenditure of money for an initiative does not necessarily correspond with its success or failure. From 1972 through 1976 six of the eight measures on which advocates spent more than their

[27] Baus and Ross, *Politics Battle Plan*, p. 61.

[28] *San Francisco Chronicle*, March 23, 1978.

[29] Baker, "American Conceptions," p. 13.

[30] Roger Jon Diamond et al., "California's Political Reform Act: Greater Access to the Initiative Process," *Southwestern University Law Review*, vol. 7 (Fall 1975), p. 562.

[31] Legislative constitutional amendment campaigns are an entirely different phenomenon. In June and November 1976 nineteen constitutional amendments were placed on the ballot by the legislature. Of these, most involved campaign expenditures of only a few hundred dollars; in several instances no money was spent at all in opposition to the amendment. In contrast, supporters of a measure on the June ballot, which would have raised an existing interest rate ceiling on certain types of business loans, spent $467,492 against only $268 spent by opponents. The measure lost. In November 1976 a similar measure was placed on the ballot, and this time supporters spent $661,767, while the opposition campaign reported expenditures of $48,051. The measure still lost!

opponents were defeated. For all sixteen measures from 1972 to 1976 the side spending more money was successful in only eight races. For example, opponents of the coastal conservation act in 1972 outspent proponents by more than three to one, yet the initiative passed. In contrast, state employees spent $1.8 million in the same election attempting to secure passage of a salary measure, against the minuscule $38,000 spent in opposition, but the initiative failed. The opponents of marijuana liberalization spent only $5,000 but were able to offset expenditures by its supporters amounting to $214,000. In general, opponents of initiatives who spent the most tended to be successful in defeating the measure; on the other hand, high-spending advocates most often found their cause go down to defeat.

Campaign funds are, however, not unimportant. As noted, they are often critical when proponents are at the stage of circulating the petition, and they may be decisive for either side in a closely contested contest. But other factors are important as well. For a question like the death penalty, on which opinions are clear-cut and little technical expertise is required, a formal political campaign may not have much impact. On the other hand, a lengthy and complicated issue, like that of nuclear power safety on which technical experts disagree, puts a heavy burden on campaign publicity to educate the voter.

In 1972 the high cost of initiative campaigns was dramatically illustrated. Nearly $11 million was spent in the primary and general elections on some thirty-two measures (including constitutional amendments and bond issues proposed by the legislature). Billboards, bumper stickers, and—most of all—television commercials drove home to the voter the role of money in the politics of the initiative, although most of the big spenders lost. In partial reaction, the authors of the political reform initiative measure adopted by the voters in 1974 included an overall limitation on future spending for a proposition campaign of 8 cents for each member of the existing voting age population, subject to future cost-of-living adjustments. In 1976 the limit amounted to $1,159,680. An additional ceiling, noted above, covered petition circulation. The act also included an elaborate provision which would prohibit one side from outspending the other by more than $500,000. The rationale for this approach was set forth by Daniel Lowenstein, chief author of the act and subsequently the first chairman of the Fair Political Practices Commission, the agency to enforce the act: "It seemed more important to limit the inequality of spending than merely to limit the total amount."[32] This provision of the act was immediately challenged in court, however, and was never enforced.[33]

What may one conclude about initiative campaigns and their financing? Certainly, they are risky investments, as clearly demonstrated by the 1972 experience in which millions of dollars were spent on losing causes. Between 1964 and 1976 no major economic group was able to enact an initiative measure. Realtors and land developers, state employees, agri-business, farm labor, and greyhound racing interests all failed in their attempts to bypass the legislative process. Instead, victories were achieved by groups with minimum economic clout but with the ability to capitalize on high public interest in such contrasting issues as coastal conservation and the death penalty, and —in the case of environmentalists and civic reformers—the ability to mobilize effective political campaigns without massive funding.

The character of most initiative campaigns—reliance on sloganeering and emotional appeals, on propaganda and sixty-second television spots—is not unique, of course. It seems to parallel "the new style of campaigning, the decline of party and the rise of candidate-centered technology," described by Robert Agranoff.[34] In fact, it would appear that the politics of the initiative was a precursor of these broad developments. Although the "new politics" owes much to the more recent advent of television, it was in California that the current form of political campaigning began to take shape. As the distinguished historian, Walton Bean, noted:

> The "publicity" for American political campaigns had previously been handled, as Carey McWilliams put it, by "broken-down politicians and alcoholic camp followers." But in the 1930's an organization called Campaigns, Inc., a remarkable partnership of two Californians, Clem Whitaker and Leone Baxter, revolutionized political campaigning by making carefully planned use of mass media and of the commercial techniques of the advertising industry. It was natural that

[32] Diamond et al., "California's Political Reform Act," p. 485.

[33] In overruling the spending limitation, the California Supreme Court cited the language of *Buckley* v. *Valeo*, 424 U.S. 1 (1976): "A restriction on the amount of money a person or group can spend on political communication during a campaign necessarily reduces the quantity of expression by restricting the number of issues discussed, the depth of their exploration and the size of the audience reached. This is because every means of communicating ideas in today's mass society requires the expenditure of money." (*Citizens for Jobs and Energy et al.* v. *Fair Political Practices Commission*, 16 Cal. 3rd 671 [1976].)

[34] Robert Agranoff, *The New Style in Election Campaigns* (Boston: Holbrook Press, 1976), p. 471.

> the first full-fledged professional campaign management firm in the United States should have developed in California, because of the state's lack of party organization, its constant influx of new voters, and its extraordinarily frequent use of the initiative and referendum. . . .
>
> For the next 20 years [following a successful campaign by the new firm in 1933 to defeat a referendum against the state's Central Valley Project] their support decided many of the key issues of California politics. They usually managed the campaigns for or against five or six initiative or referendum propositions in every state election.[35]

The *New York Times'* California correspondent, Gladwin Hill, commented:

> They [Whitaker and Baxter] flourished because they filled a need. The important electoral device of the initiative was becoming a far bigger affair than the simple citizen-petition operation the Progressive reformers had envisioned. Many of the issues were multi-million dollar matters. Consequently expenditures by contending forces were running into hundreds of thousands of dollars. It was sensible to have such outlays handled with professional skill.[36]

By the 1950s dozens of campaign-counseling firms had been established in the state. For many of these organizations, the initiative provided their introduction into professional political management, and the techniques and tools devised for that arena were quickly extended into candidate campaigns.

The Voter

Whether campaigns are in support of a candidate or a ballot measure, voters are the target. It remains to discuss their participation, understanding, and behavior in the initiative process. At least three questions must be asked: To what extent do voters participate? Do they understand the measures on the ballot? What are the major factors that shape their decisions?

Participation. Voting on initiative measures almost always coincides with a general or primary election. Under the state constitution the

[35] Walton Bean, *California: An Interpretive History,* 2nd ed. (New York: McGraw-Hill, 1973), pp. 470-471.

[36] Gladwin Hill, *Dancing Bear: An Inside Look at California Politics* (Cleveland: World, 1968), p. 194.

governor may call a special election to consider an initiative, but this has been done only three times, in 1939, 1949, and 1973. Thus, participation in direct legislation is heavily influenced by the size of the turnout for presidential and gubernatorial contests[37] and for congressional and legislative races occurring at the same time. An initiative campaign itself is but one among several factors shaping the turnout on election day.

As noted in Table 5-3, more than 90 percent of those casting a ballot typically vote on initiative measures. In the 1976 general election, for example, 94 percent voted on the greyhound racing proposal and 95 percent on the agricultural labor relations measures. In 1972 between 90 and 95 percent of those voting cast a ballot on each of the nine initiative measures. (Only 88 percent voted on the wild and scenic rivers measure in 1974—the lowest figure since 1962.) Initiative voting almost always involves a drop-off from the vote for president or governor, which is generally around 98 percent of the total vote cast, but approximates that for state legislators or congressional representatives.

A notable exception occurred in June 1978, when some 6.5 million persons voted for or against Proposition 13, the hotly contested property tax limitation initiative, compared with only 5.7 million who voted in the gubernatorial primary held at the same time. The latter figure was undoubtedly depressed because of the absence of a serious contest in the Democratic primary. Nevertheless, it is clear that many citizens went to the polls primarily to vote on the initiative measure.

In general, the vote on initiatives—reflecting their more controversial nature—almost always exceeds by several percentage points the vote for constitutional amendments proposed by the legislature.

The electorate differs in character from the total adult population. Typically, lower socioeconomic groups—minorities, the poor, the uneducated—vote in smaller relative numbers than do more privileged members of society. The electorate is also skewed in the

[37] In California, as in most other states, governors are elected in the middle of the presidential term. Presidential elections typically draw a larger number of voters to the polls than do contests for governor. In the special election of 1939 the voter turnout was 82 percent of registration. This was a hotly contested election involving two initiative measures and three referendums. In contrast, the special election of 1949, which involved two initiatives, a bond issue, and nine constitutional amendments submitted by the legislature, attracted only 61 percent of the registered voters to the polls. The special election called by Republican Governor Ronald Reagan in 1973 for the sole purpose of considering his tax limitation initiative drew an even smaller proportion, only 48 percent of registrants.

direction of older voters. A recent census bureau report concluded that "A significant part of the decline in the voting rate since 1964 can be attributed to an increase in the proportion of the electorate under 35 years old—traditionally a low-turnout age group . . . this segment of the voting-age population increased from 28 percent to 40 percent in the period from 1964 to 1976," in part a result of the lowering of the voting age to eighteen prior to the 1972 elections.[38]

These differences between the character of the electorate and that of the adult population have led William J. D. Boyd of the National Municipal League to speculate whether or not "since the arrival of one man, one vote, state legislatures do not represent the *entire* population (not just those who vote) more accurately than the voters at any single election." From this specific perspective, he asks whether the initiative and referendum are in fact, "less democratic" than representative institutions.[39] Whatever the case, the size and internal composition of the electorate are important factors in the politics of the initiative process.

In short, voting on initiatives is reasonably high among those going to the polls, but low as a proportion of the adults eligible to vote. As is also true of statewide candidates, no initiative ever receives the approval of a majority of California adults. Millions of Californians in effect delegate their vote to their fellow citizens.

A recent development has made the matter more complicated. Under amendments to the elections code made in 1966, at the time the legislature moved to annual sessions, ballot propositions—including initiatives—can now appear on the June primary ballot if the petitions qualify in time. From 1966 through 1978 five initiatives so qualified. The primary election involves from 0.5 million to 1.5 million fewer

---

[38] As reported in the *Los Angeles Times*, April 14, 1978.

[39] Letter to the author, February 28, 1978. Boyd continues: "Black or Mexican-American districts (or Puerto Rican in New York) have exactly the same number of people in their district as do any other group. Now they may not turn out and vote in large numbers, but even if they do not vote they do have a representative in Sacramento (or Albany or wherever). Thus, in the legislature they and their numbers are reflected in almost exact ratio to their numbers in the *total* population. (Naturally, gerrymandering, the concentration of minorities in ghettoes, and so on, throw off the 'exactness' of this representation.) That would be *much* better representation than they actually get at the polls. This may or may not be their own fault, but it is a fact. . . . Also, I am curious to see what happens as the demography of the nation changes. We have been a 'youth cult' nation for many years. Now the emphasis is shifting and fast. Our population is aging, and they are the very group that have the higher voter turnout. Could we not see the older people represented in far greater numbers in the voting booth than they are in the population at large? (Even in the entire population they will become a larger voice.) Will they begin to turn toward more status quo or even conservative (at least fiscally) measures?"

registrants than the ensuing general election and an even greater fall-off in the number of voters. In 1976, in fact, the difference between the primary and general election turnout exceeded 1.8 million. Since 1960, at least, a primary election has never involved more than half the eligible citizenry. In 1976, for example, only 44 percent of California adults voted in the primary; in 1974 the figure was even lower—36 percent.

In the politics of the initiative process, these differences are highly significant. The lower the turnout, the easier it will be for a well-mobilized group to dominate the election process. Instead of having to obtain a vote of over 4 million to insure success, a primary ballot proposition might pass with a million fewer votes.

Not only do the total numbers of voters differ in a primary and general election, but the character of the electorate also varies. Although patterns from election to election are not consistent, a larger share of registered Republicans tend to vote in both primary and general elections than is true of Democrats. (Democrats outnumber Republicans by about a three-to-two margin in California.) Primary election turnout is also affected by the character of the contests for the particular party. In the 1978 gubernatorial primary noted above, for example, the incumbent Democratic governor, Jerry Brown, did not face serious opposition, while the race for the Republican nomination was hotly contested by five candidates. As a result, the Republican turnout was stimulated. This, in turn, undoubtedly increased the margin of victory for the property tax initiative, which Republicans tended to favor in significantly greater proportion than Democrats.

Whether these differences between primary and general elections in absolute voter turnout and the internal character of the electorate will prove influential remains to be seen. It is clear that they have only recently become relevant to initiative strategists in the timing and conduct of their campaigns.

Voter Understanding. The nine out of ten voters who cast a ballot on initiative measures often make up their minds how to vote on the eve of the election, particularly in the case of complex, technical issues. Over the years, this is the pattern of behavior reported by Mervin Field's distinguished *California Poll* in its preelection surveys:

> An initiative ballot proposition as it is first presented to voters in summary form appears to fill a need or correct a situation with which a large segment of the public is in sympathy. Initially, while not many people fully grasp all

> the details and ramifications, their instinctive reaction is generally favorable. Then the issue is joined by the opposition usually well after the initiative qualifies and is placed on the ballot. Typically, the public only becomes fully aware of the opposition to the measure relatively late in the campaign, sometimes only a few weeks before Election Day. Then if the force and extent of opposition to the proposal is considerable, public awareness of the measure increases dramatically. And more times than not the original instinctive support of the idea is replaced by a negative view.[40]

This description is illustrated by the 1976 elections. During the campaigning on an initiative to restrict construction and operation of nuclear power plants, 54 percent of those polled—a sample of the registered electorate—indicated an awareness of the measure in late January. By April this figure had increased to 65 percent, with the June election some two months away. By early May, 37 percent of the sample polled believed they knew enough about the measure to vote, while 63 percent said they would like to wait until they heard more about the proposal. On election eve, 58 percent of those polled said they knew enough to vote. Among this group 52 percent had "definitely" made up their minds, and only 3 percent were undecided. Among those "still waiting for more information" 42 percent were undecided, and only 15 percent had definite intentions.[41] On general election day, however, 95 percent of those actually participating in the June primary voted on the measure. (It is probable that a disproportionate number of those who were undecided did not vote on the measure or, perhaps, did not vote at all.)

A parallel development occurred in the fall election, when the voters were faced with a controversial agricultural labor relations act, sponsored by Cesar Chavez and the United Farm Workers and opposed by growers and farming corporations. As of late September, the *California Poll* indicated that only 46 percent of the California public had seen or heard anything about the farm labor measure.[42]

Field suggests that the voter then gets his cues concerning these types of issues by looking "to what other people say, to what respected institutions and leaders say, and to the advertising and other information about the measures that is made available."[43] Wolfinger and Greenstein made a similar observation in analyzing the 1964

---

[40] Mervin Field, *The California Poll*, June 3, 1972.

[41] Ibid., March 4, 1976; April 16, 1976; May 18, 1976; June 4, 1976.

[42] Ibid., October 12, 1976.

[43] Ibid., October 13, 1978.

anti–fair housing initiative: "Voting choices in such contests are likely to be more responsive to leadership group influence than those in general election voting, where party identification guides most voters. . . . Campaign activity and the positions taken by community leaders may have had considerable impact upon voting patterns."[44]

An important source of information is the pamphlet mailed by the state to every voter, in which each ballot measure is objectively summarized, and arguments are presented by proponents and opponents.[45] The state League of Women Voters assumes a responsibility for objective publicity concerning propositions, even those which the league officially opposes. Major newspapers of the state attempt to play a similar role as do, to a much lesser extent, the radio and television. In short, voters who are reasonably alert may well be confronted with more information than they can absorb.

Whatever the case, a large body of voters appears to know what it is doing. For example, although respondents were not always familiar with the details of the pro-labor farm worker initiative in 1976, there was a clear congruence between their attitudes toward Chavez and the growers and their views on the measure: 89 percent of those who felt that they would like to see Chavez "win out" favored the proposition, while 78 percent of those favoring the growers associated that view with opposition to the measure.[46]

The campaign over the tax limitation initiative on the June 1978 ballot was exceptional. Only 9 percent of those polled were "undecided" or "unaware" on election eve, and supporters and opponents alike possessed clear and logically consistent views backing their voting intention. Those voting yes focused on two main themes: "Taxes are too high" (51 percent) and "The time has come to cut government costs, waste, and inefficiency" (46 percent). Comments offered by those voting no included "Would mean too big a cutback for schools" (27 percent) and "Would put too many teachers, firemen, and policemen out of jobs" (19 percent).[47]

[44] Raymond E. Wolfinger and Fred I. Greenstein, "The Repeal of Fair Housing in California: An Analysis of Referendum Voting," *American Political Science Review*, vol. 62 (September 1968), pp. 762-763.

[45] In the state of Washington a study revealed that "the official voters pamphlet is mentioned by the most persons as their first choice of information on ballot propositions, followed by newspapers, family, friends, and television, then various other sources. What is most important perhaps is that the voters mentioning the pamphlet as their first choice for information exhibited significantly better knowledge of the issues." (Hugh A. Bone, "The Initiative in Washington: 1915-1974," *Washington Public Policy Notes*, University of Washington, Institute of Governmental Research [October 1974].)

[46] Field, *The California Poll*, October 12, 1976.

[47] Ibid., May 17, 1978.

The highly technical nuclear initiative was very different. Of those persons stating they favored the proposal, 24 percent offered reasons associated with a vote of no, while 16 percent of those opposed to the measure provided a rationale for their choice associated with a yes vote.[48] These findings are paralleled by a separate open-ended postelection survey in Sacramento County. Twenty percent of the respondents who had voted for the measure, when asked "Why did you vote as you did?" had clearly voted for the wrong reasons, for example, "saying that they voted yes because there was a need for more nuclear energy no matter what." Similarly, 8 percent of those voting no were similarly confused, providing statements such as, "I voted no because I don't want nuclear power under any conditions."[49]

Ballot propositions not infrequently involve such confusion. In 1972 a vote *for* farm labor required a vote *against* a collective bargaining measure supported by growers. In 1974 a vote *against* construction of a dam required a yes vote in support of "wild and scenic rivers." Skillful campaigners can use such ambiguity in support of their cause. However, Wolfinger and Greenstein concluded from their analysis of the 1964 initiative, which repealed the state's fair housing act and which involved a no vote for those in favor of the act, that "the number of 'wrong' votes resulting from confusion about the proposition's impact on fair housing legislation does not seem to have been great. . . . [There is] no support for the contention that the election was significantly affected by the wording of the proposition or by ignorance of its meaning."[50]

The 1976 nuclear initiative involved a highly technical issue, with scientists and engineers arguing on both sides and a high degree of voter confusion and uncertainty. In contrast, an issue like the death penalty presented the voters with a problem which they had confronted over the years and on which opinions were crystallized. Thus, although a *California Poll* in early October 1972 indicated that 80 percent of the public had not heard of the death penalty initiative, only 13 percent of the persons polled were undecided as to how they would vote when told about the measure. Their views coincided almost exactly with those already cognizant of the initiative and were overwhelmingly in support of restoring the death penalty.[51]

[48] Ibid., April 16, 1976.

[49] Alexander J. Groth and Howard G. Schutz, "Voter Attitudes on the 1976 Nuclear Initiative in California," University of California, Davis, Institute of Governmental Affairs (December 1976), p. 10.

[50] Wolfinger and Greenstein, "The Repeal of Fair Housing," p. 757.

[51] Field, *The California Poll*, October 24, 1972.

An almost identical result was found with respect to a proposal to decriminalize the use of marijuana. A month before the election, three-fourths of the public had either not heard about the proposition or wanted more information before making up their minds. When pressed for a decision, however, only 11 percent indicated they were undecided. Here, too, their preferences coincided almost exactly with those already aware of the proposition, 60 percent of whom opposed the measure. In both instances, the *California Poll* indicated that the public's views on the propositions were consistent with findings about the death penalty and marijuana conducted in previous years. The death penalty advocates were riding a tide "when the public's feelings seem to be growing more strongly disposed toward the desirability and necessity of capital punishment," and, confirming a 1971 survey, "a majority were still not tolerant of the use of marijuana, and were against liberalizing legalization of it." [52]

Voting Behavior. Since 1960 there have been almost no close initiative contests. Of the twenty-six measures from 1960 to 1976—seven of which were adopted—only three involved a vote split closer than 55 to 45 (senate reapportionment, 1962; tax and expenditure limitation, 1973; wild and scenic rivers protection act, 1974). Four other measures—most recently the coastal conservation and agricultural labor relations initiatives of 1972—involved a vote split between 55-45 and 60-40, but for the remaining nineteen the winning side was able to capture a vote in excess of 60 percent.

No less than in presidential or gubernatorial races, initiative voting decisions are influenced by currents of conservatism and liberalism, by socioeconomic status, by age and race, by urban or rural residence, and—related to all of these—by party affiliation. Issues such as school busing, the death penalty, environmental controls, and tax measures involve themes which have long divided the public in familiar ways. In contrast, the salaries of state employees or greyhound racing cut across normal political lines. Other factors affecting the vote on these initiatives are the absence of the party label on ballot measures and a general lack of party activity, an often relatively low level of voter awareness, and frequent last-minute decision making, "subject to quick change under the pressure of a massive campaign and emotional appeals." [53]

---

[52] Ibid., October 24 and 25, 1972.

[53] Mervin Field, quoted in "A Feature in California, More than 140 Proposals since 1912," *Los Angeles Times*, October 23, 1972.

A glimpse at the distribution of voter attitudes concerning the nuclear power plant and agricultural labor relations measures of 1976 reveals some of the underlying bases for initiative voting. In the Sacramento postelection survey, "Party affiliations and differences seemingly related to conservative-liberal political preferences proved highly significant in relation to the vote on the nuclear initiative." Of the Democratic identifiers, 54 percent favored the measure, as contrasted with only 28 percent of the Republicans.[54] Going beyond party, the study concluded that the conflict over nuclear power could be generalized as one between specific groups: an older, more conservative, and more affluent stratum of society, more suburban, more concerned with maintaining a high standard of living and national energy independence, and less worried about the risks associated with nuclear power, arrayed against a younger, more liberal, less affluent stratum that was less favorably disposed to the status quo, more oriented to conservation policies, and less concerned with energy consumption in relation to social well-being.[55]

With respect to the agricultural labor relations initiative sponsored by Cesar Chavez and the United Farm Workers in 1976, the *California Poll* reported that Democrats were evenly split on the measure, whereas Republicans were overwhelmingly against it. Blacks and Latinos, representing about one in seven voters, favored the measure by a three-to-two margin, while the rest of the population was against it by a two-to-one ratio.

Proposition 13, the 1978 tax limitation measure, met with overwhelming support in the electorate as a whole, but there were marked differences among particular groups. For example, 63 percent of homeowners favored the measure in contrast to only 42 percent of those living in rented properties. An election eve poll showed that 61 percent of whites supported the initiative, while 65 percent of blacks opposed it. These differences were reflected in party statistics: Republicans favored the proposition by more than two to one, as contrasted with a bare majority of Democrats.[56]

In the California context, such political differences may also involve local or regional voting patterns. Indeed, Wolfinger and Greenstein suggested on the basis of their study in the 1960s that with respect to propositions, "where political stimuli are not so

[54] Groth and Schutz, "Voter Attitudes," p. 24.
[55] Ibid., p. 54.
[56] Field, *The California Poll*, June 6, 1978.

mediated by party identification, those influences associated with the regional political cultures are likely to have more impact."[57] The pattern is a very mixed one, however. The well-known liberalism of San Francisco was clearly demonstrated by its 51 percent vote against the 1972 death penalty initiative, in contrast to a 25 percent vote in conservative Orange County. But these sharp county distinctions did not reflect a north-south split in the state; California's northern counties outside the San Francisco Bay Area voted nearly as strongly as Orange County for the death penalty measure, while even the other Bay Area counties voted 61 percent for the initiative.

Governor Reagan's 1973 tax and expenditure limitation initiative illustrated a similar but less pronounced pattern. In this instance, San Francisco voted 64 percent against the measure, while Orange County—long regarded as "Reagan country"—voted 59 percent for it. The measure was only narrowly defeated (50.4 percent) in southern California as a whole, compared with a 59 percent negative vote in the north, clearly reflecting political currents different from those involved in the death penalty controversy.

A final example, the coastline preservation measure of 1972, suggests there are no easy answers to summarizing initiative voting patterns. San Francisco—the home of the Sierra Club and other environmental causes—voted 62 percent for the measure, but a favorable vote was cast in all other sections of the state as well, including a majority—albeit slim—in Orange County.[58]

What does this evidence suggest? Voters participate in the initiative process in large numbers. They frequently make up their minds at the last minute. Although they are occasionally confused as to the meaning of an initiative and vote contrary to their intentions, they

[57] Raymond E. Wolfinger and Fred I. Greenstein, "Comparing Political Regions: The Case of California," *American Political Science Review*, vol. 63 (March 1969), p. 82.

[58] In a survey of eight initiative measures on the ballot from 1972 through 1976 (dealing with the death penalty, obscenity, marijuana, coastline conservation, school busing, political reform, nuclear power regulation, and farm labor), Elizabeth LaMacchia divided California's fifty-eight counties into five categories on a liberal-conservative spectrum, based on whether the county voted for or against the measure. San Francisco was the only county to follow the liberal line on all but one issue—the nuclear power measure. Alameda County, across the bay from San Francisco, fell into the center of the spectrum with four liberal votes. Thirty counties, including Los Angeles, Orange, and San Diego, were classed as moderately conservative with five conservative votes out of eight, while twenty-four counties voted the liberal line on only two of the eight issues—against more stringent laws controlling obscenity and for political reform. Two small rural counties voted conservatively on all issues except political reform. ("The Deceptive Contradictions of County Voting Patterns," *California Journal*, vol. 8 [October 1977], pp. 351-353.)

generally vote in accordance with their underlying beliefs and attitudes. Partisan and regional influences are sometimes, but not consistently, evident. And most often, as noted by Baus and Ross, electors tend to vote no—regardless of the liberal or conservative nature of the measure—leaving the fate of most legislation to their representatives and not to themselves.

Conclusion

From 1960 through 1976, only two of the seven initiative measures approved by the California electorate were not struck down by the courts, in whole or in part, as unconstitutional.[59] Of the two remaining, the railroad anti-featherbedding act can hardly be classed as a critical public issue. The coastal conservation act was, under the terms of the initiative, brought to an end in 1976, although its major provisions were implemented in a coastline preservation act passed by the legislature in the same year, an action that was clearly the result of the prior initiative. In 1978 a major shift in the structure of state and local finance resulted from the passage of Proposition 13, although it was possible that court action might alter some of its features.

There were of course the highly praised initiatives of the 1920s and 1930s—civil service, judicial reform, and the executive budget—and public school funding in the 1940s and 1950s. But since World War II virtually no major public policy measure other than those noted has been placed in the constitution or statutes as a direct result of the initiative.[60]

A small output? Perhaps, although the successful measures include some of the most important policy issues enacted in the state. Whatever the case, consideration of the initiative is growing. Over 120 proposals were submitted to the attorney general from 1970 through 1978, although few qualified for the ballot. The success of the highly publicized tax limitation measure in 1978 will almost surely stimulate interest in the initiative. If this proves to be the case, these conclusions seem clear:

[59] For a more detailed review of these decisions, see Gordon E. Baker, "Judicial Review of Statewide Initiatives in California: Proposition 13 in Recent Historical Perspective," paper presented at the annual meeting of the American Political Science Association, New York, August 31, 1978.

[60] Writing in 1939, Key and Crouch described the success of direct legislation up to that time: "It seems certain that the initiative and the referendum have not had a very profound effect on the great body of legislation, although it cannot be denied that through these means, decisions of great significance to particular groups have been made." (*Initiative*, p. 575.)

- The initiative will continue to be a permanent part of the California political scene, complementing if not supporting weak political party organizations whose leadership is dominated by personalities and issues rather than resting on formal structure.
- The high costs of the initiative process both in petition circulation and in campaigning will continue. Legal attempts to curtail these expenditures have been declared unconstitutional, although campaign disclosure laws have been tightened to provide complete records of interest-group participation in the funding of campaigns.
- While these high costs are identified primarily with economic special interest groups—including not only business but also labor unions and public employees—grass-roots organizations will continue to compete successfully in the initiative process with relatively modest financial resources.
- The "new politics" of the 1970s, with its emphasis on professional campaign management, targeted direct mailings, and the sophisticated sloganeering of the sixty-second television commercial will dominate most initiative campaigns, just as it has increasingly become a feature in presidential and gubernatorial races.
- Successful initiatives will generally be adopted by a vote of no more than 25 to 30 percent of the adult population of the state. Whether such a decision is more or less "democratic" than an action by a state legislature, itself the product of a limited electorate and generally safe districts, is an open question.
- The initiative will continue to permit "flashes of prejudice and emotion to sweep legislation onto or off the statute books,"[61] but the increased role of the courts in ruling on the constitutionality of such measures would appear to provide a protection against the dangers of such actions with respect to questions of civil liberties and civil rights.
- The initiative process is often not "a particularly efficient means of enacting new legislation. Lawmaking requires hearings, debates, compromise and deliberation, whereas the initiative process is inherently arbitrary."[62] Such failures of the initiative appear in ambiguous or contradictory legal draftsmanship, in patently unconstitutional language, or in measures that would clearly have benefited from the give-and-take of the legislative process.

[61] Winston W. Crouch, John Bollens, and Stanley Scott, *California Government and Politics*, 6th ed. (Englewood Cliffs, N. J.: Prentice-Hall, 1977), p. 127.
[62] Carey McWilliams, "The Initiative: A Vehicle for Eccentric Reform," *Los Angeles Times*, April 2, 1978.

- Reforms addressing these problems will continue to be introduced but will be unsuccessful if seen by interest groups as barriers to the direct access to the electorate that now exists.
- Despite the obvious complexities of the ballot, "California's well-educated voters [seem] far more able to cope with intricate initiatives than had been presumed by political scientists. . . . The easy assertions about the apathy, indifference, and susceptible nature of voters can at least be questioned by the California experience."[63]
- The initiative will be employed by candidates for public office as a part of their personal campaign strategy. In fact, this will be the prime motivation behind the drafting and sponsorship of some measures. This activity may increase as issues and personalities fill the vacuum left by increasingly weak party ties.
- The initiative will continue to be used as an educational tool. Even when the chance of success is small, as in the case of the marijuana decriminalization measure, proponents hope that their views will gain a wider airing through the process of petition circulation and ballot campaigning.
- Most important, the initiative will remain a critical part of the politics of the legislative process. The very existence of an alternative to the legislature and the governor, whether it is used or not, influences the pattern of legislative behavior. Examples have been noted where the legislature has acted to defeat an initiative on the ballot or to forestall one under consideration. Even an unsuccessful initiative may stimulate legislation in the direction desired by the measure's sponsors, but—equally—failure may lead to legislative inaction, as legislators respond to a public decision against a proposal. And legislative inaction may also lead to an initiative. Indeed, legislators and governors themselves may use the threat of an initiative to gain passage of a bill and, failing to do so, take the lead in sponsoring a ballot measure. Although it will be infrequent—if for no other reason than that initiatives fail far more often than they succeed—legislative leaders will confront the centrifugal pressures of members willing and able to go outside the capitol in pursuit of their goals. Interest groups and campaign contributors will be standing in legislative halls to make this point, if anyone forgets.

What then of the vision of the Progressives noted in the opening paragraphs of this essay? Unquestionably, California political life has

---

[63] Price, "The Initiative," pp. 260-261.

been dominated by their "reforms"—a weak party structure, a direct primary and nonpartisan local elections, a strong civil service. Unquestionably, too, the state has prospered, albeit in fits and starts. There have been periods of reaction and lobbyist domination as well as times of forward-looking programs in almost every field of public activity, times of economic progress and racial intolerance, and times of unparalleled growth coupled with inadequate control of that development. But what of the initiative, which it was alleged in 1911 would neutralize special interest groups, curtail corruption, provide a vehicle for civic education, create pressure on state officials to act in the public interest, and ultimately make "every man his own legislature"?

The answer is assuredly mixed. We cannot isolate this one institution and attribute to it either the blessings of progress or the sins of omission and commission which have featured in California's public life in this century. Nor can we even answer whether California would be better or worse off if the Progressives had not been successful in 1911. Special interests in the state are as active and powerful as anywhere in the nation, but their numbers include effective grass-roots environmental protection and civic reform groups as well as dominant economic forces. Corruption is relatively rare, but the power of campaign contributions is strong and, although fully reported, unrestricted. Civic education is high, but millions of Californians do not participate politically at all.

Yet, if every person is far from being his or her own legislature, it is equally true that the initiative has become so deeply rooted in the political culture of the state that no public figure in memory has suggested that it be eliminated—or even substantially modified—and none is likely soon to do so. Attempts to restrict its use, by reintroducing some form of the indirect initiative, cannot even clear a legislative committee. The initiative's appeal for young and old, for liberal and conservative, is pervasive and compelling. There is every reason to believe it will continue to be so—an imperfect but useful institution in a world of imperfections.

Bibliography

Baker, Gordon E. "American Conceptions of Direct vis-à-vis Representative Governance," *Claremont Journal of Public Affairs* 1 (Spring 1977): 5–18.

Baker, Gordon E. "Judicial Review of Statewide Initiatives in California: Proposition 13 in Recent Historical Perspective." Paper presented at the annual meeting of the American Political Science Association, New York, August 31, 1978.

Bean, Walton. *California: An Interpretive History.* 2nd ed. New York: McGraw-Hill, 1973.

Berg, Larry L. "The Initiative Process and Public Policy-Making in the States: 1904–1976." Paper presented at the annual meeting of the American Political Science Association, New York, August 31, 1978.

Bone, Hugh A. "The Initiative in Washington: 1915–1974." *Washington Public Policy Notes.* University of Washington, Institute of Governmental Research, October 1974.

Bone, Hugh A., and Robert C. Benedict. "Perspectives on Direct Legislation: Washington State's Experience, 1914–73." *Western Political Quarterly* 28 (June 1975): 330–351.

Brestoff, Nick. "The California Initiative Process: A Suggestion for Reform." *Southern California Law Review* 78 (March 1975): 922–958.

Casstevens, Thomas W. "Reflections on the Initiative Process in California State Politics." *Public Affairs Report.* University of California, Berkeley, Institute of Governmental Studies, February 1965.

Crouch, Winston W. *The Initiative and Referendum in California.* Los Angeles: Haynes Foundation, 1950.

Crouch, Winston W., John Bollens, and Stanley Scott. *California Government and Politics.* 6th ed. Englewood Cliffs, N.J.: Prentice-Hall, 1977.

Diamond, Roger Jon, and others. "California's Political Reform Act: Greater Access to the Initiative Process." *Southwestern University Law Review* 7 (Fall 1975): 454–602.

Dziublenski, Joe. "The Continuing Campaign to Inhibit the Initiative." *California Journal* 7 (August 1976): 280–281.

Field, Mervin. *The California Poll,* various issues.

Greenberg, Donald S. "The Scope of the Initiative and Referendum in California." *California Law Review* 54 (October 1966): 1717–1748.

Groth, Alexander J., and Howard G. Schutz. "Voter Attitudes on the 1976 Nuclear Initiative in California." University of California, Davis, Institute of Governmental Affairs, December 1976.

Haynes, John Randolph. "Direct Legislation." *Transactions of the Commonwealth Club of California* 6 (September 1911): 286–290.

Hill, Gladwin. *Dancing Bear: An Inside Look at California Politics.* Cleveland: World, 1968.

Key, V. O., Jr., and Winston W. Crouch. *The Initiative and Referendum in California.* Berkeley: University of California Press, 1939.

LaMacchia, Elizabeth. "The Deceptive Contradictions of County Voting Patterns." *California Journal* 8 (October 1977): 351–352.

League of Women Voters of California. "Constitutional Revision—Focus on Direct Legislation." February 1966.

Lutrin, Carl E., and Allen K. Settle. "The Public and Ecology: The Role of Initiatives in California's Environmental Politics." *Western Political Quarterly* 28 (June 1975): 352–371.

Matthews, Linda. "The Ballot Initiative: Whom Does It Serve." *Los Angeles Times*, October 22, 1972.

McWilliams, Carey. "The Initiative: A Vehicle for Eccentric Reform." *Los Angeles Times*, April 2, 1978.

Mueller, John E. "Voting on the Propositions: Ballot Patterns and Historical Trends in California." *American Political Science Review* 63 (December 1969): 1197–1212.

Owens, John R., Edmond Costantini, and Louis F. Weschler. *California Politics and Parties.* New York: Macmillan, 1970.

Price, Charles M. "The Initiative: A Comparative State Analysis and Reassessment of a Western Phenomenon." *Western Political Quarterly* 28 (June 1975): 243–262.

Tallian, Laura. *Direct Democracy: An Historical Analysis of the Initiative, Referendum and Recall Process.* Los Angeles: People's Lobby, 1977.

Wolfinger, Raymond E., and Fred I. Greenstein. "The Repeal of Fair Housing in California: An Analysis of Referendum Voting." *American Political Science Review* 62 (September 1968): 753–769.

Wolfinger, Raymond E., and Fred I. Greenstein. "Comparing Political Regions: The Case of California." *American Political Science Review* 63 (March 1969): 74–85.

6
Australia

Don Aitkin

The referendum is all that is left in Australia of the three instruments of popular control widely accepted by democratic theorists in the nineteenth century—the initiative, the referendum, and the recall. The referendum might have shared the fate of the other two had it not been that the makers of the Australian constitution at the turn of the century finally adopted it as the means by which their constitution was to be amended. As a result, Australians have taken part in thirty-six national referendums since the first in 1906. In addition, the referendum process has been used on three other occasions in national politics to ascertain public opinion about non-constitutional matters: in 1916 and 1917 whether Australian men should be conscripted for military service, and in 1977 the preferred national song. With these exceptions, however, Australian referendums are understandable only in the context of the politics of the constitution.[1]

The role of the referendum in both constitutional and non-constitutional politics has been repeated in the several states. Local option referendums were common in the late nineteenth and early twentieth centuries when electors voting in general elections would also cast a vote as to whether the district should allow the sale of liquor on licensed premises. More recently, statewide referendums have been used to help determine whether part of a state should become a new state (New South Wales, 1967), whether hotels should be allowed to trade after a certain hour or on Sundays, and whether a state should secede from the federation (Western Australia, 1933).

[1] The best guide is Geoffrey Sawer, most especially his two-volume work, *Australian Federal Politics and Law, 1901-1929*, and *Australian Federal Politics and Law, 1929-1949* (Melbourne: Melbourne University Press, 1956 and 1963).

In these cases the referendum has had no legal force, since the government of the day has retained the power to make up its own mind. But some states have followed the Commonwealth example and employed the referendum as a device for controlling constitutional change. Although each state had in colonial days a version of the Westminster system, with Parliament sovereign, New South Wales, Queensland, and South Australia have each passed laws requiring the assent of the electors at a referendum to any proposed variation in the basic institutions of Parliament (including a change in this provision itself). For all that, referendums in state politics are much less common than is the case in federal politics.[2]

The process needed for constitutional amendment is set out in section 128 of the Commonwealth constitution. In brief it requires that the proposed change receive the approval of an absolute majority of both houses of the Parliament, after which (not earlier than two months nor later than six) it must be submitted to the voters in each state. The proposal succeeds if it gains an absolute majority of all the votes cast as well as a majority in each of a majority of states (that is, at least four of the six states of the federation). If one of the houses of Parliament objects to the proposed change, and the other approves it a second time, then the governor-general may submit the proposal to the electors.

The framers of the constitution wanted one that would last, and they had to guess at the height of the hurdles that would trip the badly thought out or the ephemeral but would still allow useful changes—and of course they disagreed as to the desirability of change in principle. But it is unlikely that they intended the test to be as difficult as it has proved to be. Of more than eighty proposals that have been raised in Parliament, only thirty-six have gone to the people; of those thirty-six only eight have been approved by the electors, and only one of them was at all controversial (see Table 6-2). In a comparable length of time the Swiss constitution was amended by referendum forty-seven times. What has made constitutional amendment in Australia such a difficult business? Retrospective analysis of the thirty-six referendums suggests that there have been three broad factors at work: the high level of partisanship in Australian politics, the lack of an informed and interested electorate, and the procedural hurdles themselves. Let us begin with the last.

---

[2] The use of referendums at the state level has varied from state to state, with no obvious pattern save a general preoccupation with drinking hours and a greater use of the device in the two most populous states (see Table 6-1).

TABLE 6-1

Australian Referendums at the State Level

State (No.)	*Date*	*Subject*	*Percent Voting Yes*
New South Wales (11)	16 Dec. 1903	Reduce size of legislative assembly to ninety	72.9
	10 June 1916	6 P.M. closing hour for bars	62.4
	1 Sept. 1928	Prohibition of liquor sales	28.5
	13 May 1933	Reform legislative council	51.5
	15 Feb. 1947	6 P.M. closing hour for bars	62.4
	13 Nov. 1954	10 P.M. closing hour for bars	50.3
	29 Apr. 1961	Abolish legislative council	44.7
	29 Apr. 1967	Create new state in northeast New South Wales (referendum held only in proposed new state area)	45.8
	29 Nov. 1969	Open bars on Sundays	42.0
	1 May 1976	Daylight saving time	63.0
	17 June 1978	Direct election of legislative council	84.8
Victoria (7)	1 June 1904	Keep public education secular	58.6
	1 June 1904	Provide scripture lessons in schools	53.0
	1 June 1904	Use of certain prayers and hymns	51.2
	21 Oct. 1920	Local option on sale of liquor	52.9
	29 Mar. 1930	Abolish liquor licensing	42.9
	8 Oct. 1938	Abolish liquor licensing	33.6
	24 Mar. 1956	10 P.M. closing for bars	39.7
Queensland (1)	5 May 1917	Abolish legislative council	39.3
South Australia (3)	26 Apr. 1911	Increase parliamentary salaries	32.5
	27 Mar. 1915	6 P.M. closing hour for bars	56.3
	20 Nov. 1965	Establish state lottery	65.7
Western Australia (4)	8 Apr. 1933	Secede from the Commonwealth	66.2
	8 Apr. 1933	Call constitutional convention	42.5
	9 Dec. 1950	Prohibition of liquor sales	26.5
	8 Mar. 1975	Daylight saving time	46.4
Tasmania (2)	25 Mar. 1916	6 P.M. closing hour for bars	58.7
	14 Dec. 1968	Establish Wrest Point Casino	50.6

TABLE 6-2

NATIONWIDE REFERENDUMS IN AUSTRALIA

Subject	*Date of Referendum*	*Government Party*	*States with Majority Vote in Favor*	*Percent Voting Yes*	*Percent Turnout*
Senate elections	12 Dec. 1906	Non-Labor	All	82.7[a]	50.2
Finance	13 Apr. 1910	Labor	Q, WA, T	49.0	62.2
State debts	13 Apr. 1910	Labor	All except NSW	55.0[a]	62.2
Legislative powers	26 Apr. 1911	Labor	WA	39.4	53.3
Monopolies	26 Apr. 1911	Labor	WA	39.9	53.3
Trade and commerce	31 May 1913	Labor	Q, SA, WA	49.4	73.7
Corporations	31 May 1913	Labor	Q, SA, WA	49.3	73.7
Industrial matters	31 May 1913	Labor	Q, SA, WA	49.3	73.7
Railway disputes	31 May 1913	Labor	Q, SA, WA	49.1	73.7
Trusts	31 May 1913	Labor	Q, SA, WA	49.8	73.7
Nationalization of monopolies	31 May 1913	Labor	Q, SA, WA	49.3	73.7
Conscription for overseas service[c]	28 Oct. 1916	Non-Labor	V, WA, T	48.4[b]	82.7
Conscription for overseas service[c]	20 Dec. 1917	Non-Labor	WA, T	46.2[b]	81.3
Legislative powers	13 Dec. 1919	Non-Labor	V, Q, WA	49.7	71.3

Nationalization of monopolies	13 Dec. 1919	Non-Labor	V, Q, WA	48.6	71.3
Industry and commerce	4 Sept. 1926	Non-Labor	NSW, Q	43.5	91.1
Essential services	4 Sept. 1926	Non-Labor	NSW, Q	42.8	91.1
State debts	17 Nov. 1928	Non-Labor	All	74.3[a]	93.6
Aviation	6 Mar. 1937	Non-Labor	V, Q	53.6	94.1
Marketing	6 Mar. 1937	Non-Labor	None	36.3	94.1
Postwar reconstruction and democratic rights	19 Aug. 1944	Labor	SA, WA	47.0	96.5
Social services	28 Sept. 1946	Labor	All	54.4[a]	94.0
Organized marketing of primary products	28 Sept. 1946	Labor	NSW, V, WA	50.6	94.0
Industrial employment	28 Sept. 1946	Labor	NSW, V, WA	50.3	94.0
Rents and prices	29 May 1948	Labor	None	40.7	93.6
Powers to deal with Communists and Communism	22 Sept. 1951	Non-Labor	Q, WA, T	49.4	95.6
Parliament	27 May 1967	Non-Labor	NSW	40.3	93.8
Aboriginals	27 May 1967	Non-Labor	All	90.8[a]	93.8
Prices	8 Dec. 1973	Labor	None	43.8	93.4
Incomes	8 Dec. 1973	Labor	None	34.4	93.4
Simultaneous elections	18 May 1974	Labor	NSW	48.3	95.5
Mode of altering the constitution	18 May 1974	Labor	NSW	48.0	95.5

TABLE 6-2—Continued

Subject	*Date of Referendum*	*Government Party*	*States with Majority Vote in favor*	*Percent Voting Yes*	*Percent Turnout*
Democratic elections	18 May 1974	Labor	NSW	47.2	95.5
Local government bodies	18 May 1974	Labor	NSW	46.9	95.5
Simultaneous elections	21 May 1977	Non-Labor	NSW, V, SA	62.2	92.3
Senate vacancies	21 May 1977	Non-Labor	All	73.3 [a]	92.3
Territory franchise for referendum	21 May 1977	Non-Labor	All	77.7 [a]	92.3
Retiring age for judges	21 May 1977	Non-Labor	All	80.1 [a]	92.3
National song [c]	21 May 1977	Non-Labor	—	— [d]	92.3

NOTE: The full names of the states, in the order of their appearance in the table, are: Queensland, Western Australia, Tasmania, New South Wales, South Australia, and Victoria.

[a] Referendum carried.

[b] Electors in territories also voted.

[c] Not a constitutional referendum.

[d] Electors were asked to choose one of four songs. "Advance Australia Fair" won 43.4 percent of the first preference vote, and 65.2 percent of the voters selected it as a second choice after "Waltzing Matilda."

[e] Compulsory voting was introduced in 1924 and has been in force ever since.

SOURCE: Commonwealth of Australia, *Commonwealth Parliamentary Papers* (published for each session of Parliament by the Commonwealth government).

The Height of the Hurdles

The Australian constitution was an agreement between the political leaders of six independent colonies. It was not forged in the fires of a revolution, and it was not itself agreed to by an overwhelming popular vote. Although there were comfortable majorities in all the colonies, the turnout was not impressive, and the yes vote represented less than 43 percent of the enrolled electorates. Indeed, the federation was something of an oddity. The Australian colonies had very similar demographic, economic, and social characteristics, and the federal form made sense only because of the distances involved, which were huge by nineteenth-century standards.

Those who set up the Commonwealth of Australia saw the need for a new political institution which would deal with questions such as defense, communication, immigration, and customs and excise, but they saw no need to transfer all or most powers to the new federal body. For one thing, each colony had well-developed political institutions and economic and social structures. For another, it would be absurd, given the communications available in 1900, to try to administer an education system, for example, or the sale of Crown lands from the national capital. Then too, no politician is ever likely to do away with his own power base. Although most of the new federal politicians had come up through colonial politics, their places were at once filled with others who saw their own futures in state politics. From the beginning, therefore, tension was built into constitutional amendment. All proposed changes to the federal constitution involve the transfer of power from the states to the federal sphere or the creation of new powers to be held by the Commonwealth where none had existed before. In either case constitutional amendment involves the relative diminution of the power of the six states and is therefore likely to be resisted by state politicians.

In practice national referendums have often become the battle ground between alliances of federal and of state politicians. In 1977, for example, the federal government and opposition were united in their view that the four proposals going to the people should be passed, while the principal opposition to the proposals came from the premiers (chief ministers) of Western Australia and Queensland. In the event, the proposal most objected to—that elections for the House of Representatives and for the Senate should always be held together—was defeated. Although there was a most comfortable national majority (62 percent), the question was approved in only three rather than four states.

The 1977 result and its parallels in the past point to the severity of the requirement that there be an approving majority in four of six states. Two referendums in 1946 gained national majorities but found only three states in favor, and an earlier referendum in 1937 produced an approving national result but with only two states in favor. There have been another nine in which the national approval was greater than 49 percent though less than 50 percent, but still only three states were in favor. An all-party Parliamentary Joint Committee of Constitutional Review suggested in 1959 that the requirement be reduced to half the states rather than a majority, but the electors rejected this when it was put to them in 1974.

There is no technical requirement that proposed amendments to the constitution be put forward by the government of the day, and in fact motions urging constitutional change, and even bills with the same end, have been sponsored by the opposition or private members. But in practice the government has such control over parliamentary business that without its support a proposed change has little chance of receiving the approval of both houses of Parliament.[3] When the Senate is in the hands of the opposition (which is not uncommon because of the different terms and methods of election of senators), it may try to embarrass the government by moving for a referendum under the proviso clause in section 128. This has happened once, in 1914, when the governor-general refused to exercise his discretion (on the advice of the Cabinet). On the other hand, rarely have governments been prepared to spend the time and energy necessary to ensure that the electorate is as well informed about the referendum as it might be or ought to be. In part this is owing to the sheer pressure of business that faces any government and the difficulty of campaigning effectively in a nation as large and scattered as Australia (although this problem has lessened somewhat with the advent of television). In part the failure to educate the public stems from a common failure of resolve close to polling day as governments decide that the referendum is lost anyway. Many referendum campaigns have been quite perfunctory.

In any case, a referendum is a more perplexing business for the electorate than is a general election. Australians are well used to elections. On average they take part in one (for the House of Representatives, the Senate, or the state legislature) each year, and the consequences of elections are familiar or at least predictable. But a

[3] Australian parliamentary practice is well explained in L. F. Crisp, *Australian National Government* (Melbourne: Longmans, 1974), and David Solomon, *Inside the Australian Parliament* (Sidney: George Allen and Unwin, 1978).

referendum offers a difficult constitutional question which must be answered by an unqualified yes or no. The Australian constitution is a legal rather than a political document, and even lawyers are rarely familiar with it. The question to be resolved concerns the modification, deletion, or addition of words or sentences, and the consequences of approval are simply unknowable. Undoubtedly many electors, puzzled by the wording, bemused by the complexity of the issue, and battered from both sides by the antagonists, shrug their shoulders and vote no.

The very form of the referendum ballot paper may put off some voters. The question asks "Do you approve the proposed law for the alteration of the Constitution entitled . . ." followed by the short title of the bill. In 1974, for example, the first question related to "A Bill for an Act to facilitate alterations to the Constitution and to allow electors in the Territories, as well as in the States, to vote at referendums on proposed Laws to alter the Constitution." Not only are the words unfamiliar to most electors, but the wording obscures the fact that the principal aim of this bill was to reduce from four to three the number of states registering approving majorities. Fiddling with the wording is not common because of the standard form of the ballot paper. But the two conscription referendums of 1916 and 1917 were strangely worded indeed. The 1916 question ran as follows:

> Are you in favour of the Commonwealth having, in this grave emergency, the same compulsory powers over citizens in regard to the requiring of their military service for the term of this war, outside the Commonwealth, as it now has in regard to military service within the Commonwealth?

This was narrowly defeated, and the Hughes government tried again at the end of 1917, with a question that was more terse but no more helpful to the elector: "Are you in favour of the proposal of the Commonwealth Government for reinforcing the Australian Imperial force oversea?" This was defeated by a rather larger margin.

There can be no certainty as to the effect of compulsory voting, introduced in 1924 for elections to the Commonwealth legislature and for referendums. In the first twenty years of the Commonwealth the turnout for referendums was very similar to the turnout for elections, even when the two events were not held simultaneously. Only half the enrolled electorate voted in the referendums of 1906 and 1911, although six in ten voted in 1910, and more than seven in ten in 1913 and 1919. It is hard to believe that the increase to 91 percent which occurred in 1926 had no effect at all on the outcome of the vote, for the most plausible a priori reasoning suggests that the dragooning of the uninterested and ignorant to the polls would have increased the number of those likely to vote no. There have been more successes in referendums since 1924 than before, however, and there has continued to be a large number of near misses. No finding can be returned.

Much the same conclusion results from an examination of the effects of the timing and number of referendums. Governments have abandoned the omnibus referendum, in which a large number of questions is subsumed in a single yes or no choice. This strategy was last tried in 1944, no more successfully than on three previous occasions (1911, 1919, and 1926). Recently either two or four separate questions have been asked simultaneously (two in 1967 and 1973; four in 1974 and 1977). Since four out of the twelve questions were passed, it is tempting to explain this relative success by the small number of questions. But the record of similar offerings from 1910 to 1946 is not equally encouraging (only one of seventeen was passed).

Governments are always tempted to hold a referendum at the same time as a general election because of the pressure of business and the cost of holding them separately. It seems pretty clear, however, that this timing is likely to result in the referendum's failure because of the high party temperature at election times. Only two of eighteen proposals asked in a general election have succeeded. One of these was a minor and uncontroversial machinery measure, while the other gave the Commonwealth power to distribute social welfare benefits to the electorate.

In general, although the procedural hurdles of Australian referendums have added to the difficulty of gaining the necessary majorities to approve proposals, the more basic explanations for the lack of success lie elsewhere—in the levels of partisanship in Australian politics and the education and involvement of the electorate.

Referendums and Party Politics

The Australian party system is old and extremely stable.[4] It developed between the years 1890 and 1910 from an earlier period of factional politics; in the 1910 election the Labor and Liberal parties between them won 95 percent of the vote and all but one of the seats.

[4] See Don Aitkin, *Stability and Change in Australian Politics* (New York: St. Martin's Press, 1977).

Although there has been some readjustment in the party system (principally a division on the non-Labor side occasioned by the entry of the Country party in 1919) and both sides have known savage internal fighting and splits, the images, rhetoric, ideology, and electoral support of the parties have changed little during the greater part of the twentieth century. The party system has been characterized by high levels of partisanship. Not only are 90 percent of the electorate more or less loyal to one party (and tend to retain that loyalty for long periods), but the parties themselves display high levels of cohesion and party discipline. Members of Parliament rarely cross the floor, and coalitions across the main party divide are unknown, even during war.

Such partisanship is exacerbated by frequent elections. The constitution requires a new election for the House of Representatives not much more than three years after the last, but in practice elections are more frequent than this (there were thirty-two elections to the House of Representatives between 1901 and 1977). Since the term of a senator is six years and half the Senate retires every three years, it is not uncommon for the elections for the Senate to be held at different times from those of the House of Representatives. (Two referendums designed to synchronize these elections failed to pass in 1974 and 1977.) It is fair to say that Australian parties are perpetually thinking about elections; it is also fair to say that Australian elections are tough contests in which everything is geared to party victory.

This is not a promising environment for national referendums. It is beyond question that no proposal will pass unless there is at least a fair measure of agreement between the major parties that the change is necessary. Even then some have been lost when opposition has been led by minor parties. In 1967, for example, a combination of Democratic Labor party and Country party politicians successfully defeated a proposal to break the nexus between the sizes of the House and the Senate, which the constitution fixes at two to one. The federal structure of Australian politics complicates the matter, for the parties at the federal level are not able to compel their state counterparts to follow their line in a referendum campaign. Several times (notably in 1926, 1937, and 1977) state party leaders have opposed their federal colleagues in a referendum and helped secure the defeat of a proposal that had at least some sort of agreement at the federal level.

Agreement among federal politicians has usually been short-lived; indeed, parties have often opposed extensions of powers which they themselves had sought previously when in government. The causes are twofold: the short-term focus of party warfare makes an opposition reluctant to be seen to agree with anything the government seeks, and each party is suspicious of the use the other would make of the powers if granted. It was not always so. For the first thirty years of the Commonwealth there was something of an understanding among federal politicians that federal power was inadequate and ought to be expanded. Here the cause lay principally in the unlucky timing of federation—the constitution was drawn up before the great increase in the extent of government activity which has characterized the twentieth century. As elsewhere, the pressure on government was felt mostly at the center, but the Australian constitution provided only a defined set of powers to the central government, and residual powers remained in the hands of the states. In 1911, 1913, 1919, and 1926 various Australian governments put to the people proposals aimed at increasing Commonwealth powers with respect to trade and commerce, monopolies, wages and industrial conditions, and corporations. None of these was approved, usually because of the party battle which surrounded the referendums.

But many of these proposals resembled those of another time. The Hughes national government's proposals of 1919 were essentially those of the Fisher Labor government in 1911 and 1913. The Bruce-Page government's corporations and arbitration referendum of 1926 represented yet another attempt to get approval for changes in the status quo which had not been given in 1919, 1913, and 1911. On almost every occasion there was some agreement between parties that the powers sought were necessary, but that agreement vanished once the campaign began if it had not already disappeared over the questions of wording during the preceding parliamentary debate. After 1926 there was little consensus about extensions of power in the economic area, most probably because of Labor's increasing commitment to notions of centralization (adopted as part of the party's platform in 1918). Indeed, the Whitlam government's attempt to secure powers over wages and prices in 1973 suffered the worst defeat of all: There were majorities against the proposals in every state and only one voter in three approved the wages question. The Liberal and Country parties fought hard and successfully in 1974 against a proposal that elections for the House and the Senate be synchronized, and then in government three years later put forward essentially the same proposal themselves. Although the Labor party in opposition supported them, the question was narrowly lost.

The parties' track record in the conduct of referendums has been so bad that one might wonder why they bother to continue with these polls. But the constitution gives them no choice. If the High Court rules that a given Commonwealth law is invalid (as happens from time to time) or a federal government finds that its powers (or indeed those of the state governments) are inadequate to deal with what seems to be a major national problem, the recourse to referendum is irresistible. The opposition of the day, for its part, sees a heaven-sent opportunity to show up the inadequacies of its rival. In an ideal world it would be possible for the Commonwealth to achieve its end through the transfer of the desired powers from all the states. This strategy was attempted in both World War I and II, in order not to divide the nation during a crisis. The Labor party in government was in both cases the sufferer, since it might well have been successful at referendums: the agreed-upon transfers of power were so tardily accomplished that nothing of substance occurred.

The Problem of the Electorate

Enough has been said to make it clear that the task of the citizen at an Australian referendum is not an easy one. At the same time, however, the citizen is not well equipped for his task. Australians combine high levels of partisanship with generally low levels of political interest. As a result, the party position on a given question tends to determine that of the citizen. Not only is the Australian constitution a legal document of some aridity, but there is no tradition of teaching it in the schools. In contrast to the United States, Australia is a nation which takes its constitutional past very much for granted, and the great majority of citizens grow up with only the vaguest understanding of the constitutional arrangements of their polity. A referendum on the constitution is therefore something of a crisis.

For the most part, referendums follow pretty closely upon the decision to hold them, and the referendum campaigns have tended to be short affairs. By law each citizen is provided with statements written on behalf of the parliamentary supporters and opponents (if any) of the proposal, and these have in recent years served as the basis of the campaigns. The tradition of all-out party warfare has carried over into referendums. When the questions are seen as important both sides employ exaggeration and distortion in attempts to capture the electorate; the intellectual level of referendum debates is often appalling. In 1977, for example, the writers of the case against simultaneous elections for the House of Representatives and the Senate managed to suggest that the very existence of the Senate was in question, that in some unexplained way the powers of the smaller states in the federation were to be reduced, and that the right to vote was somehow threatened because the proposal would reduce the number of elections a citizen might have to participate in. Forty years earlier, those who opposed the referendum on federal control of aviation argued that it would lead to a reduction in railway services to country people. In these cases and others the arguments were so bad that any citizen who had troubled to find out about the proposals would surely have dismissed them as preposterous; the questions were, however, defeated. In many referendum campaigns the issue becomes one of more powers to politicians versus less powers, or of centralism versus federalism. The citizens may, as has been argued, display their good sense in voting no, but the process of making up their minds must be mostly an intuitive one; there has been no serious public debate of these questions since at least the 1940s.

The fundamental paradox is that the referendum process assumes an interested and educated body of citizens and one which is likely, on balance, to make judicious decisions. This is not an accurate description of the Australian electorate, although there is some hope that the description is becoming less inaccurate. For the referendum process to work well there needs to be a measure of agreement between the political parties that the proposed changes are necessary, and then a long, leisurely, and cool campaign—one which allows the issue to be thrashed out within an electorate that is not much interested in constitutional questions. The six months allowed by the constitution as the maximum between the passage of the proposal through the Parliament and its appearance in a referendum is barely enough, and the usual breathing space is much less than six months.

Prospects for the Future

The story of the referendum in Australian politics is on the whole a dismaying one, but there are cheering signs. In the 1970s the political parties seemed to reach a tacit agreement that the constitution had become outmoded in many of its provisions, and that somehow or other the politicians would have to find an efficient means of amending it. As has been said already, such understandings have occurred in the past. Not only were many similar proposals to revise legislative powers put to the people in the first thirty years of the Commonwealth, but two later inquiries into the constitution and its workings produced a great measure of consensus among the parties. A royal commission of 1929, which consisted of members of all parties with a distinguished constitutional lawyer as chairman, proposed a series of changes to the constitution including some new federal powers; its findings were not acted upon. In 1959 the Joint Committee on Constitutional Review proposed even more changes—including altering the method of amendment to reduce the number of approving states from a majority to half—with an even greater measure of agreement; again nothing was done.

In 1970 the Victorian parliament resolved that the other states be invited to join in constitutional discussions, which should eventually include the Commonwealth.[5] Constitutional conventions had been held before, notably in 1934 and 1942, but had come to nothing. The Victorian initiatives led to a large constitutional convention in Sydney in 1973, with local government bodies represented as well as the Commonwealth and the states. This convention saw itself as the start of a new process of constitutional debate and set up standing committees on a wide range of subjects. Subsequent conventions in Melbourne in 1975 and Hobart in 1976 paid attention among other things to the question of referendums.

After the discussions in Hobart the Fraser government in 1977 sent four questions to the people, all of which had been canvassed at the convention, though not all of them had been agreed to in the form in which they went to referendum. This 1977 referendum had the distinction of being the most successful since federation: three of the four questions were approved, and the fourth lacked only the majority of states. For the first time in ten years, the political parties at the federal level campaigned together. Some of this unusual togetherness can be attributed to the constitutional crisis of 1975, in which the governor-general dismissed the Whitlam government because of its failure to secure supply—the appropriation of money to carry out its functions—the result of a deadlock between the houses. One of the 1977 questions sought to ensure that a midterm vacancy in the Senate would be filled by a member of the retiring senator's party, a matter which had been critically important in the 1975 crisis. For all that, the continuing series of constitutional conventions and the apparent determination of the present federal and state parliamentarians to improve the referendum process offer some hope that future Australian referendums will be more successful and a better example of intelligent democracy in action than they have been in the past.

[5] Constitutional change in the 1970s is discussed from a number of points of view in Gareth Evans, ed., *Labor and the Constitution 1972-1975* (Melbourne: Heinemann, 1977).

7
France

Vincent Wright

The referendum has a long and controversial history in France, although in the late eighteenth century and throughout the nineteenth century the word was never used. Indeed, in the main French dictionaries and encyclopedias of the time there are lengthy descriptions of the "plebiscite" and its use in France and frequently no mention at all of the "referendum." All the French "referendums" which took place between 1793 and 1870 are referred to by contemporaries and by present historians as "plebiscites." As in the rest of the book, the word "referendum" is used in this chapter, but it should be remembered that the French still make a distinction between the two, with the plebiscite denoting a Caesarist device for eliciting a vote of confidence.

The Precedents and the Intentions

The use of the referendum was first widely advocated during the trial of Louis XVI, and during the First Republic there was a full-scale debate on its nature and desirability between the supporters of direct democracy and those of representative democracy. Their basic arguments differ little from those heard during the Fifth Republic, more than 160 years later. The referendum was first employed to ratify the constitutions of Year I (August 1793), Year III (September 1795), and Year VIII (August 1799), and its use to veto legislation voted in parliament was envisaged in the stillborn Montagnard constitution of Year I. The referendum was also used by Bonaparte to ratify the constitutional arrangements which made him consul (February 1800), consul for life (May 1802), and emperor (May 1804). The restoration of the empire in 1815 was also ratified by a referendum in May 1815. The reputation of the referendum as a Bonapartist device was reinforced in the nineteenth century when Louis Napoleon, nephew of Napoleon I, used it to legalize and legitimize his coup d'état of December 1851 (vote of December 21 and 22, 1851), his restoration of the empire (vote of November 21, 1852), his annexation of Nice and Savoy (votes of April 15 and 22, 1860), and his liberal constitutional amendments (vote of May 8, 1870).

The referendum was totally abandoned during the Third Republic (1870–1940). Although the law of July 10, 1940, which conferred constituent powers on Marshal Pétain, provided for its use to ratify the new constitution (which never appeared), it was not until October 21, 1945, when General de Gaulle was head of the provisional government established after the liberation of France, that it reentered French political practice. On that occasion the French were asked whether they wished the new Assembly (which they were electing that day) to draw up a new constitution (thus putting a legal end to the Third Republic) and whether it should have unlimited powers to do so. The referendum procedure was used again in May 1946 when the electors rejected the proposed constitution, and in October 1946 when they voted, by a small margin, to accept a modified constitution. There were no further referendums during the Fourth Republic (1945–1958) even though the constitution provided for their use as a mechanism for constitutional amendment. The politicians of the Fourth Republic thus emulated their predecessors of the Third by rejecting the referendum as a procedure of government.

When General de Gaulle returned to power in May 1958 the referendum was given a renewed lease on life. He used one to ratify his new constitution, and in the following three years he organized two referendums on Algeria and one on the method of electing the president of the republic. It was clearly President de Gaulle's intention to make the referendum a normal mechanism of government.

At the time of the April 1962 referendum on Algerian independence he announced that "henceforth, on a subject which is vital for the country, every citizen may be called upon, as now, to judge for himself and assume his responsibilities. No one can doubt that the character and operation of the institutions of the republic will be profoundly marked by it." The vote, he argued, would "definitely consecrate the practice of the referendum."[1] As though wishing to drive home the point, he held a referendum six months later, October

[1] This and all other unattributed quotations and figures are taken from the work of the Paris Fondation Nationale des Sciences Politiques or the Grenoble Institut d'Etudes Politiques (see bibliography).

1962, on direct election to the presidency of the republic, a measure which was profoundly to alter the nature of the French political system. By late 1962 the regime was being described as a "plebiscitary democracy," and to most political observers it appeared that the referendum had become part of the presidential arsenal, a weapon to be wielded whenever circumstances demanded. It was certainly never perceived as a parliamentary procedure.

Since October 1962 the referendum has been used at the local level to determine the merging of communes into bigger territorial units (a stipulation of the Local Government Act of 1971) and by a few mayors anxious to buttress their negotiating position against Paris or to legitimize their own intransigence in dealing with other local authorities. In recent years there has been talk of holding referendums on President Giscard d'Estaing's "charter for an advanced liberal democracy" and on the principle of direct elections to the European Parliament, and there were rumors that it might be employed on the issue of transforming the present legislative electoral law into one based on proportional representation. In 1977 François Mitterrand, leader of the Socialist party and a bitter critic of previous referendums, proposed one on French nuclear energy policy.

Successive opinion polls taken by the Institut Français de l'Opinion Publique (IFOP) have attested to the continuing popularity of the principle of the referendum as a means of eliciting the nation's sentiments on major issues.

As can be seen from Table 7-1, there has always been a majority in favor of the referendum, although it was not substantial during the politically controversial campaigns of the autumn of 1962 and the spring of 1969. Since the popularity of electing the president by

TABLE 7-1

RESULTS OF OPINION POLLS ON THE REFERENDUM IN FRANCE
(percent)

Response	*July 1945*	*September 1962*	*October 1962*	*March 1969*	*March 1972*
In favor of referendums	66	51	45	51	67
Against referendums	20	24	32	27	19
No opinion	14	25	23	22	14
Total	100	100	100	100	100

SOURCE: Institut Français de l'Opinion Publique (IFOP).

universal suffrage is even higher, it may be suggested that the French have no particular aversion to the mechanisms of direct democracy.[2]

Since October 1962, however, there have been only two national referendums in France—in April 1969 and in April 1972. President Pompidou held only one referendum during his five-year presidency, and his successor, Giscard d'Estaing, elected in May 1974, had not used it by mid-1978. Although, to use de Gaulle's words, "No one can doubt that the character and operation of the institutions of the republic [have been] profoundly marked" by the referendum, it would be hazardous to claim that the practice of the referendum has been "consecrated." Why the referendum has fallen into abeyance serves as the underlying theme of this chapter. It will be suggested that the reasons must be sought in a number of interrelated institutional, political, and personal factors and in the increasing recognition of the defective nature of the referendum itself.

The Referendums of the Fifth Republic: Issues and Results

Since the collapse of the Fourth Republic in May 1958 six national referendums have been held in France.[3] The first referendum of the new regime was devoted to its own establishment. The government headed by General de Gaulle, who had been invested as prime minister on June 1, 1958, drafted a constitutional text and submitted it to the nation for approval. The referendum also invited electors in the French overseas territories to choose between total independence (the answer given only by Guinea, which was then deprived of all French aid) and membership of the now defunct French community (the choice of all the others). Nearly four-fifths of the voters approved the new constitution, and there was a majority for it in every *département* of France.

The second and third referendums of General de Gaulle related to the Algerian war, which had poisoned French politics since its outbreak in November 1954. On January 8, 1961, three-quarters of

[2] The figures are given in Jack Hayward and Vincent Wright, "Les Deux Frances and the Presidential Elections of May 1974," *Parliamentary Affairs*, vol. 27 (Autumn 1974).

[3] For a general list, see Appendix A. I have excluded the referendum of July 1, 1962, which concerned only the voters in Algeria (which was, strictly speaking, still part of France at that time), and asked, "Do you wish Algeria to become an independent state cooperating with France under the conditions defined by the declaration of March 1962?" It was massively answered in the affirmative. I have included the September 1958 referendum on the new constitution, even though the Fifth Republic was not officially promulgated until the outcome of the referendum was known.

the French voters accepted a government bill on Algerian self-determination, and on April 8, 1962, nine French voters in ten accepted the peace settlement signed between France and Algeria at Evian the previous March. The fourth referendum to be held after the collapse of the Fourth Republic was much more controversial than its predecessors. The electorate was asked, "Do you approve the bill submitted to the French people by the president of the republic dealing with the election of the president of the republic by universal suffrage?" According to the 1958 constitution the president of the republic was elected indirectly by an electoral college comprising 80,000 local notables. De Gaulle wished to modify the constitution on this very important point, and 61.8 percent of the voters backed him in the referendum. The result was interpreted as unsatisfactory by many, since only 46.5 percent of the total electorate approved.

The last referendum of General de Gaulle was also his last act as president of the republic, for its failure led to his immediate resignation. On April 27, 1969, the electors were asked to adopt or reject a government bill directly inspired by de Gaulle, dealing with "the creation of the regions and the transformation of the Senate." The regional reforms envisaged the setting up of regional councils composed of representatives of social and economic interests as well as of members of the established local councils. They were in response to de Gaulle's claim, made in 1968, that "the centuries-old centralizing effort required to achieve and consolidate France's unity is no longer necessary. On the contrary, it is its regional development that will provide the motivating force of its future economic power."[4] His desire to reform the Senate dated from his celebrated Bayeux speech of 1946: He wished to give it a largely consultative role and to change its recruitment to include members elected on a socioprofessional basis. Of those who voted in the April 1969 referendum (and they represented more than four-fifths of the electorate) 53.2 percent rejected the proposals, and de Gaulle resigned immediately, for he had made the outcome an issue of confidence.

The last national referendum of the Fifth Republic took place on April 23, 1972. President Pompidou asked the French to approve the entry into the European Community of Great Britain, Ireland, Norway, and Denmark. In an election campaign in which the voters "bristled with indifference," two-fifths of the electors stayed at home

[4] Quoted in Jack Hayward, "Presidential Suicide by Plebiscite: de Gaulle's Exit," *Parliamentary Affairs*, vol. 22 (Autumn, 1969).

—the highest abstention rate in any national election since the war.[5] The presidential victory (67.7 percent of the voters said yes) was thus somewhat soured by the pervasive odor of indifference.

The Referendums of the Fifth Republic: Presidential Aims

General de Gaulle's intentions in holding his referendums were many, interrelated, sometimes confused, frequently conflicting, seldom clear, rarely specified, and never entirely pure. They were often as complex, as convoluted, and as implausible as the plot of a Verdi opera. They also varied in time, and a full understanding of the motives and aims of the referendums requires an awareness of the political context in which they were held.

Gaullist apologists of the referendum produced several arguments in its defense. First, it was a method of increasing citizen participation in public affairs—one of the cherished doctrines, if not practices, of the Gaullist regime. It was argued that one of the basic weaknesses of the Fourth Republic was that decisions had been taken as the result of back-room bartering in the French parliament by governments which were formed by undisciplined, unstable, and short-lived coalitions. The referendum was seen, therefore, as a means of reestablishing the link of accountability and political responsibility between the governed and the government. The second justification for the use of the referendum resided in its capacity to reveal the existence of a national consensus which was disguised and often perversely hidden by the political parties which had every interest in emphasizing the divisions of French society. Third, the referendum was an educational device, an intense pedagogical exercise, designed to inform the people of the substance of major policy options. Fourth, the referendum was viewed as a mechanism to inhibit political aggression by siphoning such aggression into agreed institutional electoral channels. The Algerian referendums of January 1961 and April 1962, which took place in an atmosphere of incipient civil war, were certainly regarded as a means of defusing highly charged, emotive, and even traumatic political situations. The same could be said of the referendum on the "renovation" of the state proposed by de Gaulle in the midst of the May events of 1968, but which was "postponed" until April 1969. The fifth and final function of the national referendum was its ability to provide a political counterweight to the excessive localism of French politics. Members of the French parlia-

[5] Michael Leigh, "Linkage Politics: The French Referendum and the Paris Summit of 1972," *Journal of Common Market Studies* (December 1975).

ment were depicted by the Gaullists (with some justification) as essentially brokers of constituency interests and the prisoners of powerfully organized local pressure groups. They were thus frequently politically paralyzed and prevented from taking badly needed action. The notorious alcohol lobby, for example, blocked vital legislation for many years by bringing pressure to bear on electorally sensitive members of the National Assembly. It was thought that by raising such problems to the national level they were more likely to be tackled.

A close examination of the referendums of the Fifth Republic suggests that they were also expected to fulfill other, less enlightened functions.

Bring about Catharsis. The referendum was intended to contribute to a dramatic assertion that a new political era was about to begin. Thus the people were invited to participate in the destruction of the Fourth Republic—"the regime of chaos and confusion," in the words of Michel Debré—to assist in the political liquidation of the Algerian war which had contaminated French politics for so long, and to help the president to renovate and modernize the state after the political and social upheaval of May 1968.

Establish and Consolidate the Regime. The function of the constitutional referendum of September 1958 was clearly to base the new regime on widespread public consent, thus underlining the contrast with previous Republican constitutions. The constitutions of the Second Republic (1848) and of the Third (1875) were drafted and voted in parliament and were never put to the public vote. That of the Fourth, which emerged from the constituent assembly elected in 1945, was accepted in the October 1946 referendum in which 9 million voted for, 8 million voted against, and over 8 million abstained. (The first draft of the constitution had been rejected in May 1946 in the first referendum in French history to produce a negative vote.) In spite of the big favorable vote for the constitution of the Fifth Republic the legitimacy of the regime had to be reaffirmed in later referendums, since many politicians of the left continued to assert, however unfairly, that the Fifth Republic, like the First and Second Empires, had extracted assent from a people traumatized by a military coup d'état, the menace of civil war, and the prevailing atmosphere of violence and political blackmail.

Strengthen the Legitimacy of the Presidency. The constitutional settlement of 1958 was a compromise between competing political actors, and as a result the constitution distributed functions, powers, and responsibilities between different and potentially conflicting public authorities: the president, the prime minister, the government, and the two houses of parliament were all given their share of political power, but in an imprecise and obscure way. It certainly did not create presidential government—that was to be the task of General de Gaulle, using all the weapons at his disposal. The referendum was one such weapon and was used in October 1962 for direct election to the presidency. Henceforth, any president of the republic could claim to be the *élu du peuple*—the representative of the entire people—a claim which would considerably strengthen his hand in any conflict with a hostile prime minister, government, or parliament. The referendum was also used to assert and highlight the political responsibility of the president of the republic (which was specifically denied in the constitution). Like all other referendums, it was deliberately turned into a vote of confidence in order to emphasize the key position of the presidency in the decision-making process. It had the added advantage of relegating the French parliament to the role of helpless spectator. In the October 1945 referendum General de Gaulle, as head of the provisional government, already had won from the electorate an affirmative and binding reply to a government (not parliamentary) proposal—a clear breach of the sacrosanct Republican principle that parliament was the only sovereign body in France. De Gaulle always saw the referendum as a means of correcting the "distortion of the representative principle," which was the inevitable consequence of granting parliament excessive powers and a monopoly of political sovereignty.

Finally, the referendum provided the French president with a badly needed direct link with the French people. It must be remembered that it was not until December 1965 that the president of the republic was elected directly by the people, and until then the referendum was his only direct access to the mass electorate: the press conferences, the television appearances, and the regal visits to the provinces were but poor substitutes. It has also been argued that since the presidential mandate lasts seven years, a very long time in politics, a president needs occasionally to "recharge his electoral batteries." The referendums of 1962 and 1969 (and the 1972 referendum of Pompidou) became, therefore, pretexts for seeking a midterm vote of confidence; they were, in the words of Jean-Luc Parodi, "the referendums of confirmation."[6]

[6] Unpublished thesis, quoted in John Frears, *Political Parties and Elections in the French Fifth Republic* (London: C. Hurst, 1977), pp. 246-247.

Strengthen de Gaulle's Position. Although it must be admitted that, for the general, office and man were inseparable, de Gaulle always felt a strong need for direct communion with the people. Nowhere was this need more clearly defined than in his speech just before the January 1961 referendum, in which he said, "I need, yes I need, to know how things stand in your minds and hearts. And therefore I turn to you, over the heads of the intermediaries . . . the question is one between each man and woman amongst you, and myself." The first president of the Fifth Republic may have felt secure in his sense of innate legitimacy—a legitimacy born in the dark days of June 1940 when he alone upheld the honor of his country—yet he always craved a democratic legality to underpin, to complement, or to reinforce that legitimacy. And the referendum could somehow supply that legality. It was as though the rebel against legally constituted authority in 1940 and in 1958 was intent on establishing the impeccability of his legal credentials. In that limited yet important sense the referendum may have responded to a deep-felt psychological need.

At a more mundane level, the referendum was also a means of seizing the initiative in a compromised political situation. François Goguel has written that it is impossible fully to understand the January 1961 referendum on Algerian self-determination without taking into account the prevailing political climate:[7] The Algerian peace negotiations were in an impasse after the breakdown of discussions at Melun; the extreme right was violently hostile to de Gaulle's peace moves; the army was divided and restless; there was a vague fear of impending civil war; parliament was opposed to the government's agricultural and defense policies; the economic austerity program was unpopular with the unions; the centrists were against de Gaulle's anti-American, anti-European, and anti–United Nations posturings; all the opposition parties were highly critical of the presidential drift of the regime. Yet de Gaulle was convinced that the mass of the people were with him, and a referendum was an admirable means of demonstrating this fact. Not only would a successful outcome be a striking vote of confidence in the regime, his office, and himself, but it would also deliver a blow against parliament, the parties, his left-wing and centrist opponents, the extreme right, and the potentially rebellious elements in the army. In that respect, the January 1961 referendum must be considered as an agent of calculated confrontation, a method of disarming and neutralizing the opposition. It was also a method of dividing and confusing the opposition, for de Gaulle forced the Communists to choose between

[7] François Goguel, in *Le Référendum du 8 janvier 1961* (Paris, 1962), p. 17.

rejecting a progressive measure or backing him and his government. He also forced the non-Communist left (then very hostile to the Communists) to follow the Communist party in its rejection of Algerian self-determination or to support the government.

The October 1962 referendum affords the best example of de Gaulle exploiting the procedure to seize the political initiative. He feared, not unjustifiably, that with the Algerian problem now solved, the politicians would no longer consider him indispensable and would take the first opportunity to get rid of him. His referendum on direct elections to the presidency was, therefore, a defiant preemptive strike, and its success guaranteed his survival.

In 1969 General de Gaulle's position was equally vulnerable. The fragility of his regime had been exposed during the events of May 1968; the health of the French franc—an obsessive concern of the general—was parlous; there were disquieting signs of inflation; his foreign policy based on rapprochement with the U.S.S.R. had been seriously weakened after the Soviet invasion of Czechoslovakia the previous year; his controversial outbursts in Quebec and his position on the sale of arms to Israel were both unpopular. More significantly, the elections of June 1968 had been a triumph not for himself but for *le parti de la peur*, a very conservative coalition led by his own prime minister. De Gaulle's position was sadly reminiscent of that of Napoleon III in May 1870: in both cases, the providential and enlightened leader saw his power being contested by the unruly mob outside parliament and politely subverted by his own conservative supporters within parliament. De Gaulle's response (like that of Napoleon III) was recourse to a referendum as a dramatic means of redressing the situation.

Serve as an Act of Revenge. De Gaulle also used the referendum as a means of settling old scores not only with parliament and the parties but also with the traditional political elite which he despised for its pusillanimous opportunism during World War II and for its resistance to the charms of Gaullism after the war. It is revealing that two of his referendums—those of October 1962 and April 1969—were designed specifically to weaken the power of the elite. In October 1962 he asked the French to take the election of the president of the republic out of the hands of the 80,000 local notables who then constituted the presidential electoral college, and in 1969 he proposed reforms designed to diminish the power and prestige of the traditional elite which was entrenched in the Senate and the local assemblies—both obdurate bastions of anti-Gaullism.

Impose "A Revolution from Above." On May 24, 1968, at the height of the biggest social and political upheaval of the Fifth Republic, President de Gaulle announced his intention of holding a referendum on the reform of the Senate and the creation of regional assemblies to give to "the state and above all to its leader a mandate for renovation." For General de Gaulle this was to impose a modernizing revolution on the traditional elite (including members that politically supported him), which was characterized by deep-seated conservatism and intellectual sclerosis. In the eyes of de Gaulle, this referendum, by increasing citizen participation, would unleash and harness new political forces—*les forces vives de la nation.* As in the referendums of 1961 and 1962, he wanted to force conservatives to swallow policies they had opposed and confront the left with the dilemma of choosing him or rejecting reforms. The 1968 referendum was "postponed" (de Gaulle's own word) on prime minister Pompidou's advice, and it was not held until April 1969.

Buttress the Diplomatic Position of France and Enhance Its Prestige. There are countless statements made by General de Gaulle which indicate that he was conscious of the international repercussions of his referendums. Massive votes of confidence would inform foreigners that the new regime was well established and that its leadership was secure. In a speech on December 20, 1960, just before the first referendum on Algeria, he stated that if the result were "positive and striking . . . foreigners will be given clear notice that France knows what she wants." It is also clear that in the two referendums on Algeria he was aware of the impact that favorable votes would have on opinion in North Africa and on the Algerian freedom fighters of the Front de Libération Nationale (FLN), for they would be interpreted as manifestations of French goodwill and the desire for peace.

The Objectives of President Pompidou

Like de Gaulle's referendums, the one held by Pompidou in April 1972 on the entry of four new countries into the European Community was motivated by several interconnected desires:

- to indicate the extent of national consensus on a major policy
- to restore the prestige of the regime, which had been badly tainted by a series of recent financial and property speculation scandals
- to reassert the president's authority, which had been shaken by his inability to push through some constitutional modifications

- to demonstrate to his popular and dynamic prime minister, Jacques Chaban-Delmas, that the president was the sole master of the executive
- to manifest his independence from the hard-line Gaullists who were opposed to British entry (as General de Gaulle had been) and to confound them by effecting the change of policy by the irreproachably Gaullist device of the referendum.
- to attract the opposition centrists who were keen Europeans, in the hope of smoothing their path into the government coalition
- to drive a wedge between the parties of the left which were divided on the issue
- to create conditions favorable for the forthcoming general election[8]
- to strengthen France's diplomatic position at the Paris summit meeting which was to be held in the autumn of 1972.[9]

The aims of the referendum during the Fifth Republic may be summarized by an inelegant and contrived alliteration: It was an instrument of consultation, consensus, consent, consecration, confirmation, crisis, confrontation, and confusion. It purported to consult the people on major decisions, to articulate a national consensus on such decisions and elicit the consent of the people for their implementation, to give official consecration to the new regime, to confirm the popular mandate of the president, to correct the "distortions" of the political system owing to excessive localism, to solve the crises of Algeria and of the state, to induce a confrontation with parliament, the parties, and the traditional notables, and to confuse the opposition. It was intended to be both constructive and destructive, creative and nihilistic, consolidating and iconoclastic, infrequent in its use yet enduring in its impact. But above all, it was intended to be a powerful weapon of the president to be used whenever he thought the circumstances demanded.

The Referendums of the Fifth Republic: Problems and Prospects

Why, given the many properties and possibilities of the referendum, has so little use been made of it in the 1970s? There appear to be

[8] Pierre Messmer, later prime minister, was to admit that Pompidou intended to bring forward the date of the election (scheduled for June 1973) had the referendum ended, as anticipated, in triumph (*Expansion*, September 1974, p. 169).

[9] As Prime Minister Chaban-Delmas noted, "What would our [European] partners say if the referendum were greeted with widespread indifference and opposition? . . . What would be France's position?" (Quoted in Leigh, "Linkage Politics.")

five basic reasons. First, the referendum itself has become controversial and is contested by important and influential sections of opinion. Second, from the president's point of view, it has proved to be a somewhat defective weapon. Third, the present president of the republic does not share the views of his predecessors on the desirability of the referendum. Fourth, there may be some difficulty in finding an appropriate and acceptable subject for a referendum. Fifth, the referendum has been rendered superfluous by changes in the French political system.

The Controversies Surrounding the Referendums. The use of the referendum in France has always roused passionate controversy and criticism. This is scarcely surprising, for as Gordon Smith has pointed out, it enshrines those basic first principles of belief in equality, popular sovereignty, and majority rule.[10] The debate has continued unabated since 1791, fed by the disputed use of the referendums of the First Empire (1804–1815), the Second Empire (1852–1870), and the Liberation (1945–1946). So the arguments on both sides are well rehearsed. The anti-Bonapartist parliamentary right, which was associated with the Orléans monarchy (1830–1848) and which dominated the early years of the Third Republic (1870–1940), feared the arbitrary and fickle nature of the referendum, which could always be used by the demagogue to dupe a gullible people. The traditional Republican view was that parliament alone was sovereign and that the task of the electorate should be limited to choosing representatives who were responsible for constructing a coherent program based on the selection of available options. Both the moderate right and the Republican left were haunted by their own historical experience, inasmuch as referendums were associated less with the annexation by France of Nice and Savoy in 1860 than with the legalization of Bonapartist coups d'état and the legitimation of imperial despotism.

The parliamentarians' visceral hatred of the referendum was manifested at the beginning of the Fourth Republic when most political parties unsuccessfully opposed General de Gaulle's plan to introduce the referendum procedure into French public law as a means of effecting constitutional amendments. It resurfaced in the early 1950s when the parties agreed that any modification of the constitution (then under discussion) could take place only if there were a majority in parliament sufficiently large to avoid recourse to a

---

[10] Gordon Smith, "The Functional Properties of the Referendum," *European Journal of Political Research*, no. 4 (1976), p. 1.

referendum. After the three referendums of October 1945, May 1946, and October 1946, which were all concerned with the foundation of the Fourth Republic, no other took place until September 1958 when de Gaulle was back in power. During the Fifth Republic the hatred of the referendum has not diminished: Each one held has merely exacerbated the anger and indignation. The 1972 referendum, which was arguably the least controversial, was nevertheless described as "a trap" (Michel Rocard), "a mystification" (Pierre Mendès-France), and "a masquerade" (Edmond Maire). The October 1962 referendum on direct election to the presidency and the April 1969 referendum on the reform of the Senate and the creation of the regions particularly provoked the wrath of the political elite: that of 1969, for example, was denounced by Jean Lecanuet, then an opposition centrist, as "unconstitutional, oblique, inopportune, illogical, illusory." Perhaps the dislike of the referendum was best summed up by Pierre Mendès-France in mid-1968 when de Gaulle declared his intention of holding one: "Plebiscites? You do not discuss them: you fight against them."

Not only were the objections of the parliamentary and party critics rooted in an apprehensive interpretation of French history and in their perfectly natural reluctance to be bypassed by way of referendums, they also were justified and sustained by the abuse and misuse of the referendum during the Fifth Republic. Objections to the referendum took many forms. Its opponents disliked its Manichaean nature, its crude invitation to vote yes or no on highly complex issues disguised by misleadingly simple questions. They also denied that the results of referendums could ever accurately register the intensity of feeling on a particular issue. But their principal objections focused on its constitutional impropriety, on the arbitrary, illogical, and dishonest choice of questions and on the political immorality of the whole operation.

Constitutional issues. A score of constitutional controversies have surrounded the use of the referendum during the Fifth Republic, but two have dominated all others. The first relates to the power of initiative, and the second concerns the nature of the subjects put to a referendum. Both controversies have involved an interpretation of articles 11 and 89 of the constitution:

> Article 11. On the proposal of the government during parliamentary sessions, or on the joint proposal of the two Assemblies, published in the *Journal Officiel*, the president of the republic may submit to a referendum any government bill dealing with the organization of the public au-

> thorities, approving a [French] Community agreement or authorizing the ratification of a treaty which, although not in conflict with the constitution, would affect the working of institutions.
>
> If the result of the referendum is favorable to the adoption of the bill, the president of the republic promulgates it within the time limit laid down in the preceding article.
>
> Article 89. The right to propose amendments to the constitution belongs concurrently to the president of the republic, on the proposal of the prime minister, and to members of parliament.
>
> The amending project or proposal must be passed by the two assemblies in identical terms. The amendment becomes effective when it has been approved by referendum.
>
> However, the amending project is not submitted to a referendum when the president of the republic decides to submit it to parliament, meeting as convention; in this case, the amendment is accepted only if it obtains a majority of three-fifths of the votes cast . . .

Article 11 clearly indicates that the president of the republic has no power directly to initiate a referendum: the initiative rests with the government or with parliament. Michel Debré, the constitutional alter ego of General de Gaulle, assured the Council of State in April 1958 that the president would have discretionary powers to refuse a referendum but none to initiate one. Article 89 on constitutional amendment specifies that any such amendment requires the intervention and agreement of both houses of parliament. In fact, General de Gaulle violated both articles of the constitution—a venial sin in the Gaullist catechism, since *raison d'état* took precedence over constitutional niceties.

The initiative for holding all the referendums of the Fifth Republic lay squarely and manifestly with the president of the republic. The referendum of January 1961 on Algerian self-determination was announced by General de Gaulle on November 16, 1960, and the "proposal of the government" was made on December 8.[11] The referendum of October 1962 on direct election to the presidency was announced by de Gaulle as early as August 29—three weeks after an unsuccessful attempt on his life—when he declared his intention of modifying the constitution "to ensure the continuity of the State."

[11] The official communiqué of the Council of Ministers of November 16, 1960, reads: "General de Gaulle made known his intention of submitting, at the appropriate time, to the country, by way of referendum, a bill concerning the organization of the public authorities in Algeria."

He made his intention officially known to the Council of Ministers on September 12, and "the proposal of the government" was made on October 2. Similarly, the referendum of April 1969 was "proposed" to the president of the republic by Prime Minister Couve de Murville on April 2, but it had already been announced by de Gaulle in a speech in Brittany the previous month. President Pompidou was no less culpable of constitutional impropriety when he underlined the personal nature of his initiative in the April 1972 referendum. He announced the referendum at his press conference of March 16, 1972, and the government formally proposed it to him three weeks later.

The second clear violation of the constitution related to the subjects raised in the referendums. As already noted, any amendment of the constitution should have been governed by article 89, which requires the consent of parliament. In fact, all the referendums of the Fifth Republic were proposed under article 11, which does not provide for constitutional amendment. Supporters of *Algérie française* argued at the time of the April 1962 referendum that Algerian independence was a clear breach of the principle of territorial inviolability contained in article 2 of the constitution: Algeria was legally part of France and could not, therefore, be ceded except by proper constitutional amendment. That issue exercised only a small minority of the politicians of the extreme right. The same could not be said of the controversies surrounding the October 1962 and April 1969 referendums. All the constitutional lawyers (with the exception of a few Gaullists whose ingenuity was matched only by their intellectual defensiveness) agreed that altering the method of electing the president of the republic (October 1962) and radically changing the structure and the powers of the Senate (April 1969) constituted profound modifications of the constitution and that they should therefore be carried out under the provisions of article 89. It was quite clear that article 11 was totally inappropriate.

The October 1962 referendum was denounced by Gaston Monnerville, president of the Senate, as "a deliberate, calculated, and outrageous violation of the constitution," and neither he nor the constitutional lawyers were placated by André Malraux's retort that "for most Frenchmen the violation of the constitution means a coup d'état not an electoral consultation." The chorus of criticism was joined by the Constitutional Council (although it declared itself incompetent to judge Monnerville's request to have the referendum declared unconstitutional) and by the prestigious Council of State. Paul Reynaud, one of the leaders of the moderate right in the National Assembly, openly accused the president of the republic of breaking a promise made to the Constitutional Consultative Committee in 1958, while the influential Club Jean Moulin demanded that the Constitutional Council be given greater control over the use of the referendum.[12] But the chorus of criticism was to no avail. Indeed, General de Gaulle defiantly declared that the success of the referendum had endorsed the constitutional right of the president to hold a referendum on similar subjects. This claim was later specifically rejected by the Council of State in its highly publicized secret judgment on the 1969 referendum—a referendum which provoked renewed passionate, angry, and hostile reactions.

Choice of questions. It was never made clear why certain subjects were put to a referendum and others were not. Not put to a referendum were such important decisions as whether to continue with the construction of an independent nuclear defense force in 1960, to withdraw from NATO in 1963, to precipitate a major crisis in the Common Market in 1965, to reform the social security system in 1967, to restructure the entire university system in 1968, to modify the laws on divorce, abortion, and contraception in 1974 and 1975, and to lower the voting age to eighteen in 1974. Curiously, most Gaullists—erstwhile ardent defenders of the referendum—ridiculed François Mitterrand's suggestion that a referendum be held on France's future nuclear energy policy.

There was also something illogical about the choice of certain subjects. Thus General de Gaulle's decision to keep Britain out of the European Community was never put to a referendum—in contrast to his successor's decision to allow Britain in. Similarly, the creation of the French regions in 1960 and their reform in 1964 and 1972 were felt to be unworthy of a referendum, but de Gaulle's regional proposals of 1969 were not.

It was argued that the questions posed in the referendums were ambiguous, misleading, obscure, and unfair. The referendums on Algerian self-determination (January 1961) and independence (April 1962) asked two separate questions: in essence, "Do you agree with the policy proposed, and do you want General de Gaulle to implement it?" The April 1972 referendum asked the electors to give a single reply to a question about the entry of four different countries into the Common Market. But the worst example of the dishonest and obscure question was that put in the April 1969 referendum. It was deceptively simple: "Do you approve of the bill dealing with the creation of regions and the reform of the Senate?" The bill mentioned

---

[12] *L'Etat et le citoyen* (Paris: Le Seuil, 1962), p. 25.

in the question was 8,000 words long, covered fourteen tightly printed pages, comprised sixty-nine articles, and involved the modification or replacement of nineteen articles of the constitution. Moreover, the constitutional experts of the Council of State described the bill as "one of the worst drafted ever to come before the council." The electors were invited to give a single reply to two very distinct questions, while the important issue of the change in the interim presidency which was envisaged in the bill was not even specified in the question put to the electorate.[13] Opinion polls indicated that even government supporters wanted the right to give separate answers —which had been the case in the October 1945 referendum when two distinct questions were asked. They also revealed that the electorate had different reactions to the two issues (see Table 7-2).

Political immorality. The accusations about the political immorality of the referendums centered on several issues. The first related to the amount and nature of the information given to the electors. The official campaigns on television and radio were generally fair—their regularity was supervised by the Constitutional Council (article 28 of the constitution), but the official campaigns were always very short and were always preceded and accompanied by unofficial campaigns which were monstrously biased in favor of the regime and the government. In the October 1962 and April 1969 referendums every elector was sent, at government expense, not only the details of the proposed changes but also a copy of General de Gaulle's defense of them; they were sent no opposition literature. Furthermore, the announcement of every referendum triggered off measures designed to mollify disgruntled groups such as farmers, shopkeepers, and hoteliers. In addition, the zeal of the tax collectors was always tempered on government instructions.

No referendum campaign was an educative exercise—a claim made by the apologists. The basic issues were rarely discussed at length by either the government or the president, who generally limited his television appearances to impassioned appeals for a personal vote of confidence. Opinion polls revealed the electorate's ignorance of the issues. An IFOP poll taken just before the 1958 referendum disclosed that half the electorate (49.5 percent) had not even looked at the copy of the constitution that had been sent to them, and 56.5 percent of the electors had never discussed the text of the constitution. It is unclear how many of those who claimed to

[13] The bill wished to confer the interim presidency (in the event of the death, resignation, or incapacity of the president) on the prime minister—a presidential appointee—rather than on the president of the Senate.

TABLE 7-2

POLLS ON 1969 REFERENDUM ON REGIONAL REFORM AND SENATE REFORM
(percent)

Issue	*March 14–18*	*March 29–31*	*April 11–12*	*April 21–22*
Regional reform				
For	54	55	52	43
Against	20	21	22	25
No reply	26	24	26	32
Total	100	100	100	100
Senate reform				
For	26	28	30	23
Against	33	30	31	33
No reply	41	42	39	44
Total	100	100	100	100

SOURCE: SOFRES.

have read the constitution actually understood it. Since it was the most badly written, most muddled, most contradictory, and most obscure constitution in French history (and the competition is considerable) the numbers could not have been great. Similar ignorance was revealed by an IFOP poll of April 10, 1972, less than a fortnight before the referendum voting day. It showed that half (49 percent) of the electorate did not even know the question that was being posed, and most of those who did know the question thought it unclear.

The second major accusation of political immorality laid against the referendums of the Fifth Republic was that they were deliberately turned into votes of confidence, that under the pretense of consulting the people the president of the republic was, by changing the nature of the consultation, hypocritically exploiting them. And it is certainly true that both de Gaulle and Pompidou linked the questions of the referendum to wider issues. General de Gaulle always made a referendum an issue of personal confidence. In January 1961, for example, after requesting a "frank and massive" affirmative vote he warned that "a negative or uncertain" result "would prevent me from pursuing my task." Not unnaturally, the statement was denounced by the critics as an act of political blackmail, since it was tantamount to asking the electors whether they wanted the president of the republic (who was also commander in chief of the armed forces) to resign in the middle of a bloody colonial war. During the referendum campaign of October 1962 he told television viewers (October 4) that "your replies will tell me whether I may and whether I must continue my task," and in the 1969 campaign he told them (April 10) that "there cannot be the slightest doubt . . . the continuation of my mandate or my departure obviously [*sic*] depends on the country's answer to what I ask . . . What kind of man would I be . . . if I sought ridiculously to stay in office?" President Pompidou was more reticent about making his referendum an issue of confidence, although Maurice Schumann, the minister of foreign affairs, announced during the campaign (March 18, 1972) that "if disapproved by the people, it is up to them to designate another president and we shall have another government."

Presidents de Gaulle and Pompidou and their governments also attempted deliberately to blur the issues. In 1958 the opposition to the referendum was cynically equated with Communism, and opponents were accused of lack of patriotism and of wanting civil war; in a television speech on October 18, 1962, they were accused by de Gaulle of wanting "to return to the regime of misfortune," his disparaging description of the Fourth Republic. In the 1969 campaign (March 11) he accused opponents of the referendum of wishing to destroy the currency, the economy, and the republic—a somewhat dubious dramatization and a fudging of the real issues. President Pompidou was less unscrupulous than his illustrious predecessor. Nevertheless, in a public declaration (April 5, 1972) he represented the referendum on the entry of the new members into the European Community as a means by which the electors could approve the whole of his European policy.

The opposition was frequently as guilty as the government in trying to confuse the referendum issues. For instance, the Communist party argued in 1958 that to vote yes was "to acquiesce in the murder of the republic," in 1961 that "our no is also a no vote to the monopolists," and in 1969 that the referendum was "an opportunity to put Gaullism on public trial."

The electors were not completely impervious to the prevailing political climate when making up their minds. In the October 1962 referendum, for example, de Gaulle was able to exploit several factors: gratitude to the man who had put an end to the Algerian war; the sympathy which followed the unsuccessful attempt on his life at Le Petit Clamart the previous August; the widespread desire not to revert to the crisis-ridden regime of the Fourth Republic; the insecurity engendered by the wave of OAS[14] violence and heightened by the Cuban crisis. By the time of the 1969 referendum, however, the political situation had radically altered. The fear created by the events of May 1968 had largely passed; de Gaulle's threat to resign no longer conjured up a grim picture of chaos and confusion, especially since the reassuring Pompidou had declared indirectly his willingness to take over; and there was a feeling that the regime needed roots not only in consent but also in legality and constitutionality, that the charismatic variety of Gaullism no longer seemed appropriate to the new political situation.

The confusion of issues was perhaps inevitable, and the opinion polls revealed the impact of the confusion in the minds of the electors. Motives became very mixed and often had only a distant bearing on the questions being asked. In the January 1961 referendum on Algerian self-determination, for example, it emerged that some voters were voting for or against de Gaulle, some for peace in Algeria, some against the Fourth Republic, some against the government's economic and social policies, some against Communism—and some for or against the proposals contained in the referendum bill. The 1969 referendum provides another very good example (see Table 7-3).

To summarize, the controversies which raged over the referendums of the Fifth Republic turned on their unconstitutionality, on their arbitrary choice of questions, on their dishonest presentation, and on their inevitable transformation into presidential votes of confidence, with the results being influenced by partisanship, unrelated issues, and the prevailing political climate. No president of the republic could be unaware of the controversial and politically divisive nature of the referendum—a factor which perhaps helps explain the caution with which it is now approached. It was certainly highly revealing that Pompidou when prime minister dissuaded de Gaulle from using the referendum at the height of the May 1968 events, recognizing that its use would prove too divisive and was more likely to exacerbate than to calm the troubled situation.

The Referendums of the Fifth Republic: A Defective Presidential Weapon. Some of the presidential aims of the referendums were undoubtedly fulfilled. The early referendums helped enhance the prestige of de Gaulle, his office, his regime, and even his country. The referendums on Algeria, for example, exposed the weakness of the North Africa lobby that had been so powerful during the Fourth Republic,

[14] Organisation de l'Armée Secrète, a fanatical pro–French-Algeria military faction.

TABLE 7-3

VOTER MOTIVATION IN THE 1969 REFERENDUM

Motivation	*Percent (multiple replies)*
Reasons for voting yes	
To support de Gaulle	60
To avoid crisis	46
To support regional reform	36
To support the government	22
To support Senate reform	19
Reasons for voting no	
To bring change of regime	47
To oppose de Gaulle	32
To oppose the government	31
To oppose Senate reform	27
To oppose regional reform	24

SOURCE: SOFRES poll, based on sample of 2,000 votes, reported in *Nouvel Observateur*, April 21, 1969.

isolated the extremists, helped ensure the loyalty of a restless army, and prevented the kind of myth making that bedeviled the politics of the German Weimar Republic. After the massive yes vote for Algerian independence in April 1962, no one could claim that the patriotic and unwilling masses had been stabbed in the back by a handful of cowardly politicians. The October 1962 referendum on direct elections to the presidency conferred "a profound legitimacy" upon the post by giving it an impeccable democratic source—the people—and it also clearly indicated to the political parties that presidential government was not merely an unpleasant interval but a lasting reality.

For the president, the early referendums had other profound and often unexpected beneficial effects, for they helped to crystallize and to accelerate favorable political changes that were only dimly emerging. They must be counted as one of the factors which contributed to the bipolarization of French politics in the 1960s and early 1970s, to the breakup of the unstable multiparty system of the Fourth Republic, and to the success of the Gaullist party based on the electoral apostasy of moderate right and center-right voters who deserted their parties when they were hostile to de Gaulle. Finally, it must be recalled that it was the October 1962 referendum which helped to forge the progovernment party coalition that was to secure the parliamentary base of presidential government: A small group of influential notables led by Valéry Giscard d'Estaing quit the Centre National des Indépendants, which was hostile to the referendum, and formed their own Independent Republican Party which then entered into alliance with the Gaullists.

Not all the presidential ends of the referendums were, however, attained. The 1972 referendum, for example, failed to prevent the Communists and Socialists (who were divided in their attitudes to the referendum) from concluding an agreement on a joint program of government and on electoral strategy barely three months after the referendum. Furthermore, not all the consequences of the referendums were beneficial to the presidency. A referendum is a dynamic instrument, and although it may be exploited in an attempt to sanctify the status quo, it frequently opens up new and unpredicted options, thus escaping the control of the manipulator. For instance, the October 1962 referendum eased the path of the Communist party out of its political ghetto, hardened Socialist opposition to the president, and facilitated the first steps toward left-wing unity. The 1969 referendum, which was designed to destroy the old Senate, had the unexpected result of enhancing its prestige: henceforth, it would be viewed with greater respect by both the population and the government.

For the president, the referendum became a double-edged weapon, to be used only with the utmost caution. It could easily end, as in April 1969, in political defeat and resignation; or it could easily be interpreted as a failure. Although two-thirds of the voters said yes in April 1972, there was a very high abstention rate, and an IFOP poll taken just after the vote showed that only 26 percent thought it had been a success for the president, 46 percent thought it a failure, and 28 percent gave no reply. The political reputation of Pompidou was clearly tarnished by the "failure."

Changing Presidential Views. General de Gaulle's attachment to the referendum was already clear when he was head of the provisional government established after the liberation in 1944. He insisted on its use in 1945, and against the wishes of most of the political parties he had it introduced as a mechanism for constitutional amendment. In his celebrated speech at Bayeux in 1946 he advocated the use of the referendum for major bills on which the government had suffered defeat in parliament. In 1948, at a press conference, he stated that "in France, the best supreme court is the people" and declared that in the event of constitutional deadlock or parliamentary paralysis the people should be asked to decide: "that would be a truly functioning democracy."[15] For de Gaulle, the referendum was the clearest, the frankest, the most democratic of procedures, and, perhaps more important, as already seen, a political weapon with immense potential.

Although President Pompidou frequently asserted (notably in his speech of January 4, 1972) that the referendum was a useful and even essential instrument of government, he called only one during his five years as president. Several factors may be advanced to explain his reticence: (1) He was by temperament much more conservative and much more cautious than his predecessor. He was less of a gambler, less imbued with the sense of his own charisma, less attracted to the dramatic gesture, and less obsessed with his need for direct communion with the people. (2) He represented not "personalized Gaullism" but "institutionalized Gaullism." He had reached the presidency because of his ascendancy in parliament, in the Gaullist party, and in the government party coalition—all bastions of the intermediaries and the notables with whom he had a perfectly healthy working relation. (3) Although not a lawyer by training, he had spent part of his career in the Council of State and in the Constitutional Council—bodies which had always expressed great reservation about the referendums of his predecessor. (4) The failure of the April 1969 referendum and the relative failure of his own in April 1972 must have been very sobering experiences.

President Valéry Giscard d'Estaing has proved even more resistant than his predecessor to the charm of the referendum. Probably his skepticism about its efficacy is not the only explanation of his reluctance to use it. The aversion may go much deeper. Giscard d'Estaing is heir to a long line of great notables: His family belongs precisely to that category of intermediaries that de Gaulle exploited, despised, defied, and tried to bypass. The French president also belongs to an influential parliamentary dynasty of the conservative Republican right which had always been deeply distrustful of vulgar Caesarist devices such as the referendum. Finally, he has always expressed his disquiet about the bitterness of French political dialogue. His political style is quiet, conciliatory, relaxed, and persistent: he avoids divisive and dramatized confrontation. The use of the referendum—an eminently controversial and contested procedure—would merely reactivate the old divisive demons of French politics and must therefore be avoided. It is instructive that all the social, political, and even constitutional reforms of Giscard d'Estaing have been voted in parliament.

---

[15] Quoted in Henry W. Ehrmann, *Politics in France*, 3rd ed. (Boston: Little, Brown, 1976), p. 103.

Finding an Appropriate and Acceptable Referendum Subject. As already noted, article 11 of the constitution enables the government to propose bills involving the organization of the public authorities, the approval of a French Community agreement, and the ratification of a treaty which, although not in conflict with the constitution, would affect the working of institutions. The first category excludes any constitutional revision (that is, almost anything of real importance), the second category is completely out of date since the French Community no longer exists, and the third (as the 1972 referendum demonstrated) is unlikely to interest the masses. Moreover, the electorate must feel that the referendum exercise is somehow politically justified and genuine and not merely manipulative. The early referendums were perceived as important in creating, stabilizing, and consolidating the new regime and presidential power and in solving the Algerian crisis. Those of April 1969 and April 1972 were viewed as unnecessary by large sections of the electorate: a SOFRES poll of 1969 indicated that a majority of the voters thought that the regional and Senate reforms fell more properly within the competence of parliament.[16]

At bottom, there is a fundamental dilemma in choosing subjects for a referendum. In the French political context, for a referendum to be perceived as important it has to be turned into a general vote of confidence or linked to larger and more important questions; otherwise it will be greeted with boredom and indifference. On the other hand, if it becomes too clearly a plebiscite it may subvert its democratic intention and arouse passionate resentment and controversy. It is difficult to see how the present president of the republic, who is somewhat squeamish about openly violating the constitution, can choose a subject which will be at once interesting, constitutionally proper, perceived as politically valid and morally untainted, and capable of avoiding the plebiscitary dilemma.

Pressures for Abandonment. A number of factors have combined to render the referendum politically and institutionally redundant. First, the regime is now much more established. The tumultuous years of the Algerian war and the turbulent days of May 1968 are firmly in the past. The Fifth Republic has proved its endurance by outliving every other French regime, with the exception of the Third Republic, since the Revolution. There is thus no obvious need for a crisis-solving mechanism. Moreover, the regime's legitimacy is no longer

[16] *L'Express*, April 28, 1969, quoted in Lowell G. Noonan, *France: The Politics of Continuity in Change* (New York: Holt, Rinehart, and Winston, 1970), p. 292.

questioned, and its political longevity will be based not on theatrical, arbitrary, and divisive demands for public support but on predictable rules, settled procedures, and acceptable conventions. Second, the presidency itself is now much more secure, much more formalized and institutionalized, and more generally recognized as the locus of political decision making. Its position no longer needs propping up by dramatic appeals to the public. Third, the president now has a direct link with the people—his own election by universal suffrage introduced by the October 1962 referendum—and the referendum is therefore less important in that respect. Paradoxically, the success of the early referendums in strengthening the regime and the presidency has helped render the referendum procedure superfluous. Moreover, the regime has succeeded in turning not only every referendum but also every general election into a presidential vote of confidence. Fourth, as already noted, the presidency under Giscard d'Estaing has been occupied by a man who is reluctant to use it. Fifth, since the election of Giscard d'Estaing in 1974 an important element of the government coalition has been the moderate right-wing and centrist notables who have always displayed their animosity toward "Caesarist contrivances" (Jean Lecanuet). Sixth, the regime has made its peace with the notables, with parliament, and with the parties—the intermediaries over whose heads the referendum was designed and employed to appeal. The final, but by no means the least important, factor has been the improbability since 1974 of winning a referendum vote. The left won sweeping gains in the by-elections of 1974 and in the local elections of 1976 and 1977 and was given a majority by every opinion poll. Although it lost the March 1978 elections it polled as many votes as the government coalition at the first ballot. To win half the votes in a country as finely divided as this is a politically risky operation.

The Balance Sheet of the Referendums of the Fifth Republic

The balance sheet of the referendums since 1958 is not entirely negative, since the early ones unquestionably helped to put the regime on a firm foundation, to establish a stable executive authority based on the presidency, and to give a boost to the emergence of a reasonably coherent and disciplined center-right coalition—three factors sadly lacking during the Fourth Republic. The Algerian referendums legitimized a badly needed surrender, isolated the extremists, and helped ensure the loyalty of the army. In the exceptional and crisis-ridden circumstances of the first years of the Fifth Republic they played an important role in stabilizing and strengthening the regime.

Their misuse and abuse, especially in October 1962, April 1969, and April 1972, brought about their disuse, by rendering them suspect and unacceptable as a normal constitutional procedure. In truth, the referendums of the Fifth Republic were shot through with contradictions rooted in the conflicting aims of the presidents of the republic, especially those of General de Gaulle. For example, he wished it to be an instrument of both revolution and conservation, a means of both dramatizing and defusing a situation, a device for creating both consensus and confrontation, a method of both clarifying and confusing the issues, a device used illegally to establish his legality and that of his office. The consequences also were often contradictory and paradoxical. The referendums were used to marshal public support for the presidents, yet that of April 1969 led to de Gaulle's resignation and that of April 1972 politically and diplomatically weakened Pompidou. They were employed as a legitimizing agent, but their partisan and illegal exploitation led to the undermining of their own legitimacy as an instrument of democratic government. They were used, too, to register and publicize an underlying consensus on certain key issues, but in 1969 and 1972 they actually prevented the articulation of that consensus on decentralization and on Europe. Finally, they sought to impose change—"a revolution from above"—but the failure of the 1969 referendum, for example, prevented any future attempt radically to reform the Senate and the French regions.

Given the political and institutional evolution of the regime, the temperament of the present president of the republic, the controversial nature of the device, and its intrinsic weakness as a reliable instrument of presidential government, it seems likely to be used again only in exceptional circumstances. Before the March 1978 general elections it was argued that it might be used to resolve a conflict between the president of the republic and a left-wing government backed by a sympathetic majority in the National Assembly, but the argument was never seen as worthy of serious consideration. Before the referendum is totally dismissed and relegated to France's vast constitutional museum, however, it is worth recalling that the history of that "effervescent," "undocile," and "unpredictable" people—three adjectives used by General de Gaulle about the French—is rich in the kind of exceptional circumstances that might again provoke the use of that much contested procedure.

Bibliography

The general political background to each referendum is discussed in the *Année politique* of the appropriate year. *Sondages* of 1958, 1962, 1969, and 1972 contains the IFOP opinion polls concerning the various referendums. The constitutional controversies surrounding the referendums are debated at length in the *Revue du droit public* (notably in the articles by Georges Berlia, Pierre Lampué, Loïc Philip, and Jean-Marie Garrigou-Lagrange in 1962 and 1969).

Several invaluable articles appeared in the *Revue française des sciences politiques* of 1959, 1961, 1963, and 1970. In addition, see Jack Hayward, "Presidential Suicide by Plebiscite: de Gaulle's Exit," *Parliamentary Affairs*, vol. 22 (1969), pp. 289–319; and Michael Leigh, "Linkage Politics: The French Referendum and the Paris Summit of 1972," *Journal of Common Market Studies* (December 1975), pp. 157–170.

Studies of the early referendums were published by the Association Française de Science Politique as Cahiers de la Fondation Nationale des Sciences Politiques: (*L'Etablissement de la Ve République: Le Référendum de septembre et les élections de novembre 1958* [Paris, 1960]; *Le Référendum du 8 janvier 1961* [Paris, 1962]; *Le Référendum du 8 avril 1962* [Paris, 1969]; *Le Référendum d'octobre et les élections de novembre 1962* [Paris, 1965]). They provide the basic reading on the subject.

The Institut d'Etudes Politiques of Grenoble produced a useful volume in 1970 on the referendum of April 1969 entitled *La Réforme régionale et le Référendum du 27 avril 1969* (Paris: Editions CUJAS, 1970).

Works of a general nature containing some useful information and insights include:

Avril, Pierre. *Le Régime politique de la Ve République.* 2nd ed. Paris, 1967.

Braud, Philippe. *Le Comportement électoral en France.* Paris, 1973.

Chapsal, Jacques. *La Vie politique en France depuis 1940.* 3rd ed. Paris, 1972.

Charlot, Jean. *Le Phénomène Gaulliste.* Paris, 1970.

Charnay, Jean-Paul. *Les Scrutins politiques en France de 1815 à 1962.* Paris, 1964.

Chevalier, Jean-Jacques. *Histoire des institutions et des régimes politiques de la France moderne, 1789–1958.* Paris, 1967.

Denquin, Jean-Marie. *Référendum et Plébiscite.* Paris: Librairie générale de droit et de jurisprudence, 1976.

Ehrmann, Henry W. *Politics in France.* 3rd ed. Boston: Little, Brown, 1976.

Gicquel, Jean. *Essai sur la pratique de la Ve République.* Paris, 1968.

Frears, John. *Political Parties and Elections in the French Fifth Republic.* London, 1977.

Viansson-Ponté, Pierre. *Histoire de la République Gaullienne.* 2 vols. Paris, 1970–1971.

Williams, Philip. *Crisis and Compromise.* London, 1964.

Williams, Philip, David Goldey, and Martin Harrison. *French Politicians and Elections, 1951–1969.* Cambridge, 1970.

Some useful background works on French referendums include:

Bayle, M. *Le Référendum: Etude historique et critique.* Lyons, 1900.

Bortoli, Gilbert. *Sociologie du référendum dans la France moderne.* Paris, 1965.

Debacq, J. *Le Référendum: Etude de législation comparée.* Paris, 1896.

Husson, Raoul. *Les Elections et le référendum des 21 octobre 1945, 5 mai et 2 juin 1946.* Paris, 1947.

Husson, Raoul. *Les Elections et le référendum des 13 octobre, 10 novembre, 24 novembre et 8 décembre 1946.* Paris, 1947.

Salmon, A. *Théorie et pratique du référendum.* Paris, (*Documentation française*) 1962.

Sicard, G. "Référendums et plébiscites dans l'histoire de France." *Revue des sciences politiques* (February–March 1964), pp. 85–116.

8
Scandinavia

Sten Sparre Nilson

Referendums have taken place in all the Nordic countries, but not frequently. Denmark has had thirteen, Norway six, and Sweden three. Only in Denmark are they constitutionally required, and only there is the verdict mandatory in certain cases. Nevertheless, it can be said that the use of the institution has been important in Norway and Sweden as well as in Denmark, but not in Finland (one referendum) and Iceland (four referendums).

In the light of the Scandinavian experience it seems possible to offer tentative answers to certain questions: Do referendums prevent or promote social change? Can referendums increase citizen participation? If the constitution does not require a referendum, why do politicians nevertheless choose to hold one? What are the consequences of the referendum for political parties and for the parliamentary system of government?

Prevention and Promotion of Change

Public opinion is seldom influenced by political parties in a referendum to the same extent as in an election. Nonparty organizations often take over the campaigning function to some degree, but it appears that the people's verdict is laregly unstructured by either political parties or organized interest groups. This seems to encourage conservative outcomes. When people are asked whether they want to change their accustomed patterns of behavior, most instinctively stick to the things they know, to whatever is familiar. Two Scandinavian referendums illustrate this psychological tendency.

In Sweden the question of switching from driving on the left-hand side of the road to driving on the right-hand side was placed before the voters in 1955. Experts on transportation strongly favored the change, but it was rejected by a large majority of voters (15.2 percent yes to 84.8 percent no). They disliked the idea of making such a drastic change in their daily habits.[1]

The referendums on lowering the voting age in Denmark provide somewhat different examples. A majority in parliament proposed in 1961 to change the limit from twenty-three to twenty-one years of age, and this was duly ratified by the electorate with a vote of 55.0 percent yes. In 1969 parliament adopted by a large majority a measure to lower the voting age still further from 21 to 18 years. But this time the reaction of the voters was not the same; they defeated the new proposal, as shown in Table 8-1.

The enormous increase in turnout in 1969 came as a surprise. It is true that lowering the age limit from 21 to 18 was not quite the same thing as lowering it from 23 to 21.[2] But the force of the reaction seems to indicate that another factor must also have been at work. Apparently Danish voters regarded the question of letting youth take part in politics as much more important in 1969 than they had in 1961. The proposal had been endorsed by the political parties and was not opposed by any organizations or news media of importance in 1969. Observers agreed that propaganda activity was conducted in a very low key right up to polling day. Yet voters turned out in large numbers. The conclusion seems almost inescapable that they did so largely in order to express their displeasure with the youth rebellion of the late 1960s. Teenagers started exhibiting most unusual haircuts, clothes, and manners, while certain groups of young people, especially students, took leading parts in radical political movements. This happened not only in Denmark but also in other countries, most strikingly in France during the semirevolutionary weeks of May 1968, as well as in the United States, Germany, and elsewhere. All this was brought home to Danish voters by the mass

[1] Politicians may have wished to avoid making an unpopular decision, but in the end they found they had to make it anyway: The switch to right-hand driving was carried out in 1967 without another referendum. In their 1955 propaganda campaign, the advocates of left-hand driving stressed the advantage of preserving what everyone was used to; see the posters reproduced between pages 72 and 73 of *Upplysningsverksamhet vid folkomröstningar,* Swedish Official Reports (Statens Offentliga Utredningar, 1956), no. 35. Organizations like the Transport Workers Union and the Taxi Drivers Association argued that the cost of the reform would fall disproportionately on people in the lower income brackets. This may explain why only 15.2 percent of the voters voted yes.

[2] A Gallup poll indicated that lowering the age limit from twenty-one to twenty years might have stood a chance of being accepted by a slight majority of voters (H. Jörgen Nielsen, "Voting Age of 18 Years," *Scandinavian Political Studies,* vol. 5 [1970], pp. 301-305).

TABLE 8-1

REFERENDUMS ON LOWERING THE VOTING AGE IN DENMARK, 1961 AND 1969

	Yes		*No*		
Lowering Voting Age	Number	Percent	Number	Percent	*Turnout*
From 23 to 21 (1961)	580,000	55.0	475,000	45.0	37.2
From 21 to 18 (1969)	445,000	21.2	1,650,000	78.8	63.6

SOURCE: *Oekonomi og Politik*, vol. 35 (1961), p. 152; and *Scandinavian Political Studies*, vol. 5 (1976), p. 304.

media, especially the press and television. Most of them seem to have been unfavorably impressed by what they saw. The new currents among the younger generation were unfamiliar and disturbing.

A third, more controversial referendum took place in Denmark in 1963, when a set of laws limiting property rights by extending public regulation had been passed by a majority of some twenty-five votes in parliament (the votes of the three leftist parties against the votes of the three rightist parties).[3] The adherents of the left, apparently less interested, turned out in smaller numbers than the adherents of the right. The rate of participation was 73 percent, as against 86 percent in the previous parliamentary election of 1960. There were four different laws, and they were all rejected by varying majorities—on the average 1.3 million no to some 900,000 yes.

The conservative function of the referendum appears to depend to a large degree on the specific form in which the institution is adopted. In Denmark the constitution used to provide for referendums not as a regular feature of political life but as a strong requirement in the case of constitutional amendments. A favorable majority had to include no less than 45 percent of the entire electorate for an amendment to come into force. In other words, indifference, apathy, or uncertainty among voters could be almost as important as active opposition. The result was, in practice, to make constitutional change virtually impossible. For example, a set of amendments was strongly recommended in May 1939 by prominent politicians representing the major parties, which had collectively received more than 1.2 million

[3] Poul Andersen, "Dansk folkeafstemning om love" [Danish referendum concerning laws], *Nordisk Administrativt Tidskrift*, vol. 47 (1966), pp. 2-16 (English summary).

votes at the election one month earlier. Only 966,000 voters turned out to support the amendments, however, and a 91.9 percent vote of yes proved insufficient since it constituted only 44.9 percent of the Danish electorate.

When comprehensive constitutional changes were again submitted to the Danish electorate in 1953, politicians took care to include a measure believed to have great popular attraction—a change in dynastic rules making it possible for the young princess Margrethe to succeed to the throne. This seemed to do the trick. A vote of 78.4 percent yes on a 58.3 percent turnout provided just enough votes in favor of the new constitution, which relaxed the conditions for amendment although it introduced new referendum provisions.

It is not always certain, however, that referendums will inhibit change. Sometimes parties of the left succeed in promoting change by campaigning for it. When the Swedish Social Democrats in 1957 were unable to reach an agreement with either of the non-Socialist parties on the introduction of a supplementary pensions scheme, they resorted to holding a referendum. The result was to turn the previous downward trend of the Socialists into an upward one. The bourgeois opposition was badly hurt by its failure to take a common stand both at the referendum—when three different proposals were put before the voters—and at the succeeding elections.[4]

To be sure, it is not necessarily the case that parties of the right always seek to prevent change, and vice versa. For example, restrictions on the sale of liquor were introduced in several places in Norway in earlier decades on a wave of populist sentiment, often with the aid of local urban referendums. The sentiment has subsided since then, but populist elites have entrenched themselves in local power positions, and only with the aid of new referendums have adherents of the Conservative party been able to change existing regulations. The sale of liquor has been permitted in one town after the other.

Mobilization of Citizens

Mobilization of Men. Referendums open up the possibility that voters can take direct part in the making of policy decisions. But often only a relatively small segment of the electorate avails itself of the opportunity. In Scandinavia parties have been the main mobilizing agents, and voters as a rule have turned out in greater numbers to choose among parties than to answer questions posed at referendums.

[4] The possibility of more pervasive change being triggered by a referendum is discussed below.

There are some exceptions, however. In particular a clearly mobilizing effect can be noted in connection with the earliest referendums in Norway. When Frederick VI of Denmark and Norway, an absolute monarch, was forced as a result of the Napoleonic wars to cede his Norwegian kingdom to Charles XIII of Sweden in January 1814, his nephew, the viceroy of Norway, tried to raise the standard of independence. His action was endorsed by a rather informal plebiscite, and at the same time representatives for a constituent assembly were elected. Later in the year the Norwegians had to accept a union with Sweden but retained the separate constitution which had just been enacted, limiting the power of the monarch.

In 1905 the union was dissolved. It had become extremely unpopular in Norway as the result of a prolonged quarrel with the Swedes. A wave of nationalist enthusiasm swept over the country when its elected representatives took the dramatic step of unilaterally declaring that the Swedish king had ceased to reign and that the bond of union was dissolved. The Swedes on their side declared that they would accept the separation only on certain conditions. The Norwegian people were to be asked whether they agreed; and, among other things, the Swedes demanded the demolition of a number of border fortresses. The Norwegian parliament agreed immediately to the first condition, feeling sure of popular support. Its expectations were completely fulfilled. The vote was cast on August 13 and was practically unanimous in favor of secession: 368,208 for, only 184 against.[5] Several weeks' negotiations followed on the question of the border fortresses and other subjects of dispute. After they had been terminated in October, Sweden recognized Norway as a separate state, and the question of its future form of government was placed before the electorate on November 12 and 13.

Like the consultation in August, the one in November had a pronounced plebiscitarian character. The people endorsed what its leaders had done. In August the dissolution of the union was approved, in November the agreement with Sweden and the government's proposal to make a Danish prince king of Norway were considered. Formally only the latter issue was placed before the electorate, the agreement having been accepted by the Storting (parliament) in October. It seems, however, that the two issues were bound together in the minds of many voters. Most of the politicians who advocated a republican constitution had also been against the demolition of the border for-

[5] After Iceland had been granted internal autonomy in 1918, with full independence from Denmark to follow twenty-five years later, an Icelandic referendum also gave practically unanimous approval (99.5 percent yes).

tresses. They had preferred to risk war. The issue confronting the voters seemed to be not simply that of a monarchical versus a republican form of government; rather were they asked to choose between a pacific monarchy and a bellicose republic. But above all it was a question of personalities. The opposition bitterly assailed Prime Minister Christian Michelsen. At this moment, however, he was a national hero because of the leading part he had taken in dissolving the union, and when he staked his and his government's political life on acceptance of the monarchy, the popular response was overwhelming. Nearly four-fifths of the votes were in the affirmative on a very high poll—78.9 percent of a 75.3 percent turnout.

Manhood suffrage had been introduced at the turn of the century, but initially the level of participation was low: only some 55 percent of the voters took part in the Storting elections of 1900 and 1903. In the referendum of August 1905, however, no less than 84.8 percent went to the polling stations, and in November the figure was 75.3 percent.

The dramatic events of the year and the imminent danger of war, with large numbers of troops being sent to the border between August and October, aroused the Norwegian population and explains the unprecedented level of electoral participation. There also seems to have been a durable effect. While some of the voters evidently never went to the polls again after 1905, there were others to whom the experience of this year proved to be a starting point for the formation of new habits. They became politically conscious and henceforth needed no special stimulus to vote. The turnout in the Storting election of 1906 was about 65 percent, an increase of almost 10 percent from the two previous legislative contests. While the percentage of voters continued to increase from election to election, the rate of growth slowed down considerably after 1906. Participation increased by little more than 3 percent from 1906 to 1909, and only by about 1 percent from 1909 to 1912, as well as from 1912 to 1915. From 1915 to 1918 the increase was less than 0.5 percent for men, and there was a slight decrease for women, who had obtained the franchise three years earlier. But then a new big wave of mobilization occurred in connection with the referendum in 1919, this time a mobilization of women rather than men.

Mobilization of Women. The nationwide 1919 referendum in Norway concerned the prohibition of alcoholic beverages. A similar referendum was conducted in Sweden in 1922, another one in Norway in 1926, and finally one in Finland in 1931. The Scandinavian interest in prohibition was stimulated when the United States adopted it through the Eighteenth Amendment, ratified in January 1919. But it would not be correct to speak of a merely one-way influence. Scandinavian immigrants had long been active prohibitionists in the United States, particularly in the Middle West, where the movement acquired great importance. It has been said, for example: "If one can argue that a single issue was more important than any other issue in Iowa between 1885 and 1918 it was prohibition."[6] While Catholic and German populations generally opposed tough restrictions on liquor, Yankees and Scandinavians usually favored them. Aggregate voting statistics show that the Scandinavians in particular were zealous. They sided with the prohibitionist Republican party, voted for prohibition in referendums, and saw to it that saloons were closed down. Ballard C. Campbell quotes as extreme but characteristic the following examples from Iowa: While the German townships of Kneist in Carroll county and Mosalem in Dubuque county returned votes of 133 to 1 and 138 to 0 against prohibition, the three Norwegian townships of Norway, Linden, and Logan in Winnebago county totaled 120 to 0 in its support.[7]

Women were particularly interested. The part they played in the American movement has been described by authors like Ross Evans Paulson.[8] In Scandinavia their role is shown with special clarity through referendum data. In Norway the temperance societies succeeded in mobilizing a large number of women for the national referendum on prohibition in October 1919. In the southwestern third of the country, women's rate of participation in the rural districts surged from less than 30 percent to more than 65 percent.[9] Prohibition was approved by a majority of 61.6 percent, and there is no doubt that the increase in women's voting turnout greatly helped.

Although Norwegian women had to wait until the twentieth century to get the vote in ordinary elections, in earlier years they took

---

[6] Samuel P. Hays, "History as Human Behavior," *Iowa Journal of History*, vol. 58 (1960), p. 196.

[7] Ballard .C. Campbell, "Did Democracy Work? Prohibition in Late Nineteenth-Century Iowa: A Test Case," *Journal of Interdisciplinary History*, vol. 8 (Summer 1977), p. 93.

[8] Ross Evans Paulson, *Women's Suffrage and Prohibition* (Glenview, Ill.: Scott, Foresman, 1973).

[9] On regional contrasts in the referendums of 1905–1926, see Sten Sparre Nilson, "Regional Differences in Norway, with Special Reference to Labor Radicalism and Cultural Norms," *Scandinavian Political Studies*, vol. 10 (1975), pp. 123-137; and "Kvinnestemmene ved stortingsvalget 1921," *Historisk Tidskrift*, vol. 5 (1977), pp. 335-349. See also Sten Sparre Nilson, *Politisk avstand ved norske folkeavstemninger* (Oslo: Gyldendal, 1972).

part in a number of local referendums concerning restrictions on the sale of liquor. As early as 1894 the temperance societies succeeded in establishing universal suffrage for *both* sexes in municipal referendums on the issue of prohibition. In 1895, the first year this law was applied, votes were counted separately for the two sexes. In all the towns in question statistics show a consistently high rate of female participation, and women supported prohibition more strongly than did men.

In subsequent Norwegian referendums men's and women's votes were not counted separately. They were in Sweden, however, when a proposal to introduce prohibition was narrowly defeated (49.0 percent yes) in a national referendum in October 1922, and again in Finland when the only Finnish referendum of importance was held in December 1931. It repealed the prohibition of alcoholic beverages instituted some years earlier by parliament. In both Finland and Sweden women proved to be more strongly in favor of introducing prohibition, or less strongly in favor of its repeal, than were men.[10]

In both Sweden and Norway a parliamentary election was held approximately one year before the nationwide prohibition referendum, making a further comparison between elections and referendums possible. Figure 1 shows the distribution of the male and female vote in different localities in Sweden in 1922. Prohibitionist sentiment was generally weaker in towns and cities than in rural districts, and weakest of all in the central part of the country, that is, in the capital city and the area closest to it. But everywhere more women than men voted yes on prohibition. Table 8-2 shows the rates of participation in the Norwegian prohibition referendum and in the preceding parliamentary election.[11] Participation tended to decline in areas where opinion was more evenly split on the referendum issue, whereas there was a mobilization of voters in the most strongly pro- and anti-prohibitionist areas. Turnout was greatest among supporters, how-

[10] Results from Sweden are given in *Nordisk Statistisk Tidskrift*, vol. 2 (1923), pp. 292-312. The Finnish results are in *Finlands Officiella Statistik*, vol. 29 Cl (1931), where on page 5 it is stated that men and women used ballot papers of different colors. For the results in Norway, see *Alkoholstatistik 1918–1919* (NOS VI.190, pp. 34-51). The Danes' view of prohibition has been more like that of Central Europeans than of other Scandinavians: Denmark did not have a strong temperance movement, and no prohibition referendum was conducted there.

[11] The data on turnout can be compared with Figure 2 below, which shows the relation between turnout rates in the Norwegian referendum of 1972 on joining the European Economic Community (EEC) and the preceding parliamentary election of 1969. The recent voting pattern is similar to that apparent in Sweden and Norway half a century earlier, after World War I.

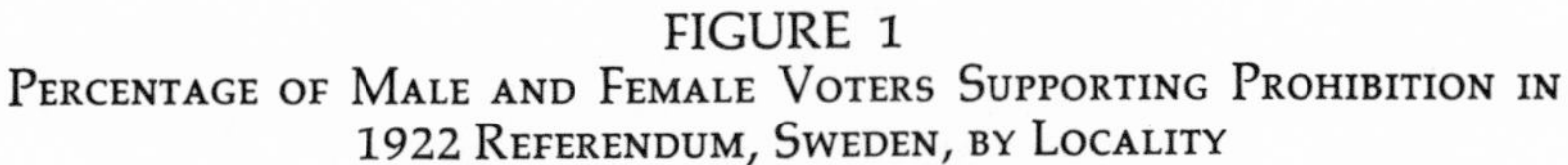

FIGURE 1
PERCENTAGE OF MALE AND FEMALE VOTERS SUPPORTING PROHIBITION IN 1922 REFERENDUM, SWEDEN, BY LOCALITY

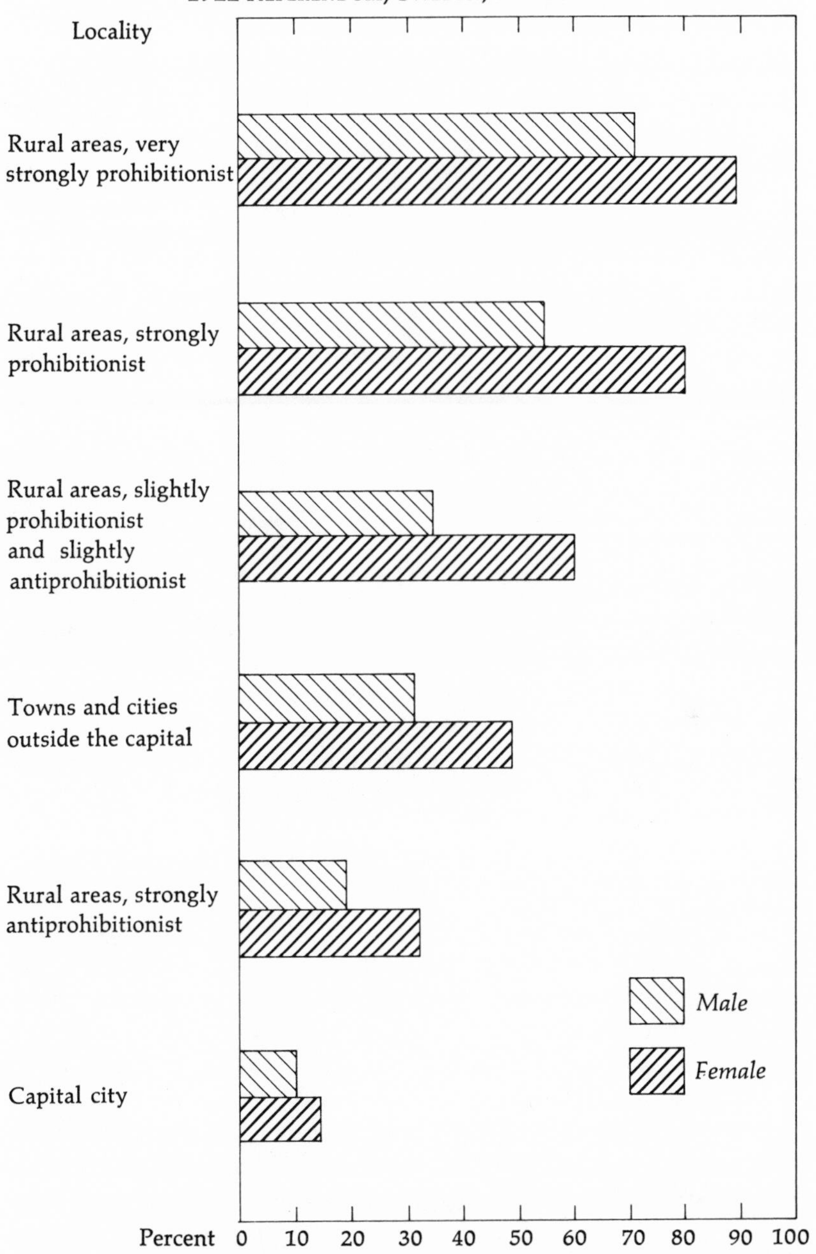

SOURCE: Calculated on the basis of figures given by Otto Gronlund in *Nordisk Statistisk Tidskrift*, vol. 2 (1923), pp. 292-312.

TABLE 8-2

TURNOUT IN ELECTIONS AND REFERENDUMS, NORWAY, 1918–1919
(percent)

	1918 Election		*1919 Referendum*		*Difference (1919 − 1918)*	
Area	Men	Women	Men	Women	Men	Women
Rural						
South and West	61.8	29.7	75.4	67.0	13.6	37.3
North	59.6	38.2	61.8	47.2	2.2	9.0
Inner East	76.9	53.8	72.3	56.1	−4.6	2.3
Oslofjord	70.4	53.2	67.6	53.6	−2.8	0.4
Urban						
Oslo	74.1	63.1	78.1	65.2	4.0	2.1
Other	78.7	71.6	76.1	68.7	−2.6	−2.9

SOURCE: Calculated on the basis of Norwegian official statistics (*Stortingsvalget*, 1918, and *Alkoholstatistik*, 1918-1919).

ever, and the mobilization of prohibitionist *women* was particularly great, above all in the Norwegian core area of teetotalism, the South and West.

Comparisons of the rates of participation in the Norwegian parliamentary elections of 1918 and 1921, the last prereferendum and the first postreferendum election respectively, give further evidence of the impact of the prohibition issue on the party system. The relative strength of the different parties remained practically unchanged from 1918 to 1921 in the towns and cities, but not in the rural districts, which made up three-quarters of the total electorate. The Liberal party, hitherto dominant in Norwegian politics, was seriously threatened, particularly by the new Agrarian party. With a strict enforcement of prohibition as the main plank in their 1921 platform, however, the Liberals saw the number of votes cast in their favor increase substantially in the South and West. This must have been due in large part to the mobilization of new female voters, who gave their support to the party of prohibition. The development of electoral participation from 1918 to 1921 was very uneven, the greatest increase appearing in the region where prohibitionist sentiment was strong and where the Liberals preserved their position as the largest party, almost as large as the others taken together.

In other parts of the country, however, they suffered heavy losses. The party had become an instrument of the temperance societies, and this proved somewhat costly. The struggle over prohibition is an illustration of "the critical role which the structure of organized group life may play in the overall level of mass political participation." Norman H. Nie, G. Bingham Powell, Jr., and Kenneth Prewitt emphasized the importance of organizational involvement which they found in a study of political life in six widely different countries: the United States, Great Britain, West Germany, Italy, Mexico, and India. They see in such involvement a great "potential for participatory democracy," but they are uncertain about the quality of organization-based political participation: "The individual mobilized by his group membership lacks the attitudes usually associated with political involvement. This may mean that the content of his effort to influence will be largely determined by the mobilizing leaders." There is a danger of too much influence accruing to "activists who do not have the attitudes usually assumed to be associated with involvement in political life." [12]

Both the potential and the danger of organizational politics can be seen in the case of Norway in 1919, where the temperance societies represented an extraordinary mobilizing force. When the movement reached its summit around 1920, the prohibitionists could claim by far the largest organized membership in the country, about twice the size of the trade unions. But their victory in 1919 cost them dearly. Prohibition did not prove a success, and a second national referendum was held seven years later after the unfortunate consequences of the policy had become apparent. The turnout decreased slightly, from 66.5 percent in 1919 to 64.8 percent in 1926; and although prohibition had been endorsed in 1919 by 61.5 percent of the participating voters, it was rejected by 55.8 percent in 1926.

The first referendum had shown the strength of the activists, while the second revealed their limitations, their lack of a sense of political realities. In the wake of prohibition came a wave of smuggling and other forms of lawlessness, but the prohibitionists did not give in. They were on a crusade. After the prolonged ordeal of World War I, 1914–1918, mankind was to be freed once and for all from the scourge of intoxicating poison—and that end could justify questionable means. For example, in a parliamentary debate in 1918, certain provisions of the electoral law to be applied in local prohibition

[12] Norman H. Nie, G. Bingham Powell, Jr., and Kenneth Prewitt, "Social Structure and Political Participation: Developmental Relationships," *American Political Science Review*, vol. 63 (1969), pp. 826-827.

referendums were attacked as grossly unfair. Prohibitionist leaders admitted that provisions like these ought not to be used in other matters but argued that it was legitimate to introduce them in the fight against alcohol—to prohibitionists a struggle against Evil itself. They were not deterred by the growth of smuggling and illicit liquor traffic, nor were they impressed by economic difficulties, which proved to be considerable for a country like Norway.

When imports of wine and liquor were stopped, the alcohol-exporting countries of southern Europe retaliated. They prohibited the importation of Norwegian fish, a move which created great hardship in the fishing districts of northern Norway. As a result, a large number of northern voters turned against the Liberals and gave their support in subsequent elections to the Conservative party. While the Agrarians were split on the prohibition issue and the Socialists somewhat reluctantly supported the Liberal government, the Conservatives opposed prohibition from the beginning. Previously they had received only a minimal share of the vote in northern Norway, but from 1921 on they advanced sharply. Their stand on alcohol policy made their party popular. While little more than one-fourth of the northerners had voted against prohibition in the 1919 referendum, there were many in that region who turned around in the following years. The antiprohibitionist share of the vote in the North was almost doubled in 1926 when the second referendum took place.

Prohibition was repealed in 1927, and almost half a century elapsed before a Norwegian governing party again called a referendum.

The Role of the Government

Most referendums in Scandinavia have been held without being constitutionally required, and the demand for such consultations has originated with the government's opponents. It is only natural for those in opposition to single out for special consideration some issue on which they hope to score a success. If groups or factions in opposition within a party or parliamentary minorities opposing a government wish to refer an issue to the voters for decision, the explanation is not hard to find. It is less evident why those in established leadership positions sometimes accede to the demand, but occasionally their motives can be gauged with a reasonable degree of certainty.

The opposition, even if it has no expectation of winning a referendum, may be motivated by the hope of strengthening its position by obtaining more electoral support than it could expect to get in a parliamentary election. On the other hand, the government may feel sufficiently confident of victory to accept the challenge or even to welcome it—there is always the possibility of having the issue laid effectively to rest with the aid of a popular verdict. This seems to have been the motivation of Prime Minister Michelsen when he accepted a referendum in the autumn of 1905, and there is no doubt that the outcome provided the new monarchy in Norway with a secure foundation.

A similar motive may have been present when the Norwegian Labor party leaders decided in 1962 to hold a Common Market referendum. NATO membership had been decided upon in 1949 without a referendum, and Labor leaders were afterward accused of manipulation. Perhaps they had come to feel that a referendum on EEC membership might forestall similar criticism. They may also have believed, as those in government often will, that they possessed certain advantages over the opposition in matters such as the timing of the referendum.[13]

But they did not act solely, or perhaps even mainly, as leaders of government. They were also very much concerned about their party, seeing the referendum as potentially beneficial.[14] This has been an important consideration with politicians whether in government, like the Norwegian Socialists, or in opposition, like the Norwegian Liberals and the Danish Socialists.

The Political Parties

Parliamentary parties play a central role in Scandinavian politics, and the referendum is an extraparliamentary institution. Yet the leaders of a party in which there is disagreement on an issue may have strong reasons to advocate or at least to accept the holding of a referendum. If it results in a strong popular majority in favor of the leaders' view, the position of the latter within the party will be

[13] If so, they made a miscalculation. In January 1963 General de Gaulle shut the door to the EEC, and the Norwegian referendum was delayed for a decade. Then the Danish government saw fit to postpone its referendum till after the one in Norway. Both delays probably worked to the advantage of the anti-EEC groups in Norway.

[14] When the Labor leaders accepted a referendum in 1962, Norwegian politicians generally regarded the opposition to the EEC as a movement of intellectuals and academics with no broad popular support. They may have been right at the time. It is my impression that they expected an easy referendum victory, which would have pacified internal party opposition. However, the motives of politicians are notoriously hard to ascertain.

strengthened. And even if they feel uncertain about the outcome, they may see the referendum as the best available means to relieve internal strain. When an election is impending, to promise to hold a referendum at a later time will have a unifying effect; those who disagree with the leadership on the issue in question can still work unreservedly for the party's electoral candidates. Such considerations seem to have weighed heavily with the Danish Labor leaders when they decided in favor of a referendum on EEC membership, much later than did their Norwegian opposite numbers, at a time when strong opposition had become visible within socialist ranks and a parliamentary election was imminent in Denmark.[15] The strategy was successful in that election, which took place in 1971.

The Social Democratic party also survived the 1973 referendum practically intact. But this was largely because the position advocated by the party's leadership obtained a solid popular majority. Had the opposite been the case, the party might have lost a good deal of its support, as the Norwegian Labor party eventually did.

Referendums can offer a good means of postponing dissension within a party, but they cannot permanently prevent it. Perhaps the clearest Scandinavian illustration of this is provided by the Norwegian Liberals. They were the first to propose a Common Market referendum. The party was badly split on the question of EEC membership. Throwing the hot potato to the electorate seemed the best thing to do, and there is little doubt that the immediate effect was to relieve the party's internal strain. When the referendum campaign finally got under way, however, the outcome seemed highly doubtful, and the strain returned with increased force: The majority of Liberal parliamentarians were in favor of membership, but the majority of the national organization were against it. A decision at the parliamentary level would certainly have led to serious internal dispute but scarcely to a complete split of the party.

Referendums regularly impose a strain on the internal cohesion of some parties. The cleavage which produces the referendum, and which in turn may be widened by it, will always cut across the existing party split to some extent. The consequences can be either temporary or

[15] Those in the British Labour party in favor of the Common Market apparently had a similar motive when they accepted the idea of a referendum. The Danish Labor leaders did not risk much, however: in the upcoming election those opposed to the Common Market were expected to win enough seats to make a referendum constitutionally mandatory in any case. But then it can be said that the British Labour pro-marketeers did not risk much either, perhaps even less. Their country had already joined the European Community Taking Britain out could have been much more of a "leap in the dark" than would staying there on improved terms.

lasting. At the Swedish pension referendum of October 1957, a number of smallholders defected from the Social Democrats and voted for the plan proposed by the Agrarians, but these voters subsequently seem to have returned to the Social Democratic fold. On the other hand, a good many former Liberal voters also preferred the Agrarian pension plan, and they seem to have voted Agrarian in later elections.[16]

Parties seldom split right down the middle, but it happened to the Norwegian Liberals over the EEC in 1972 as it had to the Swedish Liberals after the prohibition referendum of 1922.[17] The Norwegian Social Democrats also suffered a serious setback when a number of left-wing Laborites broke away after the 1972 referendum. A referendum may also lead to a fusion of parties: in 1973 the dissident Laborites joined an electoral alliance consisting of the Socialist People's party and the Communist party. These parties declared their intention of merging after the 1973 election, but in the end only a minority of Communists were willing to join the new organization, the Left Socialist party. The Left Socialists, however, seemed to constitute a serious threat to the Labor party, which until then had been the linchpin of the Norwegian party system.

The Political System

In the first section of this chapter I argued that referendums more easily prevent than promote specific changes in social or political matters. But there is also the possibility that a referendum on some major issue will set into motion a basic change in the political system as a whole.

In Norway it looked for a time as if the EEC referendum of September 24–25, 1972, would constitute a watershed in the country's political history. Though this judgment now seems to have been premature, the referendum's consequences were not insignificant. The government and three-fourths of the members of parliament were in favor of membership, but it was rejected by 53.5 percent of the

---

[16] Björn Molin, *Tjänstepensionsfragan* (Gothenburg: Akademiförlaget, 1965). See also his article, "Swedish Party Politics: A Case Study," *Scandinavian Political Studies*, vol. 1 (1966), pp. 45-58; and Bo Särlvik, "Political Stability and Change in the Swedish Electorate," *Scandinavian Political Studies*, vol. 1 (1966), pp. 190-191.

[17] The Swedish Liberals were reunited twelve years later. In Norway a minority broke with the leadership in 1921 because they considered prohibition an illiberal measure.

voters.[18] The disturbance that occurred in the smooth working of the parliamentary machinery was perhaps the least significant consequence. The Labor government, whose draft agreement with the European Community had been rejected, chose to resign and was replaced by a coalition government drawn from smaller parties. It enjoyed the support of only one-fourth of the members of parliament but was tolerated for almost a year by the majority. This abnormal situation illustrates the kind of complication that can occur when the referendum is used in a parliamentary democracy. But no insuperable difficulties arose. The minority government's main task was to negotiate a commercial treaty with the EEC. The full consequences of the referendum for domestic politics became visible only in the election of September 1973, which showed widespread voter skepticism about the established parties.

A voter who disagrees with his or her party's stand at a referendum, or who finds it internally split on the issue, may come to regard other parties in a new light. Thus, in some circumstances a referendum campaign can entail a virtual suspension of the existing party system. Such was the case in both Norway and Denmark, not least because the main traditional foes, Labor and the Conservatives, suddenly appeared campaigning together cordially in favor of Common Market membership. The temporary suspension of much that had come to be regarded as politically normal was bound to have some effect.

In Norway there was an immediate gain for the Left Socialists and Communists, who were joined by a sizable number of Labor party dissidents. Together these groups formed the Socialist Electoral Alliance, which won sixteen seats in the 1973 election, clearly a result of their strong common opposition to EEC membership. There was also a rebellion on the right, with an antitax party gaining four seats in 1973.[19] Some would argue that this phenomenon was unrelated to the struggle over the Common Market. But even if the EEC referendum did affect all results of the 1973 election, the impact was of short duration. The next parliamentary election, held in 1977, largely restored the old balance of forces and almost did away with the fledgling parties on the left and right wings of the political spectrum.

---

[18] On the Norwegian referendum and its aftermath, see Henry Valen, " 'No' to EEC," and Ottar Hellevik and Nils Petter Gleditsch, "The Common Market Decision in Norway," both in *Scandinavian Political Studies*, vol. 8 (1973), pp. 214-235; and Henry Valen, "National Conflict Structure and Foreign Politics," *European Journal of Political Research*, vol. 4 (1976), pp. 47-82.

[19] Henry Valen and Stein Rokkan, "Norway: The Election to the Storting in September 1973," *Scandinavian Political Studies*, vol. 9 (1974), p. 206.

In retrospect, it looks as if the main impact of the 1972 referendum on the party system was to bring about the virtual demise of the Liberal party. The forces loosened by the anti–Common Market campaign certainly represented a potential for greater change, but there appears to have been a failure to utilize that potential. While Labor party leaders played their cards well, the men and women of the leftist alliance played theirs badly. The leader of the antitax party died, and his movement with him, to the benefit of the Conservatives.

In Denmark the 1972 EEC referendum did not have any immediate impact on the political system. Nevertheless there may have been an indirect effect which, combined with other factors, might in the long run prove to be of lasting importance. These two Scandinavian referendums therefore present some difficult problems of interpretation, and it is not possible to make more than a tentative judgment as to their overall effect on the political systems. Some of their salient features can be described, and attention can be drawn to certain points on which there is disagreement. New light can also be thrown on certain aspects of political life with particular clarity through an analysis of referendum results.

In Norway the controversy over Common Market membership had the character of a fight between center and periphery. While there was an affirmative majority in and around Oslo, hostility to the EEC mounted with increasing distance from the nation's capital. In communities near Oslo the yes vote was 55 percent as opposed to 27 percent in distant communities.[20] People who thought that too much was being decided in faraway Oslo were reluctant to transfer authority to Brussels, which is still farther away. Some observers have contended that this struggle between periphery and center should be seen as only part of a general struggle against the political and social establishment of the country. This is doubtful, but there was something of a controversy between rural and urban establishment. Norwegian agriculture feared that it would be badly hurt by competition inside the European Community, and Per Borten, the leader of the Agrarian (Center) party, played an important role on the anti-EEC side. He had been prime minister in the coalition government of Conservatives, Liberals, Christian Democrats, and Agrarians, which had a majority in parliament and held power from 1965 until it fell apart because of disagreement over the handling of the EEC issue in 1971.

[20] As defined in the official statistics; see *Yearbook of Nordic Statistics*, vol. 11 (1972), p. 231.

The Danish economic position is different. Because of Denmark's fertile land, its agriculture stood to gain by getting access to the Common Market for its products. The Danish Agrarian party joined Labor and the Conservatives in campaigning in favor of joining, which meant that practically all Denmark's important leaders and political parties were clearly on one side. But although the Danish establishment won the referendum of October 1972, the following year saw a voter rebellion stronger and more lasting than the one in Norway. To what extent the rebellion was triggered by the referendum is an open question. The gains of the Communists in December 1973 can be linked to their party's stand against the EEC. But the most spectacular success was scored by a new party, the antitax movement led by a lawyer, Mogens Glistrup, which had not existed at the time of the 1972 referendum. As in the parallel Norwegian case, it could be said that the loosening of old party ties during the referendum campaign was a precondition for the launching of a tax rebellion, but the importance of that precondition is hard to evaluate. While the continued strength of the antitax movement, even after the election of 1977, is a main feature of Danish politics, the connection between its success and the EEC referendum remains doubtful.[21] With respect to the question of long-term consequences it seems best to sound a note of caution, but other aspects of referendums can be evaluated with less difficulty.[22]

Table 8-3 indicates what happened in the EEC referendums in Scandinavia and elsewhere. In Norway alone was there a close race. The Danish, British, and French results may seem comparable, but actually there were great differences in turnout. In France two-fifths of the electorate refused to take part in the referendum and either abstained or spoiled their ballots. Normally, in referendums and elections, between 20 and 25 percent of the French electorate do not vote, and only once since World War II had abstention been around 33 percent (in October 1946). In 1972 it was no less than 39.5 percent. People took little interest in the question of an enlargement of the

[21] The EEC cleavage "broadened during 1973," and though the referendum was only one of several factors which may explain the 1973 voter rebellion, indications are that it was not without significance. (Ole Borre, "Denmark's Protest Election of December 1973," *Scandinavian Political Studies*, vol. 9 [1974], p. 199; Jerrold G. Rusk and Ole Borre, "The Changing Party Space in Danish Voter Perceptions, 1971–1973," *European Journal of Political Research*, vol. 2 [1974], pp. 342-343.)

[22] The problems connected with an assessment of the long-term effects of referendums are discussed by Gordon Smith, "The Functional Properties of the Referendum," *European Journal of Political Research*, vol. 4 (1976), pp. 1-23.

TABLE 8-3

COMMON MARKET REFERENDUMS IN EUROPEAN COUNTRIES
(percent)

Country	*Issue*	*Year*	*Voting Yes*	*Turnout*
Norway	Entering the EEC	1972	46.5	77.6
Denmark	Entering the EEC	1972	63.3	90.1
France	Enlarging the EEC	1972	67.7	60.5
Ireland	Entering the EEC	1972	83.1	70.9
Britain	Staying in the EEC	1975	67.2	64.5

SOURCE: Appendix A.

Common Market, and many voters followed the advice of certain opposition parties to abstain or spoil their papers as a means of showing dissatisfaction with the government.[23] When Britain voted on the EEC three years later there was a turnout of 64.5 percent, a good deal less than in the two preceding general elections (78.7 and 72.8 percent, respectively). This suggested a lukewarm acceptance of membership but also showed that the active opponents made up only a small fraction of the electorate.

In Denmark things were quite different. A heated public debate took place, and the campaign has been characterized as "undoubtedly the most extensive political campaign ever undertaken in Denmark."[24] Participation had been high in the previous parliamentary elections, coming close to 90 percent a couple of times, but in the 1972 referendum it soared even higher and reached the unprecedented figure of 90.1 percent. Perhaps the established parties overplayed their hand. Sensing that the Danish population was dissatisfied with steadily deteriorating economic conditions, they stressed the advantages they thought would accrue from joining the European Community. Their effort was intense, and the voters turned out. But improved conditions did not follow immediately; on the contrary, there was further deterioration. Popular frustration was the result.

In Norway, as in Britain, participation in the referendum was lower than in a parliamentary election, but the campaign has been

[23] See the articles on Britain, France, and others in the *European Journal of Political Research*, vol. 4, no. 1 (1976), special issue on referendums. See also Chapter 7 of this book.

[24] Nikolaj Petersen and Jörgen Elklit, "Denmark Enters the European Community," *Scandinavian Political Studies*, vol. 8 (1973), p. 206.

characterized as even more intense than in Denmark. A painstaking analysis of the data explains this phenomenon. Figure 2 shows the difference between the Norwegian parliamentary election of 1969 and the 1972 referendum (that is, the difference in turnout as related to the percentage of those voting yes in the respective electoral districts). There was a mobilization of voters above the 1969 level in communities characterized either by overwhelming resistance to membership or by overwhelming support for it. But there was a clear tendency for participation to decrease below the 1969 level as local opinion became increasingly divided, and cross-pressures presumably became stronger. For the country as a whole the turnout was some 5 percent below the level of the preceding two parliamentary elections: 77.6 percent as against 85.4 and 83.8 percent.

In general, the movement opposing EEC membership contained both a streak of conservatism and a streak of radicalism. Norwegians, unlike the Danes and the British, did not see much need for a change in their country's economic position. For years its economy had been booming, and many people thought they were free now to vote in accord with their instinctive reluctance to join a group of foreign nations. In this sense the opposing vote contained an element of conservatism or traditionalism (some would speak about overtones of xenophobia or, in certain cases, of fundamentalist, anti-Catholic bigotry). In addition, many Norwegians were afraid of losing the measure of social security they had achieved under a welfare state. This attitude was to some extent combined with a more ideological radicalism, a deep suspicion that the European Community was and would remain essentially an instrument of ruthless, unreformed capitalistic and monopolistic forces.

But perhaps more important than these general attitudes were specific expectations as to the economic consequences of rejecting membership. No great fear of losing markets was evident. For more than two decades there had been, with almost no interruption, practically full employment. Only in a couple of export industries (pulp and paper, and aluminum) was the economic outlook clearly uncertain, a fact which influenced people dependent upon them to vote in favor of joining the Common Market. The fishing industry, on the other hand, proved indifferent to the prospect of better access to European markets. What counted was the European Community's obvious wish to gain access to Norwegian territorial waters. Fishermen, and almost all who had to do with the fishing industry, feared

FIGURE 2

RATE OF PARTICIPATION
(DIFFERENCE BETWEEN 1972 AND 1969 AND PERCENTAGE VOTING YES, 1972)

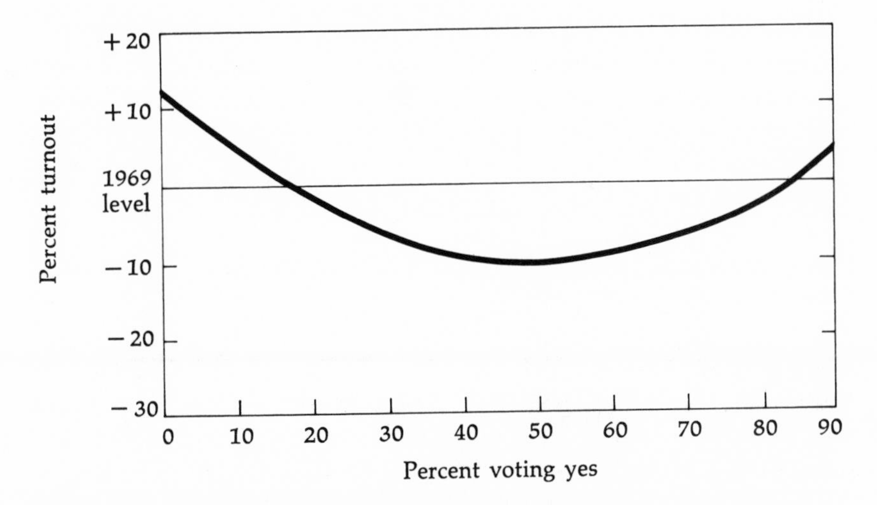

NOTE: The horizontal axis shows the percentage voting yes in the 443 communes and municipalities outside the capital and the 78 wards of Oslo; the vertical axis shows the rate of participation, expressed as the difference between percent turnout in the 1972 EEC referendum and the 1969 parliamentary election. It is positive when the turnout was higher in 1972 than in 1969, and negative when it was higher in 1969. The 1969 turnout level is marked by a horizontal line.

The U-shaped regression line ($y = 127.29 - 0.9055x + 0.0009x^2$) shows the average tendency in the relation between turnout and percentage voting yes. It is above the horizontal line in localities where yes votes constituted less than 16.5 percent of the total. Where votes were split 50-50, the curve is about 10 percent below the 1969 level. Subsequently it rises gradually once more, passing the 1969 level at the point where yes votes made up some 83 percent of the total in 1972.

SOURCE: Henry Valen, "Valgforskning og politikk," in *I Forskningens Lys: NAVF's Jubileumsskrift*, M. Sundt Mortensen, ed. (Oslo: Lyches forlag, 1974), pp. 107-108; reproduced with permission.

the depletion of the stock of fish that might well result if trawler fleets from other countries were to enter freely. This fear was clearly reflected in the fact that while 56.7 percent voted yes in the towns and suburbs, only 41.4 percent supported EEC membership in industrialized rural communities, 20.9 percent in fishing communities, and 34.5 percent in other rural areas. Survey data show similar results. Fifteen percent of farmers and fishermen voted yes in rural areas and 17 percent in industrialized communities. Moreover, only a minority of owners of shops and other small businesses, lawyers, doctors, and other professionals living in rural localities voted yes, compared with the 70 percent of their counterparts in industrialized areas.[25]

The differences between people in different occupations and localities in the Norwegian EEC referendum cannot be explained solely with reference to economic factors. Many men and women in rural areas voted no to express traditionalist convictions, such as their dislike of wine-selling Catholic countries, while among industrial workers such a vote was often meant to be an affirmation of socialist convictions.[26]

Conclusion

Referendums have been used intermittently in Scandinavia ever since the early 1900s. Some have had considerable importance, but it is difficult to say whether this will continue. There was a time when large numbers of voters could be mobilized for permanent electoral participation through the holding of a referendum, but this is no longer so, since only minor fractions of the Scandinavian electorates now fail to take regular part in ordinary elections.

One thing seems certain, however: As a result of their recent experience, many Scandinavian politicians have grown wary of using the institution. Under the Danish constitution referendums are mandatory in certain cases, and the question of lowering the voting age in Denmark to eighteen years was placed once more before the electorate September 19, 1978. But in the other Scandinavian Countries it does not seem likely that any new referendum will be held in the near future, except perhaps in Sweden. There is public disagreement within the Swedish nonsocialist coalition government on the building of atomic power installations, and the conflict between environmental concerns and industrial development appears to be one that might be settled by a referendum. The last referendum in Sweden was arranged under a coalition government of Social Democrats and Agrarians in 1957, and its outcome made the coalition fall apart. But the politicians of today may not be deterred by what happened in their country twenty years ago. And if some leading politicians think it is useful for their own purposes to propose a

[25] Henry Valen, "Valgforskning og politikk," in *I Forskningens Lys: NAVF's Jubileumsskrift*, M. Sundt Mortensen, ed. (Oslo: Lyches forlag, 1974), p. 101.

[26] To what extent the contrast between center and periphery coincided with a contrast between high and low status is discussed by Ottar Hellevik, Nils Petter Gleditsch, and Kristen Ringdal, "The Common Market Issue in Norway," *Journal of Peace Research*, vol. 12 (1975), pp. 37-53. See also Sten Sparre Nilson, "In What Sense Is a High Social Position also a Central Position?" *Journal of Peace Research*, vol. 13 (1976), pp. 67-71.

referendum, others may find it hard to resist the demand that the people be consulted.

Most referendums are said to produce a polarization of public opinion since they offer the voter only a choice between yes and no. This means the voter is pressured to vote either for or against, without the possibility of choosing some third solution. In a few Nordic referendums, however, several choices were offered to the electorate.

In Sweden in 1957 voters were asked to choose among three different pension schemes. Number 1 had the support of the Federation of Labor Unions, number 3 was supported by the Employers' Association, while number 2, endorsed by the Center party, was formulated in such a way that it might appear as a compromise between the other two—or at least its designation as "number 2" was apt to convey that impression.

In the election number 2 obtained a considerable number of votes, many more than the Center party had received in recent elections, but what this signified is unclear. The voters in the referendum may have wanted to protest against what they perceived as the schemes of big business on the one hand and big labor on the other, rather than to endorse a particular compromise. Whatever their motives, however, the referendum failed to solve the issue. None of the three schemes was backed by a majority in the final count (see Table 8-4). Had there been approximately equal support for schemes number 1 and 3, the politicians might have agreed on number 2 as an acceptable compromise.[27] But in the actual circumstances this was not regarded as appropriate. Neither side would give in. The referendum became the starting point of a protracted struggle between the parties, a struggle which was to dominate the two succeeding and bitterly fought general elections of 1958 and 1960.

In Finland in 1931 a referendum on the repeal of prohibition presented the voters with three choices: continuing prohibition of all alcoholic beverages, prohibition of all except light wine and beer, and complete repeal of prohibition. As a result of many years of intense agitation on the subject, however, the lines were drawn too tightly to admit a compromise. Public opinion had become polarized between those who wanted to maintain complete prohibition and those who wanted to repeal it entirely. In the final vote complete repeal won 60.5 percent to 37.9 percent for complete retention and only 1.6 percent for the compromise alternative.

---

[27] Björn Molin, *Tjänstepensionsfragan: En studie i svensk partipolitic* [The supplementary pensions question: A study in Swedish party politics] (Gothenburg: Akademiförlaget-Gumperts, 1965), p. 161.

TABLE 8-4

REFERENDUM ON PENSION SCHEMES IN SWEDEN, 1957

Pension Scheme	*Supported by*	*Votes Cast in Favor*	*Percent*
Number 1	Federation of Labor Unions	1,624,131	47.7
Number 2	Center party	530,576	15.6
Number 3	Employers' Association	1,251,477	36.7
Total		3,406,184	100.0

SOURCE: Appendix A.

In both the Swedish and Finnish instances, then, relatively few people preferred the "middle way," and it failed to provide the moderate solution hoped for by its proponents.

9
Ireland

Maurice Manning

The tradition of the referendum as an instrument of Irish politics goes back to the origins of the Irish Free State in 1922. Although the framers of the Free State constitution were denied the possibility of a full republic under the terms of the Anglo-Irish treaty which mandated dominion status, they nevertheless sought to incorporate some elements of democratic radicalism in their document. In particular they were conscious of a need to correct what they saw as an imbalance in the British system which favored the Cabinet at the expense of parliamentary and popular control.[1] Their solution, in part at least, was incorporated in articles 47 and 48 of the constitution, which provided respectively for referendum and initiative.

The Referendum and Initiative from 1922 to 1936

It was not totally unexpected that these provisions should find their way into the constitution. A Sinn Féin newspaper had advocated their adoption in 1919,[2] but, more significantly, both ideas were very much in vogue in the years immediately after World War I. As a result, the model used in the Irish experiment was influenced not so much by the older American, Australian, or Swiss precedents as by the postwar constitutions of the new European republics, in particular that of Weimar Germany.[3] In addition, the adoption of these devices seemed to the framers to be particularly well suited to a newly independent country, the majority of whose people had for so long been opposed to

---

[1] Leo Kohn, *The Constitution of the Irish Free State* (London: Allen & Unwin, 1932), p. 238.

[2] *New Ireland*, April 1919.

[3] Kohn, *Constitution of the Irish Free State*, p. 238.

the law and the government.[4] It was argued in the Dáil (the lower house of parliament) when these articles were being discussed that the workings of the referendum and the initiative would bring home to the people the reality of democratic control.[5]

Essentially, the referendum was envisaged as a check—a negative check—on the legislature. Under article 47 a bill which had been passed by both houses of the Oireachtas (parliament) could be suspended for ninety days on the written demand of two-fifths of the members of the Dáil or a majority of members of the Senate, presented to the president of the Executive Council (prime minister) within seven days of the bill being passed. If, within this ninety-day period, a resolution was carried by three-fifths of the Senate *or* if a petition was signed by one-twentieth of the electorate (about 100,000 voters) a referendum would be held. The outcome of the referendum would be determined by an ordinary majority of votes cast. Money bills and bills declared by both houses to be urgently necessary for public safety were exempted from this procedure. In addition, amendments to the constitution were to be submitted to referendum and were not to become law unless a majority of voters *on the register* or two-thirds of the votes recorded were cast in favor. This provision was not to become operative until 1930, however, since the constitution was to be flexible for its first eight years, during which time it could be amended by ordinary legislation.

The framers of the constitution were somewhat more tentative and cautious about the introduction of the initiative. Their caution was understandable in view of the strong possibility of civil war. They were perhaps reluctant to give full sanction to this device for extra-parliamentary legislation and merely provided for its potential adoption by the legislature whose discretion was restricted within very rigid limits. On its own initiative parliament might pass legislation for the initiation by the electorate of proposals for laws and constitutional amendments. If parliament did not do this within two years, such legislation might be introduced by a popular initiative if 75,000 registered voters petitioned (though not more than 15,000 from any one constituency). Then parliament would be obliged either to set up the machinery of the initiative or to submit the issue in question to referendum. If the machinery were set up, 50,000 voters would be enough to initiate a proposal; parliament could then either accept this proposal and pass it into law or submit it to referendum in the normal way.

[4] J. L. McCracken, *Representative Government in Ireland* (London: Oxford University Press, 1958), p. 59.

[5] *Dáil Debates*, vol. 1, cols. 1211-13, October 5, 1922.

In theory at least, the initiative made it comparatively easy for a small group to raise an issue for popular consideration. But the subsequent history of both the referendum and initiative illustrates the difficulties surrounding any form of constitutional experimentation aimed at allowing greater popular participation and decision making at a time when the basic institutions of the state and parliament itself were unacceptable to a considerable minority. Indeed, it was in part because the referendum and initiative became weapons in the post-civil war political conflict that they were eventually discarded.

Certainly the political conditions prevailing in the Free State in the 1920s ensured that neither the referendum nor the initiative would be given a fair trial. The government, which owed its majority in the Dáil to the abstention of the main opposition party, Fianna Fáil, was preoccupied with the problems of founding a state, restoring law and order, and repairing the damage of the civil war. The legitimacy of the state was questioned by Eamon de Valera's Fianna Fáil party which, after its civil war defeat, contested elections but refused to enter the Dáil because of the oath of allegiance to the king of England demanded of all members under the terms of the Anglo-Irish treaty. Overall it is not exaggerating to say that government and opposition had an almost total distrust in the democratic intentions of the other—hardly the most hopeful setting for an experiment in direct democracy. Not surprisingly, in a situation where the first priority of the government was survival, there proved to be little time or inclination to indulge in experiments which threatened the power of the executive. Before long the early hopes of a parliament free from the "tyranny" of party divisions and party whips were sacrificed to the necessity for strong and dependable parliamentary majorities. Similarly the attempt at a two-tiered cabinet soon collapsed, and against this background it was perhaps inevitable that devices such as the referendum and initiative, which could so easily be used against the government and which could give so little to government, would not long survive.

Because of the constitution's flexibility, during its first eight years sixteen amendments were passed without any need to invoke the use of the referendum. Although significant sections of the constitution were still controversial and divisive, any chance that the referendum might become an essential instrument of constitutional change after 1930 disappeared in 1929 when the period of flexible amendment was extended by another eight years.[6] Since the constitution itself did not survive past 1937 this meant that during its entire lifetime the

[6] Constitutional Amendment No. 16, Act of 1929.

referendum was never once used in what would normally have been one of its most important roles.

It seems clear that the government early on began to have serious reservations about the other possibilities for referendum envisaged in the constitution. A Cabinet subcommittee set up in 1924 recommended abolition of both referendum and initiative,[7] and this recommendation was put into effect in 1928 under circumstances of controversy and bitterness. The controversy arose out of Fianna Fáil's decision to take the oath of allegiance in 1927 and enter the Dáil. This humiliating acceptance of the oath only intensified Fianna Fáil's determination to see it removed, and the party saw in the referendum and initiative the means whereby this might be achieved—and the government severely embarrassed in the process. It began a nationwide campaign to focus attention on the issue and to raise the necessary number of signatures. In May 1928 a petition signed by 96,000 registered voters was presented to the Dáil.[8]

The position of the government was now highly embarrassing. It knew that in a referendum the vote would be strongly in favor of abolishing the oath, but it regarded the oath as an integral part of the Anglo-Irish treaty and had defended it as such in successive general elections. Furthermore it had serious reservations about the legality of unilaterally abolishing the oath (something which did become possible after the passing of the Statute of Westminster in 1929). As a result, the first reaction of the government was to stall for time. After a lengthy debate the Dáil voted to postpone allowing the presentation of the petition until the Oireachtas had prescribed the necessary procedure, possibly through the appointment of a joint committee of both houses to recommend a procedure.[9] But before this could be done the government introduced a bill, notice of which had been given before the preceding general election, providing for the abolition of the referendum and the initiative and making consequential amendments in the constitution.[10] Not surprisingly, the introduction of this bill—described as a "sharp practice" in a speech by de Valera—led to a fierce parliamentary struggle.[11] The opposition argued that the government had no authority to introduce a bill abolishing the initiative after a petition for its introduction had been signed in strict accordance with the terms of the constitution. A strong

[7] *Dáil Debates*, vol. 23, col. 1916, May 3, 1928.

[8] Ibid., vol. 23, cols. 2539 ff., June 1, 1928.

[9] Ibid., vol. 24, col. 720, June 15, 1928.

[10] Constitutional Amendment No. 10, Act 8 of 1928.

[11] *Dáil Debates*, vol. 24, col. 203, June 7, 1928.

case for the principle of direct legislation was made by opposition speaker after speaker in a spirited attempt to resist and delay the government measure. The government's position was equally adamant and probably somewhat more sincere than the opportunistic pleadings of the opposition, since de Valera in government, and later when drawing up his constitution, never showed any inclination to restore the initiative or to make the referendum accessible to the public. In fact, the real reason for the intensity of the opposition's commitment to the referendum and the initiative can be found later in de Valera's speech when he described these devices as the means whereby "the people" could remove offensive aspects and elements of subordination to Britain from the constitution.[12] Time and changed circumstances were to show that it was this, rather than any ideological commitment to direct democracy, which fueled the Fianna Fáil opposition to the proposed abolition.

The government's case was that the initiative tended to subvert the authority of parliament, destroyed the coherence of representative government, and substituted crude voting under the influence of demagogic agitation for the deliberative methods of an elected assembly. Direct government, it was argued, could become an easy means of obstruction; it was expensive to the state and had engendered the belief that it could be used for nullifying an essential part of an international settlement.[13] After bitter debates, which as often as not centered around the memories of the civil war, the bill was passed in both houses, accompanied by a declaration of urgency designed to preclude its submission to a referendum, which under the terms of article 50 of the constitution might then still have been possible.

That, effectively, was the end of the Free State's experiment with referendum and initiative. When de Valera came to power in 1932 he found he had no need for either in his task of dismantling the Free State constitution and removing all elements of subordination to Britain. The Statute of Westminster had given the Free State parliament all the powers it needed to achieve these ends, and in quick succession de Valera abolished the oath of allegience, appeal to the Privy Council, the governor-general, and all references to the king. De Valera's only real obstacle was the Senate—and this he abolished in 1934.

[12] Ibid., vol. 24, col. 1726, June 28, 1928.

[13] Kohn, *Constitution of the Irish Free State*, p. 243.

The Constitutional Referendum and General Election of 1937

By 1936 de Valera's position in domestic politics was secure. He had defeated the main opposition party, Fine Gael, in two successive elections, and that party, demoralized by election defeat and its association with the quasi-fascist Blueshirts, was in a state of decline.[14] More than that, de Valera had succeeded in removing from the constitution all the elements and references which he and his party had found offensive. But this was not enough. For de Valera the very origins of that constitution were suspect, and in 1936 he began work on a new constitution which, among other things, would owe its existence not to an act of the British parliament but to the democratically expressed acceptance of the Irish people.[15]

De Valera's new constitution, Bunreacht na hÉireann, was introduced in the Dáil in March 1937. In general, the constitution proposed a republican form of government (though without declaring a republic) with an elected president of limited powers, a bicameral parliament, and the provision of judicial review. The main differences between the old and new constitution can be seen in the incorporation by de Valera of contemporary Catholic social values in articles 40–45, special recognition for the Roman Catholic Church, the total prohibition of divorce, and a strong assertion of Irish unity.

The new constitution was opposed in the Dáil by the two opposition parties, Fine Gael and Labour. Fine Gael saw no need for a new constitution, was worried by some features of the new one, and in particular felt that the country's interests were best served by remaining unequivocally within the British Commonwealth. Labour, which till then had supported Fianna Fáil, wanted an outright declaration of a republic, while outside the Dáil the Irish Republican Army (IRA) saw the constitution as institutionalizing the "sellout" of 1922. Fianna Fáil's parliamentary majority was sufficient to withstand this opposition, and on June 14, 1937, the bill passed all stages in the Dáil.[16] Technically, at this point it could have come into effect since the second period of flexible amendment of the 1922 constitution was still in operation, and all that was needed to remove one constitution and replace it with another was an act of the Oireachtas. De Valera, however, was determined that Bunreacht na

---

[14] See Maurice Manning, *The Blueshirts* (Dublin and Toronto: Gill and Macmillan, 1970).

[15] See Earl of Longford, *Eamon De Valera*, T. P. O'Neill, ed. (Dublin and Toronto: Gill and Macmillan, 1970), chap. 24.

[16] *Dáil Debates*, vol. 68, col. 258, June 14, 1937.

hÉireann would, unlike its predecessor, owe its existence and its moral and legal basis not to an act of parliament but would instead be based upon popular acceptance. Consequently an act was passed making provision for the new constitution to be voted upon in a referendum.[17]

The referendum was fixed for July 1, 1937, the same date as the general election. De Valera still had eight months of his five-year term to run and had a secure parliamentary majority, but undoubtedly he hoped to boost the prospects of a high vote in favor of the constitution and ensure a high turnout by linking the two issues. The election campaign was the first fully peaceful election since the foundation of the state and was fought with a good humor and lack of vindictiveness that had not characterized earlier elections.[18] It soon became clear that the campaign against the constitution was not nearly as well organized or cohesive as the Fianna Fáil push for its adoption. Thus, in spite of a sizable drop in Fianna Fáil's popular vote (from 690,000 in 1933 to 599,000), the new constitution was ratified by a comfortable majority (see Table 9-1). Although 74.7 percent of the electors expressed a choice between parties, only 68.4 percent marked their referendum ballot. In spite of the drop in popular votes Fianna Fáil was still the largest single party, and de Valera was again elected head of government and soon became the first *Taoiseach* (prime minister) under his own constitution. His tactic of holding the referendum and election on the same day had clearly worked, and it was a device de Valera was to try again in a later referendum.

The constitution that came into effect on December 29, 1937, could be amended by ordinary legislation during the first three years of its existence, but after that only through referendum. Articles 46 and 47, which contain these provisions, show the extent to which de Valera had moved from his 1928 stance. There was no question now of making the referendum an easily accessible device or of subjecting governments to its use. De Valera ensured that the right to initiate a referendum lay squarely with the government of the day, and no attempt whatsoever was made to revive the initiative which de Valera had so stoutly championed in 1928.

Unlike the framers of the 1922 constitution, de Valera regarded Bunreacht na hÉireann as essentially a finished document, which should not require any further substantial amendment—even in the

[17] Draft Constitution Bill, 1937.

[18] Manning, *Blueshirts*, pp. 196-200.

TABLE 9-1

IRISH REFERENDUM AND GENERAL ELECTION, 1937

Referendum	*Votes*	*Percent*	*General Election*	*Votes*	*Percent*
For the constitution	685,105	56.5	Fianna Fáil	599,040	45.2
Against the constitution	526,945	43.5	Other parties	727,409	54.8
Total	1,212,050	100.0		1,326,449	100.0

SOURCE: W. J. Flynn, *Irish Parliamentary Handbook* (Dublin: Stationery Office, 1939), p. 52.

unlikely event of Irish unity.[19] Consequently, it was to be a rigid constitution which, after an initial three-year period of flexible amendment, could be amended only by referendum. But de Valera went further in that he confined the initiation of referendums to the government of the day. Thus under article 46 "every proposal for amendment shall be initiated in Dáil Éireann as a Bill" and having passed both houses "shall be submitted by Referendum to the decision of the people." Since it was inconceivable that such a bill could be enacted without the consent of the government of the day, de Valera was clearly laying down very restrictive ground rules for the operation of the referendum and indicating very forcefully that the referendum was unlikely to be easily available as a weapon for use against the government. In general, this was consistent with de Valera's general approach. For example, he saw the office of president as being "above politics" but devised a nomination process which ensured that in practice only the political parties could nominate candidates. And the Senate was described as being "vocational," but its electorate was drawn exclusively from party politicians, who in turn elected party politicians to the Senate. Article 47 laid down that a simple majority of votes cast would be sufficient to carry a constitutional amendment.

The constitution did make provision for a second possibility of referendum involving the Senate and the discretionary power of the president. Under article 27 a bill which has passed through both houses of the Oireachtas can be put to referendum before it has been signed into law by the president. The bill first of all cannot be a constitutional amendment. Having passed both houses of parliament it can be challenged by a petition of a majority of the members of the Senate and not less than a third of the members of the Dáil. This

[19] F. S. L. Lyons, *Ireland since the Famine* (London: Weidenfeld and Nicholson, 1971), pp. 531-543.

joint petition is then addressed to the president, who, after consultation with the Council of State but acting in his own discretion, might decline to sign the bill because it contains "a proposal of such national importance that the will of the people thereon ought to be ascertained." The president has ten days from the receipt of such a petition in which to make up his mind. If he decides not to sign there are two possible courses of action. The bill may be put to referendum within a period of eighteen months and is vetoed if a majority of votes are cast against it and if the total number of votes cast against it amount to at least a third of the votes on the register. The other possibility is that the Dáil is dissolved, a general election takes place, and the bill is reintroduced. If it passes this time, the president has no option but to sign it into law.

This elaborate procedure has never in fact been used and is unlikely to be. First, the Senate electoral system, which allows the Taoiseach to nominate eleven of the sixty members, virtually guarantees a built-in government majority and makes extremely unlikely the possibility of a petition emerging with majority support. In fact, only two measures have been defeated in the Senate in forty years. Second, there is little reason to believe that the president would support such a petition in the face of a hostile government with a secure parliamentary majority in the Dáil. In practice, Irish presidents have traditionally sought to avoid conflict with the government, and even if a majority of members of the Senate did so petition, the likelihood is that the president would not support their petition. Thus, this elaborate device has been of no consequence whatsoever since its incorporation in the 1937 constitution.

1959 Referendum to Replace Proportional Representation

The constitution was amended on two occasions during the period of flexible amendment to enable the government to deal directly with the new situation caused by World War II and especially with the threat from the IRA.[20] It was not until 1959 that the referendum was invoked in an attempt to amend the constitution.

At that time, de Valera, then seventy-seven years of age, was about to resign as prime minister to run for the presidency. He had been continuously in office from 1932 to 1948, again from 1951 to 1954, and had come back with a resounding victory in 1957. There were some, however, who doubted Fianna Fáil's ability to remain the

[20] Ibid., pp. 543-551.

dominant party without de Valera's presence and leadership. These fears were to prove groundless, for Fianna Fáil was to remain uninterruptedly in power until 1973, but in 1959 there was no certainty of this. In spite of having prescribed proportional representation with the single transferable vote in his constitution, de Valera had long had doubts about the ability of this system to produce strong governments with stable majorities. There was little evidence to support de Valera's fears, but he had voiced these doubts as far back as 1938. The same view had been held (with greater justification) by the leader of the 1922–1932 governments, W. T. Cosgrave, who had spoken out in favor of the British system of first-past-the-post voting in single-member constituencies and urged abandoning proportional representation.[21]

The issue was not actively discussed during the 1940s and 1950s, and it came as a surprise when the *Irish Independent* announced in August 1958 that the government was contemplating a campaign to abolish proportional representation and replace it with a more simplified system. By October the Fianna Fáil view had hardened and at the party's annual conference de Valera announced his intention of putting the question to the people.[22] On November 12, 1958, the Third Amendment to the Constitution Bill, which would replace proportional representation with the single-seat straight-vote system, was introduced into the Dáil. The debate on the bill was to last until the end of January 1959 when all stages were passed with a comfortable majority.

The somewhat undistinguished parliamentary debate was accompanied by an awakening of public interest in the question. The main opposition party, Fine Gael, which in the past had favored the abolition of proportional representation, now came down in favor of its retention even though some in the party (including its future leader, Liam Cosgrave) felt that the straight vote offered the best long-term prospects for Fine Gael. Once the decision was made, however, Fine Gael fought an uncharacteristically vigorous campaign against the proposed change. The Labour party had no such doubts. The proposed change could wipe it out, and right from the start it was unequivocal in its opposition. The Irish trade union movement also was quick to jump to the defense of proportional representation, as did the largest selling newspaper the *Irish Independent* and the prestigious *Irish Times*. Only the pro–Fianna Fáil *Irish Press* supported

[21] C. O'Leary, *The Irish Republic and Its Experiment with Proportional Representation* (Notre Dame, Ind.: University of Notre Dame Press, 1961), p. 30.
[22] *Irish Press*, October 20–27, 1959.

the government line. Before long the battle was joined by Enid Lakeman of the London-based Proportional Representation Society, whose indefatigable outpouring of letters, pamphlets, and lectures soon became a feature of the campaign.

Early in 1959 what the opposition groups had long suspected was confirmed with the announcement that de Valera would be a candidate for the presidency in the forthcoming June election and that he intended having the referendum on the same day. It was immediately claimed that de Valera was personalizing the issue and appealing to sentiment and emotion, and that it would be difficult for many people to refuse this "last request" of a great leader.

The first real setback for the government came from a most unlikely source, the Senate. This powerless house can merely delay bills for ninety days and can have its veto overriden by the Dáil.[23] Never in its twenty-one year history up to 1959 had it defeated a government measure, but on this occasion all six university senators voted against the government, which had two of its own supporters absent through illness. The result was a defeat for the government by twenty-nine votes to twenty-eight when the vote was taken on March 19, 1959.[24] This was an unexpected and unwelcome upset for the government, which now had to put down a motion in the Dáil to have the unaltered bill passed over the Senate veto. This was achieved on May 13 by seventy-five votes to fifty-six, and the way was now open to have the referendum on the same day as the presidential election. But the prestige of the government had undoubtedly been damaged by the incident, and the momentum of its campaign was slowed down if not adversely affected by the publicity which surrounded the Senate defeat.

By this stage it was clear that the pro–proportional representation campaign had attracted a diversity of support that the government side lacked. The newspapers and magazines were for the most part on the side of proportional representation, as were a number of usually nonpolitical voluntary organizations. Moreover, its literature was more plentiful and more substantial than that of its opponents, and some of its arguments, especially those on the rights of minorities and the dangers of arrogant government, were beginning to make an impact. Nevertheless, there was little real hope of success, and the prevailing view was that the presence of de Valera on the same ticket would be enough to win the day for the government.

---

[23] See Thomas Garvin, *The Irish Senate* (Dublin: Institute of Public Administration, 1969).

[24] *Senate Debates*, vol. 50, cols. 1669 ff.

The result, however, was a surprise. De Valera won the presidency—comfortably but not overwhelmingly with 56.3 percent of the vote, but his measure to abolish proportional representation lost with 48.2 percent of the vote. The turnout (58.4 percent) was in sharp contrast to that in 1937 when there had been a significant gap between the numbers voting in the general election and in the referendum. This time the numbers were almost identical. In the presidential election de Valera lost in only six of the forty constituencies; in the referendum there was a majority of opposing votes in twenty-one constituencies. The strongest opposition to change was undoubtedly in the Dublin region (which was also de Valera's worst area) and in Cork city. A majority of 45,000 votes against change in these areas tipped the balance of 12,000 for change in the remainder of the country.[25]

This defeat of the Fianna Fáil proposal was undoubtedly a surprise, though in retrospect it should hardly have been one. There had been no popular demand from a fundamentally conservative electorate for a change from what was by now a familiar and apparently satisfactory electoral system. There was the suspicion that the change was dictated more by party than by national considerations—something which seemed to motivate usually nonpartisan groups into joining the campaign. And there was the suspicion that not all Fianna Fáil members of parliament were enthusiastic about the change—especially those who owed their seats to proportional representation—and that as a consequence their campaigning was less than wholehearted.

1968 Referendums on Third and Fourth Amendments

It was generally expected that the 1959 result had resolved once and for all the question of the electoral system. By 1967, however, it became increasingly clear that this was far from being the case. Late that year one of Fianna Fáil's leading electoral strategists, Kevin Boland, the minister for local government, spoke out strongly in favor of the straight vote, and it became obvious that—at least in some sections of the party—support was growing for another attempt at changing the electoral system.

Why this should have happened is difficult to say. Fianna Fáil as a party was not accustomed to electoral defeat, and after the general election victories of 1961 and 1965 and the presidential victory of 1966 there may have been some in the party who relished the type

[25] Department of Local Government, official returns, Dublin.

of challenge posed by a referendum on the voting system. More important was the general belief that such a change would ensure an even bigger Fianna Fáil majority in the succeeding election.[26] In addition, some of the new young ministers in Fianna Fáil were impatient with the constraints imposed by a narrow parliamentary majority at a time of rapid economic growth and social change, and they felt that "strong" government was needed. Significant, too, was the fact that the new leader of Fine Gael, Liam Cosgrave, was known to be lukewarm about proportional representation, and it was felt that under him Fine Gael might change its mind and support the straight vote system. Whatever the reasons, the rumors were confirmed by an official announcement in January that the government intended to introduce legislation changing the voting system and widening the tolerance limits in drawing up constituencies.[27]

The two bills, the Third and Fourth Amendments to the Constitution, were introduced to the Dáil in February. The Third Amendment was new. It authorized a tolerance of up to 16 percent in drawing up constituencies to ensure that the underpopulated western region—a traditional Fianna Fáil stronghold—would be adequately represented in the Dáil in spite of its declining population. The Fourth Amendment sought the abolition of proportional representation and its replacement with the straight vote in single-seat constituencies.

Any hopes Fianna Fáil may have had of Cosgrave's supporting them or refraining from the campaign disappeared on February 28 when he told the Dáil that the issue had already been decided by the people and there was absolutely no justification for reviving it again.[28] Once again the Labour party was unequivocal in its opposition. The arguments for and against proportional representation were broadly similar to those advanced in 1959, except that this time the government emphasis was more on the need and desirability of strong stable governments, and the straight vote was advocated as the system most likely to produce this result. The arguments in favor of tolerance centered on such things as the desirability of maintaining county boundaries and on the need to see that adequate servicing could be provided for constituents in remote and inaccessible areas.

As in 1959, all newspapers with the exception of the *Irish Press* group opposed the changes. Enid Lakeman was again deeply involved

---

[26] In February 1968 on "Seven Days," an Irish television program on current affairs, two leading political scientists, Basil Chubb and David Thornley, had estimated a landslide Fianna Fáil victory in the first election under the straight vote.

[27] *Irish Times*, January 26, 1968.

[28] *Dáil Debates*, vol. 232, cols. 1959-1965.

as were the trade unions and various voluntary organizations. As the campaign continued, the vast majority of nonparty participants threw their support behind the opposition's campaign, and the extent of the government's isolation became increasingly obvious.

The referendums were fixed for October 16, 1968, and this time there was neither a general election nor the presence of de Valera to boost the Fianna Fáil campaign. Well before polling day it was clear that Fianna Fáil had made a serious miscalculation, and this impression was reenforced by the result (see Table 9-2). The turnout was considerably larger than in 1959—65.8 percent as compared with 58.4 percent. The voting on both amendments was virtually identical. Altogether only four constituencies, all in the West, voted in favor of the amendments while the remaining thirty-eight voted against.

The defeat for the government was not unexpected, but the size of the defeat was. The explanation lies in a combination of factors. Undoubtedly there was genuine anger among some sections of the public that the government should try to reverse the clear decision of the 1959 referendum within so short a time and without any evidence of a popular demand for such a change. There was a feeling that Fianna Fáil was concerned primarily with party advantage and was involving the nation in an unnecessary, expensive, and time-consuming exercise in the process. It was also felt that the tolerance issue smacked of sharp practice and amounted to a rigging of constituencies. And there was the natural conservatism of an electorate that had grown accustomed to its electoral system. On top of these factors, which help explain the paucity of independent support for the government, were the fears of some Fianna Fáil backbenchers about their

TABLE 9-2

IRISH REFERENDUMS OF OCTOBER 16, 1968

	Third Amendment (tolerance in drawing up constituencies)		*Fourth Amendment (abolish proportional representation)*	
	Votes	Percent	Votes	Percent
Yes	424,185	38.5	423,498	39.3
No	656,803	61.5	657,898	60.7
Total	1,080,988	100.0	1,081,396	100.0

SOURCE: Official returns.

own prospects under the straight vote; and there was the government's own bad image at this stage, when accusations of ministerial arrogance—and worse—were frequently made and all too often appeared to be justified.

Thus in the thirty years since the enactment of the constitution none of the three attempted amendments had succeeded, and this experience was hardly likely to enhance the referendum device in the eyes of the dominant political group, Fianna Fáil. In spite of this, the referendum was used on three occasions in the early 1970s with very different results.

1972 Referendums

The first use arose out of Ireland's decision to apply for membership in the European Economic Community (EEC). Membership in the EEC meant that legislation enacted by the Community would be applicable in Ireland. Under article 15 of the Irish constitution, however, all legislative power in Ireland was vested solely in the Oireachtas. Consequently, this article of the constitution had to be amended to enable Community legislation to apply in Ireland. As a result, yet another Third Amendment to the Constitution Bill appeared. In practice the referendum was seen by all parties as being about whether or not Ireland should join the EEC, and the arguments in the campaign covered the full range of advantages and disadvantages. Only rarely did the actual specific issue of the amendment receive much attention.

The battle was an uneven one. The two main parties, Fianna Fáil and Fine Gael, favored Ireland's entry as did the powerful farming organizations, the main business and employers organizations, and all four national daily papers. The opposition to entry was led by the small Labour party with the support of the trade unions, representatives of some of the smaller farmers, some nationalist cultural organizations, and both wings of the IRA. The only newspaper support came from the fortnightly magazine, *Hibernia*.

Even though the outcome was inevitable, there was a high level of public debate in the months preceding the referendum on May 10, 1972. The simplistic slogans of an earlier time had little place in this debate, which was wide-ranging, well informed, and free from bitterness. The main thrust of the pro-entry argument was that if Britain went in it was virtually impossible for Ireland to stay out. This campaign also highlighted the advantages to Ireland of an expanding export market and the definite prospects for Irish agriculture. The opposition focused on the loss of sovereignty, the possibility of future military involvement, the threat to some of the country's protected

TABLE 9-3

IRISH REFERENDUM OF MAY 10, 1972

	Votes	Percent
For joining EEC	1,041,890	83.1
Against joining EEC	211,891	16.9
Total	1,253,781	100.0

SOURCE: Official returns.

industries from European competition, and the inevitable price rises, especially of food.

The turnout (70.9 percent) was the highest for any Irish referendum, and an accurate indication of the level of popular interest and concern. The votes in favor were in a majority in all constituencies, and voting appears to have been fairly firmly along traditional party lines, with the 16.9 percent in opposition corresponding very closely with Labour's 1969 vote (see Table 9-3).

There were two further referendums in 1972. The first was a noncontroversial proposal to lower the voting age to eighteen, something on which all parties were agreed.[29] This involved amending article 16 of the constitution. The second proposal was somewhat more controversial and was more or less prompted by the troubles in Northern Ireland. It proposed to delete that part of article 44 which accorded "a special position to the Holy Catholic Apostolic and Roman Church as the guardian of the Faith professed by the great majority of the citizens." This had long been a controversial section of the constitution, which was seen by some as merely reflecting a statistical fact and by others as being gratuitously offensive to non-Catholics, while at the same time conferring no privileges on the Catholic church. The report of the Committee on the Constitution in 1967 had recommended the deletion of this section of article 44, and there had been little opposition to this proposal in subsequent years.

Unlike the earlier referendum on EEC entry, these last two attracted little attention. The leader of the Roman Catholic church, Cardinal Conway, made clear that his church had no objection to the proposed change, and with all three parties supporting it the result was beyond doubt. The issues at stake aroused little passion or enthusiasm, the debate was dull, and there was no evidence of any popular en-

[29] This was one of the proposals to emerge from the all-party parliamentary review committee, which had examined the constitution in 1966–1967.

TABLE 9-4
IRISH REFERENDUMS OF DECEMBER 7, 1972

	Fourth Amendment (lower voting age)		*Fifth Amendment (delete section on Catholic church)*	
	Votes	Percent	Votes	Percent
Yes	724,836	84.6	721,003	84.4
No	131,514	15.4	133,430	15.6
Total	856,350	100.0	854,433	100.0

SOURCE: Official returns.

thusiasm or interest on either issue. The turnout of 50.6 percent reflected this lack of urgency. Both amendments were carried overwhelmingly in all constituencies (see Table 9-4).

Conclusion

The referendum has proved to be a more significant political instrument in Irish politics than was generally expected in 1937. De Valera had formally and finally abandoned the easy access provided by the 1922 referendum and initiative and confined the initiation of referendums exclusively to the government of the day or in unlikely circumstances to the discretion of the president. This action was clearly seen as indicating that the use of the referendum would take place in circumstances favorable to the government and with the purpose of achieving some specific government objective. Athough this may well have been de Valera's intention, it is not how things have worked out in practice. On the three occasions when the issue could be seen as one which would benefit Fianna Fáil, the result has been an emphatic rejection of the proposed changes. Even the personality of de Valera was not sufficient to shake this independent attitude.

Of the other three issues put to referendum, two (on lowering the voting age and amendment of article 44) were uncontroversial and were issues on which there was general consensus—all of which was reflected in the low vote and overwhelming majorities for change. But it was on the question of EEC membership that the referendum was seen at its most useful. The fact of having a referendum generated one of the best informed public debates ever and provided for a high degree of popular participation. More important, it ensured that when Ireland entered the EEC—undoubtedly the most important political decision since independence—it was after the fullest popular consultation and with the unequivocal endorsement of an overwhelming majority of the population.

In the future, it is probable that the referendum will again become an important instrument of policy change in Irish politics. At present, the constitution absolutely prohibits divorce—even though all churches in Ireland, including the Roman Catholic church, have considerably relaxed their attitudes and practices in this matter. It is only a matter of time before this constitutional veto is changed, though such change will necessitate a difficult and controversial referendum campaign. Proposed changes in the structure of Irish higher education will also involve changes in the constitution. Much more contentious, however, may be the use of the referendum to change articles 2 and 3, which claim sovereignty over Northern Ireland and which are seen as an obstacle to better relations with the Protestant majority in Northern Ireland. On present evidence, such a referendum would need all-party support if it were to succeed, and such unanimity does not exist at present. In fact, above all else, the Irish experience has shown that without multiparty support few issues can hope to be carried by referendum.

10
United Kingdom

David Butler

The Precedents

A Labour government sponsored Britain's first, and only, nationwide referendum in 1975. But the idea of a referendum as a solution to particular problems had been mooted repeatedly throughout the century, usually by Conservatives who saw it as a brake on change. A. V. Dicey, its first major sponsor, argued in the 1890s that by putting Irish home rule to a United Kingdom vote it could be blocked; indeed, he regularly used the phrase "the national veto" to describe the referendum.

The idea was more seriously toyed with in 1910 when the House of Lords rejected first the Lloyd George budget and then the whole notion of Lords reform. In the protracted but abortive constitutional conference of March to November 1910, the referendum was frequently mentioned. In the ensuing general election (which the king insisted on before he would agree to bypass the Lords' obstruction by creating more peers), the Conservatives under A. J. Balfour committed themselves to establishing referendums as a means of resolving disputes between the House of Commons and a reformed House of Lords. Under a campaign challenge from the Liberal Prime Minister Asquith, Balfour agreed that the vexed issue of tariff reform should also be submitted to the people.[1]

The referendum was kept alive as an issue through the home rule crisis of 1912–1914 as a possible way of determining how much, if any, of the province of Ulster should fall under Dublin's rule, but these proposals came to nothing. So did Winston Churchill's suggestion in the 1920s that the equalization of men's and women's

[1] Two years later his successor, Bonar Law, withdrew that pledge.

franchise should be dependent on a popular vote, and so also did the Baldwin-Beaverbrook agreement of 1930 that in due course a Conservative government should hold a referendum on food taxes. In 1945 Churchill, as prime minister, raised the idea of a referendum to authorize an extension of the life of Parliament.

None of these proposals got as far as draft legislation, but they were seriously entertained by leading politicians. Indeed, few major Conservative or Liberal figures in the first half of this century did not, at one time or another, vote for a referendum at the national or the local level.

The Labour party was always more cautious. They feared the referendum as a conservative instrument of government, an extra line of defense against the changes in society that they wanted to bring about.[2] Until the 1970s they never advocated a referendum at the national level. But they too endorsed and participated in some kinds of local opinion tests.

Britain has in fact had experience with several types of local referendum. In 1850 provision was made for local polls on the establishment of free public libraries, and from 1858 until 1974 it was possible to demand a poll on municipally sponsored legislation. Since 1932 the Sunday opening of cinemas could be put to a local vote. However, there were relatively few referendums under these heads. In Scotland after 1918 there were local polls on liquor licensing, and since 1961 Welsh electors have been asked to vote every seven years, at first by county and now by district, on whether they want their public houses to open on Sundays.

But it was Northern Ireland that brought a major referendum to the British scene. In 1972 sectarian violence led to the suspension of the government and parliament of Northern Ireland by Westminster. In an attempt at a new settlement, a referendum was held on March 8, 1973, asking the voters of Northern Ireland whether they wanted the province to remain part of the United Kingdom. The great bulk of Catholics boycotted the poll, but on a 58.7 percent turnout, 98.9 percent of those who voted favored the status quo. The Northern Ireland referendum did not settle the province's difficulties, but it set a precedent that was to be important in the argument over whether to put British entry into Europe to a popular vote.

---

[2] For a classic statement of the Labour position, see Clifford D. Sharp, *The Case against the Referendum*, Fabian Tract no. 155 (London: The Fabian Society, 1911). For a different perspective on the same issues, see R J. Williams and J. R. Greenaway, "The Referendum in British Politics: A Dissenting View," *Parliamentary Affairs* (Summer 1975), pp. 250-260.

The 1975 Referendum

The question of Britain's joining the European Economic Community had been a live issue since 1961. Public opinion had fluctuated violently, and it was not till the late 1960s that opponents of entry began to see the referendum as the only defense against the pro-European consensus of the leaders of all the parties. During the 1970 election Wilson, Heath, and Thorpe each explicitly repudiated the idea of a referendum on the subject, using the constitutional argument that it was up to Parliament to decide such matters. Wilson in particular explicitly said that he would not "trim to win votes. . . . I shall not change my attitude on [having a referendum]."[3] When Labour unexpectedly lost the election, it fell to the Conservatives to take Britain into the Common Market. Heath had said that such a policy could not be carried through without "the full-hearted consent of the British Parliament and people," but the opinion polls showed an almost continuous majority against British entry from 1971 to 1973 while negotiations were completed and the formalities of entry took place. Naturally he stood firm against a referendum.

The Labour party in opposition turned sharply against the Common Market. Although from an anti-European standpoint Douglas Jay and from a populist standpoint Tony Benn had advocated a referendum from 1970 onward, the Labour leadership inside and outside Parliament at first stood firm against the idea. But once, in voting against it, Jim Callaghan described it as "a rubber life-raft into which the whole party may one day have to climb."[4] Then on March 22, 1972, the National Executive Committee switched and voted thirteen to eleven in favor of a referendum, and on March 29 the shadow cabinet voted eight to six in the same direction (reversing a ten to four decision of two weeks earlier). Roy Jenkins and two of his colleagues resigned as a matter of principle,[5] protesting such tactical shifts. But the change had been made. The Labour party went into the February 1974 election committed to renegotiate the terms of EEC membership and then to decide "the issue through a General Election or a Consultative Referendum." That pledge was repeated in the October election, with a time limit of October 1975 for the decision.

---

[3] Quoted in David Butler and Uwe Kitzinger, *The 1975 Referendum* (London: Macmillan, 1976), p. 11.

[4] Quoted in ibid., p. 12.

[5] Roy Jenkins's letter of resignation stressed three objections to referendums: (1) they cannot be limited to a single subject; (2) they must lead to divided parties and inconsistent government; and (3) they are likely to be invoked as a weapon against progressive legislation.

The renegotiations proceeded to their successful conclusion in March 1975, and the government introduced legislation for an immediate referendum. The Conservatives opposed the bill in principle but were quite helpful on matters of detail. Mrs. Thatcher's first speech as leader of the opposition was a rehearsal of the constitutional difficulties inherent in referendums. What did they imply for the legislative sovereignty of Parliament? What issues should be referred to them? Where did they leave collective responsibility? Where did they leave representative government?

Three special features of the British referendum arrangements deserve note.[6] Through historical accident, linked to the original arrangements for the secret ballot, Britain has always counted and recorded votes in larger units than any other democratic country. In 1975 the practice was carried even further. Originally the government planned to have all votes counted in London, so that the outcome should be seen as a national one, with no evidence on how different parts of the country voted. When for administrative reasons that was abandoned, they still marshaled the votes by county rather than by constituency so that no member of Parliament should be embarrassed by a demonstrated discrepancy between his voters and himself.

Second, since it was apparent that the pro-Europeans had far greater resources than did those in opposition, provision was made for a subsidy of £125,000 to each of the two umbrella organizations coordinating the campaigns for and against. Since they cut across party lines, the umbrella organizations were seen as an important device. No one, in fact, challenged the right of these self-appointed groups to speak for the two sides, though trouble could easily have arisen over who was entitled to assume such powers. They included, for example, access to free broadcast time and the writing of a pamphlet to be delivered free to every elector.

The third and most remarkable special aspect of the referendum was the government's agreement to differ: sixteen members of the Cabinet campaigned for EEC membership and seven against. The normal rules of collective responsibility, by which all ministers must support government policy or resign, were relaxed for three months with respect to this one question. It made plain a fact, of which no one could be in doubt, that the prime purpose of the referendum was to save the Labour party from tearing itself asunder while securing for the nation a firm and final verdict on EEC membership.

[6] For a full description of the 1975 referendum, see Butler and Kitzinger, *The 1975 Referendum*; Anthony King, *Britain Says Yes* (Washington, D.C.: American Enterprise Institute, 1977); and Philip Goodhart, *Full-Hearted Consent* (London: Davis-Poynter, 1976).

Of course the referendum had other functions. It served to show to Britain's European partners—as well as to critics at home—that the country did indeed feel committed to the EEC. It demonstrated the "full-hearted consent" that the opinion polls had found lacking at the time of entry. It enabled the Labour party, which had shunned the European Assembly since 1973, to send its due delegation of parliamentarians to Strasbourg, and it enabled the trade unions to abandon their partial boycott of the Brussels Commission.

It had been a gamble. Although it was only an advisory referendum, Wilson had said that he would take an adverse majority, however small, as a mandate for leaving the European Community. But it is very doubtful if his government could have survived defeat on the issue; the committed pro-Europeans in the party would not have taken a reverse as resignedly as the anti-Europeans in fact did. During the October 1974 election two leading Cabinet ministers, Roy Jenkins and Shirley Williams, had said publicly that they would not remain in the Cabinet if the referendum went the wrong way. Wilson had striven to take the referendum outside the ordinary rules of responsible Cabinet government, but it is doubtful if he managed to do so. It was, in some measure, a vote of confidence in the government, and defeat would almost certainly have meant disaster.

The campaign itself lasted only about three weeks—both sides were afraid of boring the public on this well-worn theme. It ran smoothly and inspired a great deal of ad hoc voluntary activity, enthusiastic rather than effective. Britain in Europe outspent the anti–Common Market umbrella organization by ten to one, producing glossy television programs and newspaper advertisements. The press was almost entirely pro-Europe, and some of its early coverage went beyond acceptable limits in making Tony Benn into a devil figure, but there was a moderating prudence in the final days. The battle was in fact much less bitter than had been expected, probably because from start to finish the opinion polls agreed in predicting a two-to-one victory for the pro-Europeans. (The result was 67.2 percent yes.) If the outcome had been in doubt, the campaign would have been rougher. But it is notable that the pro-marketeers made no headway over the last weeks. Despite their enormous superiority in money and organizational skill, despite the popularity of their leading figures and the support of the press, and despite the prestige of having the government on their side, the opinion polls suggested that pro-marketeers gained no additional votes. Anti–Common Market strength seems, if anything, to have increased in the final days of the campaign.

Of significance was the threat that the campaign posed to the existing party system. It demonstrated, on the one hand, that people would vote without the traditional paraphernalia of local party organization to get them to the booths—the turnout was only 8 percent below the previous general election, even though the outcome was a foregone conclusion. It showed, on the other hand, that politicians could work together across party lines. Some commentators saw the very harmonious conduct of the Britain in Europe campaign as a rehearsal for a national coalition of men of good will from the center of politics, the government of National Unity that Heath had spoken of in the October 1974 election. The Labour government felt left out. For party reasons some of its most leading figures, Wilson, Callaghan, and Healey, did not wish to get involved with Britain in Europe, but, except under its umbrella, it was hard to secure a major platform, on the hustings or on the air, from which to put their personal views on how people should vote.[7]

In the aftermath, it was not easy to find enthusiasts for referendums among the politicians. The original advocates had, on the whole, found themselves on the losing side, while those who had won had been uncomfortable at the departures they had seen from the familiar rules of the game. They understood politics in its traditional adversary form, with party loyalty regulating affairs. The potential of a referendum for disruption and unpredictability had been made plain.

But the referendum as such was not unpopular with the public. Opinion polls had repeatedly shown that voters like the idea of being consulted on major decisions. In 1968 and 1969, surveys found 69 percent of the people favored important issues being decided by referendum. The 1975 referendum won general approval before and after the event; 75 percent of the people, drawn equally from pro- and anti-marketeers, were pleased that the issue was put to the electors.

Recent Developments

But if the 1975 referendum highlighted the threat that the device could pose for orthodox British party politics, it also showed that a referendum could be conducted in a tranquil and efficient manner. It had settled a contentious issue and left no serious constitutional repercussions. It was bound henceforth to stay within the British political

[7] The government did give itself one special advantage. In addition to the pamphlets from both umbrella organizations delivered to every elector, a third pamphlet stated the government's conviction that their renegotiation had made it, on balance, in Britain's clear interest to stay in the Common Market.

dialogue, as one practicable way out of political or constitutional difficulties. In the three years after 1975, referendums were mooted in several different contexts.

To meet the challenge of Scottish nationalism the Labour government devised a scheme for devolution, involving separate Scottish and Welsh assemblies. After one bill had been frustrated in Parliament in 1977, the government brought in an amended version which sought to mollify earlier critics by providing that these assemblies should not be brought into being until they had been approved by referendums in Scotland and Wales. The revised bill was passed, but against the government's advice Parliament insisted that a majority in favor should include 40 percent of the total Scottish and Welsh electorates for it to have effect. In the debate on these measures the theology of referendums was extensively discussed, but it was accepted that, if ever referendums are justified, it is in connection with transfers of sovereignty.

The other recently mooted referendums go much nearer to the heart of British constitutional tradition, modifying the doctrines of parliamentary sovereignty and of responsible government. Not altogether surprisingly, they come from Conservatives.

After 1974 the Labour government, based on 39 percent of the popular vote and 28 percent of the nominal electorate, carried out the relatively radical proposals in their manifesto. Conservatives were alarmed that a party with so restricted a mandate could do so much to bring about "a fundamental and irreversible shift" in the distribution of power. They therefore looked for long-term defenses against the recurrence of such a situation. Some saw the answer in proportional representation, some in a written constitution, and some in a reformed House of Lords. The idea of a strengthened, elected upper chamber raised the problem of how conflict between the two houses should be resolved. Lord Carrington, the Conservative leader in the House of Lords, publicly advocated that all such disputes should be decided by referendum. The party remained uncommitted, but the fact that so influential a figure could espouse so general a use of referendums was clear evidence that the subject was again seriously on the national agenda.

It had also been put on the agenda in a different context by the leader of the Conservatives. In September 1977 Mrs. Thatcher let it be known that, in a conflict with the unions of the sort that wrecked the Heath government in 1974, she would contemplate using a referendum to solve it; she later announced that she had asked a party committee to explore a wider use of referendums.[8] Her suggestion that a referendum could be used to settle an industrial dispute excited wide, if critical, comment. Observers pointed to the time it would take to mount a referendum and to the difficulty, if the government won, of enforcing the decision of the electorate as a whole on the particular subsection of strikers. In all the discussion no one pointed out that, in the world history of referendums, they had never been used in such a context.

In June 1978 it became plain that the shadow cabinet was being asked by some of its members to promise to put the issue of capital punishment to a referendum. The idea was rejected, but it provoked Reginald Maudling, an influential Conservative, to put the case against referendums in a classic letter to the London *Times*, June 7, 1978:

> Such a referendum would raise all the grave problems of the authority of Parliaments and the position of MPs in the most acute form. . . . There can be no doubt that the majority of the public would support the restoration of capital punishment. . . . The only purpose of a referendum would be to bring pressure on MPs to vote for a proposal they would otherwise reject. . . . I do not believe that whatever the referendum disclosed Members would vote against their consciences and so there would be no practical effect but the attempt to induce them to do so would be profoundly misguided.

That letter focuses on only one of the dilemmas that referendums can pose for the supposed conventions of the Westminster model. It is part of a wider issue of parliamentary sovereignty. Even an advisory referendum can be thought to constrain the freedom of Parliament to do absolutely what it likes. A binding or constitutionally entrenched referendum would present a much more fundamental challenge to the traditional rules of the game. Moreover, any referendum on a major policy issue must also threaten the normal understandings about the collective responsibility of the Cabinet and the cohesion expected of a party that aspires to govern singlehandedly. Referendums can be grafted onto the British system of governments. But they must in some degree change its nature. Still more, they must challenge the theories and the textbook assumptions about its nature.

---

[8] The committee's report, published in September 1978, unanimously favored legislation to provide for referendums. A referendum commission would be set up to word questions and to see that the contests were fairly conducted. Referendums should be held primarily on fundamental constitutional changes but could also be held on nonconstitutional matters on the initiative of the government with the consent of both houses of Parliament.

Britain has the reputation of being a pragmatic country, skeptically building on past tradition and not easily seduced by general theory. Certainly its approach to referendums and its writings about it have been little affected by grand concepts or broad principles. Over the last three generations people frequently have advocated referendums on particular subjects because they thought that popular votes would produce the answer they favored—whether it be the rejection of Europe, the return of capital punishment, or the blocking of Irish home rule. The appeal of the referendum has usually been as a barrier to change, an endorsement of the status quo, a legitimation for doing nothing. Governments have equally regularly fought shy of referendums as a surrender of their own authority to a process that is necessarily arbitrary and unpredictable. But when government authority is not adequate to control some section of the government's own followers or of the public at large, it may be increasingly tempted to resort to referendums to endow its policies with an extra legitimacy. Because the device worked in 1975, it is more likely to be invoked again.

11
Summing Up

This book has dealt with two different worlds. On the one hand, in Switzerland, California, and a few other states of the American union initiatives and referendums are prominent strands in the fabric of political life. Their potential for making and unmaking policies is ever present in the minds of legislators and lobbyists. On the other hand, in all other countries referendums are held infrequently, usually only when the government thinks they are likely to provide a useful ad hoc solution to a particular constitutional or political problem or to set the seal of legitimacy on a change of regime. Australia alone falls into the middle ground, because the limitations of its federal constitution make recourse to a certain number of referendums inevitable. But even in Australia fifteen years could go by without a referendum, and appeals to the people are made only by choice of the government.

The incidence of referendums has increased in recent years, both in the one truly addicted nation, Switzerland, and in the rest of the world where they have merely been invoked ad hoc. In the European democracies listed in Table 1-3, as Table 11-1 shows, the slow but unmistakable growth in the number of referendums has accelerated a bit since 1960. Table 11-1 does not tell the whole story, however. Even where referendums have not been held, the possibility has been discussed more extensively in the 1970s, especially in the major English-speaking democracies, than at any time since the early 1900s. To give one example, not only did the separatist government of Quebec in 1977 announce its intention to hold a referendum on whether the province should secede from Canada, but the Canadian government in 1978 countered with more general proposals for holding national referendums. The United States offers a second example: on June 1, 1978, there were only eight congressional sponsors of legislation to estab-

TABLE 11-1

INCIDENCE OF REFERENDUMS IN WESTERN EUROPEAN DEMOCRACIES, BY DECADES, 1900–1978

Country	*1900–09*	*1910–19*	*1920–29*	*1930–39*	*1940–49*	*1950–59*	*1960–69*	*1970–78*
Switzerland	14	12	32	23	16	45	26	75
Other European democracies	2	5	5	5	8	7	13	14
Total	16	17	37	28	24	52	39	89

SOURCE: Table 1-3.

lish the initiative nationwide, but in the three months following the June 6, 1978 California referendum on Proposition 13 the number shot up to thirty-one. For a third example, after having held its first nationwide referendum in 1975, Great Britain planned to hold two more in Scotland and Wales in 1979, and the leader of its Conservative party was publicly considering using the device on other issues if she became prime minister.

In reviewing the most salient findings from this book, we want first to emphasize the distinction between the general category "referendums" and its special subset "initiatives." In most democracies, as we have seen, referendums are held entirely at the option of elected officials—parliaments and their governments—with a few minor exceptions for compulsory referendums for constitutional amendments and a few special kinds of legislation. The initiative, on the other hand, requires that if a popular petition for a referendum on a proposed or existing law contains the required number of valid signatures, that referendum must be held whether the elected officials like it or not. This helps to explain why Switzerland, California, and a few other American states have had so many more referendums than all other democratic polities. Indeed, only Weimar Germany, with two initiatives in the 1920s, and Italy with three initiatives in the 1970s (all five were defeated) offer examples of initiatives in large-scale polities.

Whether elected officials can choose the topics and times for all referendums, or can find themselves saddled with one at any moment on any subject, makes a major difference. The governments of all polities with optional referendums have chosen to invoke them only infrequently and in special circumstances—for example, when it has seemed to be the best way to resolve a particularly bitter issue without tearing apart the established political structure. Of course, governments can miscalculate: for example, the Norwegian EEC referendum of 1972, as we saw in Chapter 8, badly split both the Liberal and Labor parties, forced the Labor government to resign, and may well have led to a permanent reordering of the Norwegian party spectrum.

Governments generally prefer to keep in their own hands decisions as to whether, when, and on what issues referendums will be held, because the initiative-launched referendum is far more likely than the government-launched referendum to disrupt a polity's traditional way of politics. And an advisory referendum has less potential for disruption than one that is compulsory—although, as we saw in Chapter 10, political necessity may convert a de jure advisory referendum into one that is de facto compulsory.

Second, since in most polities the power to invoke most referendums lies solely in the government's hands, it should not surprise anyone that they are seldom allowed unless the government foresees a favorable outcome. A "favorable" outcome does not necessarily mean a resounding yes or no on a particular measure. The government may not care very much how the measure fares but may care a great deal about shunting off responsibility for the decision. It may want to demonstrate the lack of support for a given policy and to humble its sponsors. Thus most referendums, even in the most democratic countries, have to some degree been engineered to produce a popular endorsement for what those in power happen to want.

What they want may often be more than approval or rejection of a particular measure. For example, Vincent Wright's study of the French case in Chapter 7 illustrates the multiplicity of motives that can lead to the holding of referendums—legitimizing, consolidating, galvanizing, status-enhancing, opposition-dividing, authority-enlarging, and so on.

It is well to remember, in this regard, that the contemporary world differs from the world of the early 1900s in many respects. One of the most relevant developments for our purposes is the advent of public opinion polls, which make it inevitable that demands for referendums should be self-interested. No major issue can surface today without sample surveys indicating how the public feels about it. It is not surprising that referendums are generally pressed by persons and groups who firmly declare their faith in the people's judgment—while relying on evidence from the polls that the measure they favor will win. By the same token, referendums are generally opposed by people who proclaim the virtues of representative government—but are aware from the polls that their side is likely to lose. No doubt there are some idealists who support the holding of referendums without regard to their expected outcomes. There are probably rather more realists who object even to a referendum likely to yield a congenial result, on the ground that one referendum will lead to another, and the results of future referendums might not be so congenial.

This leads to our third concern: Is the referendum in effect a conservative or a progressive device—that is, does it generally produce outcomes pleasing to the right or to the left? This is usually the first—and often the only—question political activists ask about referendums, and it is not without interest for scholars as well. The evidence set forth in Chapter 4 and elsewhere is too patchy to justify a definitive answer. But our preliminary verdict would be that the referendum is a politically neutral device that generally produces outcomes favored by the current state of public opinion. Public opinion is seldom left or right on all questions at any given moment, nor is it consistently left or right on any question through all time. For example, Chapter 4 shows that in the American states in the 1960s and 1970s, it was generally liberal on questions of government spending and conservation of natural resources and generally conservative on questions of taxation and regulation of morals. In Switzerland in the same period, as Table 3-4 shows, referendums have approved both liberal measures (compulsory unemployment insurance, wage and price controls) and conservative measures (mandatory balanced federal budgets); and they have also defeated both liberal measures (free abortion, higher taxes on upper incomes) and conservative measures (reducing the number of resident foreigners, reducing the tax system's progressivity).

Such evidence inclines us to believe that partisans of either left or right would be well advised to examine carefully and in advance the state of public opinion on the issues that most concern them before they embrace the referendum as the sure pathway to the policies they want. We also believe that such considerations explain why in most polities adherents of both left and right are found among both the advocates and the opponents of holding referendums.

This, in turn, leads to a fourth question: What kinds of issues seem especially suitable for decision by referendum and what kinds seem especially unsuitable? We noted in Chapter 1 how few countries have referred moral issues, apart from liquor control, to popular votes. It is arguable that issues such as the right of the state to take life or to regulate sexual behavior are, to a peculiar degree, matters on which the public is likely to have strong views—and perhaps also an obligation to accept responsibility for official policy on matters which, like these, evoke such strong passions on both sides. Yet it is also arguable that the problems involved are so difficult and delicate that it is better to leave them to elected politicians, with their delaying, moderating, compromising, and obfuscating ways, than to the all-or-nothing confrontations that referendums so readily become. Whatever the merits of these arguments, it is true that in Switzerland and the American states in recent years there have been an increasing number of referendums on such issues as abortion, the rights of homosexuals, capital punishment, and the like.

In our judgment, the area in which referendums have most clearly been useful is in the settling of boundary issues, perhaps because the old Wilsonian principle of self-determination still strikes most people as the just basis for determining sovereignty over territories and peoples. The new development of regionalism—even separatism, notably in Spain, France, the United Kingdom, and Canada—means that nations, whether devolving power or justifying their refusal to do so, are likely to encounter the strongest pressures for holding more referendums in the future.

As students and well-wishers of Western representative democratic institutions, the co-editors of this book are most concerned with a fifth and final question: What has been the impact of referendums on those institutions? It is clear that referendums merge differently with different political systems. The Westminster model of cabinet government, with an executive collectively responsible through a parliamentary majority to the electorate, offers one classic argument for and another against referendums. If issues are decided by the voters over the heads of government and parliament, what becomes of the answerability of government to the people? How can governments be judged at each election for their overall achievements if they have not themselves made all the critical decisions?

On the other hand, the mandate theory of the Westminster model has always been unsatisfactory. General elections necessarily involve judgments on parties and personalities as well as on issues. The voter who supports a given party candidate is nevertheless regarded as having given him a mandate to implement every item in the party's lengthy and variegated platform. The voter cannot, under the current electoral system, discriminate among items in the program or even among differing general tendencies in the party. To refer some major items to popular votes would bypass some of the absurdities inherent in the mandate doctrine.

In political systems where there is a separation of powers, where responsibility for decisions is diffused through different branches and levels of government and a weak party system, there is less theoretical objection to adding one more locus of decision making, one more check to bring additional balance to the system. But the consequences of doing so will depend in good measure upon the authority attaching to the referendum verdicts and the extent to which they override the judgments of elected representatives.

Referendums disturb politicians—and us—because they tend to force the decision makers, the voters, to choose between only two alternatives: they must either approve or reject the measure referred. There is no opportunity for continuing discussion of other alternatives, no way to search for the compromise that will draw the widest acceptance. Referendums by their very nature set up confrontations rather than encourage compromises. They divide the populace into victors and vanquished. They force decisions often before the discussion process has had a chance to work itself out fully. Surely this is a great deficiency.

Yet in every polity there are times and circumstances when some decision is better than no decision, when continuing delay is itself disruptive of consensus and good temper, when the likelihood of working out a just compromise that will please everyone is slim or nonexistent. In such a situation the referendum has at least one great virtue: not only will it produce a decision, but the decision it produces is, in this democratic age, more likely to be regarded as legitimate and therefore acceptable than is a decision produced indirectly by elected officials. The people are always likely to think better of themselves than of their leaders, and thus any decision they make directly is likely to strike them as more legitimate than a decision made for them by others. Surely this is a great advantage.

Bearing all these considerations in mind, we find it impossible to take our place with either the true believers in or the irreconcilable opponents of referendums. It seems to us that to argue that *no* question should be settled by referendum is almost as untenable as to argue that *every* question should be settled thus. Referendums have often proved to be useful devices for solving or setting aside problems too hot for representative bodies to handle. They have often given legitimacy to new regimes or boundaries or constitutions that they would otherwise have lacked. In short, they have been and can continue to be valuable adjuncts to representative democracy. We would hate to see them abolished altogether, and we would hate to see them overshadow or replace representative institutions.

One thing is clear: referendums are here to stay; and they are almost certain to increase in number and importance in the years ahead.

APPENDIX A
Nationwide Referendums

In the following list an attempt is made to record all nationwide referendums in independent countries except for Australia and Switzerland, which have had more referendums than all other countries put together. (Swiss referendums are listed in Table 3-2; Australian referendums are listed in Tables 6-1 and 6-2.) The data are, in many cases, of uncertain quality. Totalitarian and managed referendums are not segregated from scrupulously reported democratic referendums. Moreover, the data are often derived from newspaper reports or uncheckable works of reference. Quite apart from possible errors of transcription, it is often unclear whether the turnout and percentages voting yes are based on all registered voters or only on valid votes. A dash (—) indicates that data are not available.

All countries which were members of the United Nations in 1978 are mentioned here, together with a few obvious additions. Appendix B lists referendums bearing on the sovereignty of subordinate or colonial territories.

Country (No.)	*Date*	*Subject*	*Percent Voting Yes*	*Percent Turnout*
Europe [a]				
Austria (1)	10 Apr. 1938	Approve Anschluss	99.7	99.7
Belgium (1)	12 Mar. 1950	Return of Leopold III	57.6	92.4
Bulgaria (3)	19 Nov. 1922	Approve trials for "war crimes"	73.1	—
	8 Sept. 1946	End monarchy	95.1	89.2
	16 May 1971	Approve constitution	99.7	99.7

Country (No.)	Date	Subject	Percent Voting Yes	Percent Turnout
Denmark (14)	14 Dec. 1916	Cession of Virgin Islands	64.2	38.0
	6 Sept. 1920	Incorporation of North Schleswig	96.9	50.1
	23 May 1939	Voting age lowered from 25 to 23; Landsthing abolished	91.9[b]	48.9
	28 May 1953	New constitution	78.4	58.3
		Voting age 23 not 21	54.6	62.2
	30 May 1961	Voting age lowered from 23 to 21	55.0	37.2
	25 June 1963	Approve agricultural acquisition law	38.4	73.0
		Approve state small-holders law	38.6	73.0
		Approve municipal pre-emption law	39.6	73.0
		Approve nature conservancy law	42.6	73.0
	24 June 1969	Voting age lowered from 21 to 18	21.2	63.6
	21 Sept. 1971	Voting age lowered from 21 to 20	56.5	83.9
	2 Oct. 1972	Join European Economic Community	63.3	90.1
	19 Sept. 1978	Voting age lowered from 20 to 18	53.9	63.4
Estonia (5)	17–19 Feb. 1923	Restore religious instruction	71.7	66.2
	19 Aug. 1932	Constitutional reform	49.2	90.5
	10–12 June 1933	Presidential government	32.6	66.5
	14–16 Oct. 1933	Presidentialism with ministerial responsibility	72.6	77.9
	23–25 Feb. 1936	Convene constituent assembly	76.1	80
Finland (1)	29 Dec. 1931	Abolish prohibition of alcoholic beverages	70.5	44.4
France[c] (10) before 1900	4 Aug. 1793	Approve constitution	99.3	26.7
	6 Sept. 1795	Approve constitution	95.6	13.7
	30 Aug. 1799	Approve constitution	63.8	3.8
	7 Feb. 1800	Approve Napoleon as consul	99.9	43.1
	Aug. 1802	Approve Napoleon as consul for life	99.8	51.2

Country (No.)	*Date*	*Subject*	*Percent Voting Yes*	*Percent Turnout*
	18 May 1804	Approve Napoleon as emperor	99.7	43.3
	30 May 1815	Restore imperial constitution	99.7	18.8
	21 Dec. 1851	Ten-year presidency	92.1	79.7
	21 Nov. 1852	Restore empire	96.9	79.7
	8 May 1870	Parliamentary rule	83.1	83.5
France[c] (10) after 1900	21 Oct. 1945	Assembly to draft constitution	96.3	79.9
		Interim power for assembly	66.8	79.9
	5 May 1946	Approve constitution	47.1	80.7
	13 Oct. 1946	Approve constitution	53.2	68.8
	28 Sept. 1958	Approve constitution	79.2	84.9
	8 Jan. 1961	Algerian self-determination	75.3	76.5
	8 Apr. 1962	Agreement with Algiers	90.7	75.6
	28 Oct. 1962	Direct election of president	61.7	77.2
	27 Apr. 1969	Senate power and regional devolution	46.8	80.6
	23 Apr. 1972	Expand European Economic Community	67.7	60.7
Germany (6)	20 June 1926	Confiscation of royal property	92.3[d]	39.3
	22 Dec. 1929	Repudiation of war guilt (reparations)	94.5[d]	14.9
	12 Nov. 1933	Approve Nazi government	93.4	92.2
	19 Aug. 1934	Approve Hitler as leader and chancellor	88.2	94.7
	29 Mar. 1936	Approve Reichstag list and führer	98.1	98.9
	10 Apr. 1938	Approve Anschluss	99	99.7
German Democratic Republic (1)	16 Apr. 1968	Approve constitution	94.5	98.1
Greece (8)	19 Nov. 1862	Election of Prince Alfred as king	95.4	—
	5 Dec. 1920	Return of Constantine I	98.6	—
	14 Apr. 1924	Institute republic	70	—
	3 Nov. 1935	Restore monarchy	97.9	—
	1 Sept. 1946	Return of George II	69	90

Country (No.)	*Date*	*Subject*	*Percent Voting Yes*	*Percent Turnout*
	29 Sept. 1968	Approve constitution	91.9	77.7
	29 July 1973	Institute republic	77.2	74.7
	8 Dec. 1974	End monarchy	69.2	75.6
Iceland (4)	19 Oct. 1918	Union with Denmark	92.6	43.8
	21 Oct. 1933	End prohibition of alcoholic beverages	57.7	45.3
	29 May 1944	Separate from Denmark	99.5	98.4
		Institute republic	98.5	98.4
Ireland (7)	1 July 1937	Approve constitution	56.5	68.3
	17 June 1959	Abolish proportional representation	48.2	58.4
	16 Oct. 1968	Increase variation in electorates	39.2	62.9
		Abolish proportional representation	39.2	63.0
	10 May 1972	Join European Economic Community	83.1	70.9
	7 Dec. 1972	Lower voting age to 18	84.6	50.7
		Remove special constitutional position of church	84.4	50.7
Italy (6)	24 May 1929	Approval of fascist regime	98.3	89.5
	26 Mar. 1934	Approval of fascist regime	99.9	99.5
	2 June 1946	End monarchy	54.3	89.1
	12–13 May 1974	Repeal divorce law[e]	59.1	88.1
	11 June 1978	Repeal state financing of parties[e]	43.7	81.3
		Repeal antiterrorist legislation[e]	23.3	81.4
Latvia (1)	Summer 1931	Minority religious rights	No	—
Luxembourg (3)	28 Sept. 1919	Confirm grand duchess	77.8	68.0
		Economic union with France not Belgium	73.0	65.3
	6 Jan. 1937	Restrictions on extremist parties	49.3	—
Norway (5)	13 Aug. 1905	Separation from Sweden	99.9	84.8
	12–13 Nov. 1905	Approve monarch	78.9	75.3
	6 Oct. 1919	Retain prohibition of alcoholic beverages	61.6	66.5
	18 Oct. 1926	Repeal prohibition of alcoholic beverages	55.8	64.8
	24–25 Sept. 1972	Join European Economic Community	46.5	77.6

Country (No.)	*Date*	*Subject*	*Percent Voting Yes*	*Percent Turnout*
Poland (3)	30 June 1946	Abolish Senate	68.0	87.6
	30 June 1946	Make economic system permanent	77.1	87.6
	30 June 1946	Approve Baltic and eastern frontiers	91.4	87.6
Portugal (1)	19 Mar. 1933	Approve constitution	99.1	97.6
Roumania (4)	2 May 1866	Approve Prince Charles Louis as reigning prince	99.9	—
	24 Feb. 1938	Approve constitution	99.9	92
	2 Mar. 1941	Approve Antonescu government	99.9	—
	9 Nov. 1941	Approve Antonescu government	99.9	—
Spain (3)	6 July 1947	Approve succession law	95.1	94.0
	14 Dec. 1966	Approve constitution	95.9	89.2
	15 Dec. 1976	Approve political reform program	94.2	77.7
Sweden (3)	6 Oct. 1922	Prohibition of alcoholic beverages	49.0	51.1
	16 Oct. 1955	Drive on right	15.2	53.2
	13 Oct. 1957	Three alternative pension plans	(1) 47.7 (2) 36.7 (3) 15.6	72.4
Switzerland (297)	Since 1866	297 national referendums (see Chapter 3)		
Turkey (1)	9 July 1961	Approve constitution	61.2	78.5
United Kingdom (1)	5 June 1975	Stay in European Economic Community	67.2	64.5
Africa and Near East[f]				
Algeria (4)	20 Sept. 1962	Approve assembly's powers	99.6	81.5
	8 Sept. 1963	Approve constitution	99.6	82.7
	27 June 1976	Approve national charter	98.5	91.4
	19 Nov. 1976	Approve constitution	99.2	92.9
Benin (Dahomey) (2)	5 Jan. 1964	Approve constitution	99.8	92.1
	31 Mar. 1968	Approve constitution	93.2	81.2
Cameroun (2)	21 Feb. 1960	Approve constitution	58.8	76.6
	21 May 1972	Unite East and West Cameroun into one republic	99.9	98.5

Country (No.)	*Date*	*Subject*	*Percent Voting Yes*	*Percent Turnout*
Comoros (1)	28 Oct. 1977	Continue Ali Soilih as president, not elect new one	56.6	92.2
Congo (2)	8 Dec. 1963	Approve constitution	86.1	91.7
	24 June 1973	Approve constitution	94.6	77
Egypt (11)	23 June 1956	Approve constitution and Nasser	99.8	—
	20 Feb. 1958	Approve union with Syria	99.9	—
	15 Mar. 1965	Reelect Nasser and approve policies	99.9	98.2
	2 May 1968	Approve statement of March 30	99.9	99.8
	1 Sept. 1971	Approve federation of Arab republics	99.9	97.2
	11 Sept. 1971	Approve constitution	99.9	—
	15 May 1974	Approve "October paper"	99.9	—
	10 June 1976	Approve extension of presidential term	99.9	95.7
	16 Sept. 1976	Reelect Sadat and approve policies	99.9	95.8
	10 Feb. 1977	Approve decree against rioters	99.4	96.7
	21 May 1978	Approve measures against opposition	97.8	85.2
Equatorial Guinea (1)	29 July 1973	Approve constitution	99	—
Gambia (2)	Nov. 1965	Approve republican constitution	62.3[g]	—
	20–23 Apr. 1970	Approve republican constitution	70.4	—
Ghana (3)	17–30 Apr. 1960	Approve republican constitution	88.4	54.3
	24–31 Jan. 1964	Approve one-party state	99.9	96.5
	31 Mar. 1978	Approve no-party constitution	55.6	—
Iraq (1)	Aug. 1921	Approve Feisal as king (consultation through headmen)	96	—
Liberia (1)	7 Oct. 1975	Limit to presidential term	90+	80+
Libya (1)	1 Sept. 1971	Approve Federation of Arab Republics	98.6	94.6

Country (No.)	Date	Subject	Percent Voting Yes	Percent Turnout
Madagascar (2)	8 Oct. 1972	Approve constitution	95.6	84.3
	21 Dec. 1975	Approve constitution	94.6	91.7
Mali (1)	26 June 1974	Approve constitution	99.7	92.1
Morocco (3)	7 Dec. 1962	Approve constitution	95.3	84.2
	24 July 1970	Approve constitution	89.7	93.1
	1 Mar. 1972	Approve constitution	98.7	92.9
Senegal (2)	3 Mar. 1963	Approve constitution	99.5	—
	2 Feb. 1970	Reinstate post of prime minister	99.9	94.9
Sierra Leone	5–12 June 1978	Approve one-party constitution	97.1	96.2
Somalia (1)	20 June 1961	Merger of two Somalias	90.6	—
South Africa (1)	5 Oct. 1960	Change to republic	52.3	90.7
Sudan (1)	3 Apr. 1977	Reelect Numeiry and approve policies	99.1	—
Syria (6)	25 June 1949	Four questions on constitution reform	90+	60+
	10 July 1953	New powers for president	99.7	86.8
	20 Feb. 1958	Approve union with Egypt	99.9	—
	1 Sept. 1971	Approve Federation of Arab Republics	96.4	89.7
	12 Mar. 1973	Approve constitution	97.8	88.9
	8 Feb. 1978	Reelect President Assad and approve policies	99.9	97
Togo (2)	9 Apr. 1961	Approve constitution	—	95
	5 May 1963	Approve constitution	98.3	90.6
Tunisia (1)	Nov. 1974	Life presidency for Bourguiba	99.9	96.8
Upper Volta (3)	27 Nov. 1960	Approve constitution	99.5	90.2
	14 June 1970	Approve constitution	98.4	75.9
	27 Nov. 1977	Approve constitution	98.7	78.6
Zaire (2)	27 June–10 July 1964	Approve constitution	92	—
	4–16 June 1967	Approve constitution	97.8	—
Zambia (1)	17 June 1969	Approve ending of entrenched clauses	91	53
Asia				
Bangladesh (1)	30 May 1977	Approve constitution and President Zia	98.9	85

Country (No.)	Date	Subject	Percent Voting Yes	Percent Turnout
Burma (1)	15–31 Dec. 1973	Approve constitution	94.4	91.1
Cambodia (4)	7 Feb. 1955	Approve Sihanouk and independence	99.8	—
	1958	Reduce number of representatives	99	—
	5 June 1960	Approve Sihanouk and his policies	99.9	91.8
	30 Apr. 1972	Approve republican constitution	97.5	75
Iran (1)	26 Jan. 1963	Approve Shah's reform program	99.9	92
Maldives (1)	Mar. 1968	Republic, not sultanate	90	—
Philippines (8)	11 Mar. 1947	Approve American business rights	88.4	40
	27–28 July 1973	Approve Marcos and martial law	90.7	—
	27 Feb. 1975	Approve restructuring of local government	69.0	90.7
	27 Feb. 1975	Approve Marcos's handling of martial law	87.6	90.7
	27 Feb. 1975	Approve continuance of martial law	86.7	90.7
	16–17 Oct. 1976	Approve continuance of martial law	97.9	97.2
	16–17 Oct. 1976	Approve constitutional amendment	90.6	97.2
	18 Dec. 1977	Approve Marcos as president and prime minister	89.5	98
South Korea (4)	17 Dec. 1962	Approve constitution	78.6	85
	18 Oct. 1969	Third term for president	65.1	75.9
	21 Nov. 1972	Approve constitution	92.2	90.0
	12 Feb. 1975	Support constitution and president	74.4	79.8
South Vietnam (1)	23 Oct. 1955	Depose Emperor Bao Dai	98.9	—
North and South America[i]				
Bolivia (1)	11 Jan. 1931	Approve constitution	—	—
Brazil (1)	6 Jan. 1963	Full power for president	84.2	66.2
Canada (2)	29 Sept. 1898	Prohibition of alcoholic beverages	51.3	44.0
	27 Apr. 1942	Military conscription	63.7[j]	71.3

Country (No.)	Date	Subject	Percent Voting Yes	Percent Turnout
Chile (2)	30 Aug. 1925	Approve constitution	94.7	86.3
	4 Jan. 1978	Approve Pinochet defense of Chile's stand	78.6	91.4
Colombia (1)	1 Dec. 1957	Approve constitution	94.6	72.3
Cuba (1)	15 Feb. 1976	Approve constitution	99.0	98.7
Ecuador (1)	15 Jan. 1978	Approve new constitution, not revised 1945 version (24.9 percent spoiled ballots)	58.1	90
Guatemala (1)	22–24 June 1935	Extend President Ubico's term of office	99.9	—
Guyana (1)	10 July 1978	Abolish referendums for constitutional change	97.4	70.7
Haiti (2)	14 June 1964	Life presidency for Duvalier	100.0	—
	31 Jan. 1971	Duvalier given power to choose his successor	100.0	—
Newfoundland (1)	Nov. 1915	Approve prohibition of alcoholic beverages	82.4	71.3
Panama (2)	15 Dec. 1940	Approve constitution	—	—
	23 Oct. 1977	Approve canal treaty with United States	67.4	94
Paraguay (1)	4 Aug. 1940	Approve constitution	92.4	—
Peru (1)	18 June 1939	Amend constitution	87.4	—
Uruguay (8)	25 Nov. 1917	Approve constitution	95.2	—
	19 Apr. 1934	Approve constitution	95.6	54.9
	27 Mar. 1938	Approve constitutional amendments	93.8	55
	29 Nov. 1942	Approve constitution	77.2	66.9
	24 Nov. 1946	Approve constitutional amendments	42.6[k]	79.9
	16 Dec. 1951	Approve constitution	54.2	36.7
	27 Nov. 1966	Return to presidential government	64.9	70
	28 Nov. 1971	Two constitutional amendments	30	92
Venezuela (1)	15 Dec. 1957	Approve President Perez's rule	86.6	—

Country (No.)	*Date*	*Subject*	*Percent Voting Yes*	*Percent Turnout*
Australasia[l]				
Australia (39)		39 referendums since federation (see Chapter 6)		
New Zealand[m] (9)	17 Nov. 1908	Prohibition of alcoholic beverages (if not continuation, 32.9 percent; reduction, 28.4 percent)	38.7[n]	79.8
	7 Dec. 1911	Prohibition of alcoholic beverages	55.8[n]	83.5
	10 Dec. 1914	Prohibition of alcoholic beverages	49.0	84.6
	30 Apr. 1919	Prohibition of alcoholic beverages	48.6	—
	9 Mar. 1949	Allow off-track betting	68.0	56.3
	9 Mar. 1949	Maintain 6 P.M. drink curfew	75.5	56.5
	3 Aug. 1949	Maintain conscription	77.8	61.5
	23 Sept. 1967	Three-, not four-year parliaments	68.1	71.2
	23 Sept. 1967	Longer drinking hours	64.5	71.2

[a] European countries that have not had nationwide referendums are: Albania, Cyprus (on June 8, 1975, a referendum in the Turkish part of Cyprus approved permanent partition, with 99.4 percent voting yes and with a 70 percent turnout), Czechoslovakia, Hungary (the constitution provides for holding referendums), Lithuania, Malta (which had a referendum before independence), Netherlands, Soviet Union, West Germany (the constitution provides for referendums at the *Land* level, and two have been held under *Land* constitutions; see Chapter 1, note 5), and Yugoslavia (the constitution provides for holding referendums). Andorra has had at least two referendums (1977, 1978); Liechtenstein has had about fifty.

[b] This referendum was lost because it secured the support of only 44.5 percent of the total electorate, not the 45 percent which was then required by the Danish constitution. In 1953 the requirement was reduced to 40 percent.

[c] The figures are for metropolitan France only.

[d] These were popular initiatives. The 1926 affirmative vote represented only 36.4 percent of the electorate, and the 1929 vote represented only 14.1 percent of the electorate. The approval of 50 percent of the electorate was required.

[e] Popular initiative.

[f] African and Near Eastern countries that have not had nationwide referendums are: Angola, Bahrain, Botswana, Burundi, Cape Verde, Central African Empire,* Chad,* Djibouti,* Ethiopia, Gabon,* Guinea,* Guinea-Bissau, Israel, Ivory Coast,* Jordan, Kenya, Kuwait, Lebanon, Lesotho, Malawi, Mauritania,* Mauritius, Mozambique, Niger,* Nigeria, Oman, Qatar, Rwanda,* São Tomé, Saudi Arabia, Seychelles, South Yemen, Swaziland, Tanzania, Uganda, United Arab Emirates,

and Yemen. Those followed by an asterisk (*) held a referendum before independence.

[g] A two-thirds majority was required, hence the 1965 proposal was defeated.

[h] Asian countries that have not had nationwide referendums are: Afghanistan, Bhutan, China, Formosa, India, Indonesia, Japan, Laos, Malaysia, Mongolia,* Nepal, North Korea, Pakistan, Singapore,* Sri Lanka, Thailand, and Vietnam. Those followed by an asterisk (*) held a referendum before independence.

[i] North and South American countries that have not had nationwide referendums are: Argentina, Bahamas, Barbados, Bermuda, Costa Rica, Dominican Republic, El Salvador, Grenada, Honduras, Jamaica (which had a referendum before independence), Mexico, Nicaragua, Surinam, Trinidad, and United States (see Chapter 4).

[j] Only 29 percent voted yes in Quebec.

[k] One alternative received 42.6 percent, another 37.2 percent, and 25.1 percent voted for "neither." The preferred proposal secured the support of only 29.1 percent of the registered voters and thus failed because it did not receive the 35 percent required by the constitution.

[l] Australasian and oceanic countries that have not had nationwide referendums are: Fiji, Gilbert Islands, Nauru, Solomon Islands, Tuvalu, Papua–New Guinea, Tonga, and Western Samoa (which had a referendum before independence).

[m] From the days before independence in 1907 New Zealand general elections were accompanied by votes on liquor licensing. In the seventeen general elections since 1919 New Zealanders have been asked to choose between (a) the status quo in liquor licensing, (b) state purchase of liquor, and (c) prohibition. In 1919 the vote was: (a) 44.4 percent, (b) 5.8 percent, (c) 49.7 percent. Support for prohibition steadily declined, and by 1975 the votes were (a) 69.2 percent, (b) 14.9 percent, and (c) 15.9 percent.

[n] A 60 percent vote of yes was required to give effect to the 1908–1914 referendums.

APPENDIX B

Referendums in Subordinate Territories

In the following list an attempt is made to list those referendums in colonial or dependent territories which affected the boundaries or allegiance of the territory, or its independence, or its pre-independence constitution. (In some of the nineteenth-century referendums in France and Italy listed here the territories were technically nations.) There have been many referendums on other questions in component states of federations and a few in colonies. For the United States, see Chapters 4 and 5; for Canada, see Chapter 4, note 7 and Table 4-3; for Australia, see Chapter 6; for Germany, see Chapter 1, notes 5 and 14.

The reservations made in Appendix A about the accuracy of the figures also apply here. A dash (—) indicates data are not available.

Territory	*Date*	*Subject*	*Percent Voting Yes*	*Percent Turnout*
Australia				
Western Australia	8 Apr. 1933	Secede from Australia	66.2	92
		Call constitutional convention	42.5	92
New South Wales (New England only)	29 Apr. 1967	Make New England a separate state	45.8	92.5
Austria				
Vorarlberg	11 May 1919	Join with Switzerland[a]	87.5	—
Tyrol	24 Apr. 1921	Join with Germany[a]	98.7	—
Salzburg	29 May 1921			

Territory	Date	Subject	Percent Voting Yes	Percent Turnout
Belgium				
Rwanda	Sept. 1961	Approve institution of Mwami[b]	20.2	—
	Sept. 1961	Approve present Mwami[b]	20.2	—
China				
Mongolia	20 Oct. 1945	Independence from China	97.8	98.4
Denmark				
St. Thomas and St. John	9 Jan. 1868	Cession to United States[c]	98.2	—
Faroes	14 Sept. 1946	Separate from Denmark[a]	50.1	66.4
Finland				
Aaland Isles	June 1919	Union with Sweden (unofficial)	45.5	96.4
France (before 1900)				
Metz, Toul, and Verdun	1552	Stay with France	—	—
Avignon	7–24 July 1791	Join with France	66[d]	—
Savoie	8–20 Oct. 1792	Join with France	99.8	—
Nice	Dec. 1792	Join with France	100.0[d]	—
Geneva	15 Apr. 1798	Join with France	—	—
Mulhouse	Jan. 1798	Join with France	97.5	—
Switzerland	May 1802	Establish Helvetic Republic[e]	43.9	49.7
Nice	15 Apr. 1860	Join with France	99.3	85
Savoie	22 Apr. 1860	Join with France	99.8	96.6
Paris	3 Nov. 1870	Approve defense government	89.9	—
France (after 1900)				
Afars and Issas (French Somaliland)	28 Sept. 1958	Stay in French Community	75.2	72.3
	19 Mar. 1967	Continue union with France	60.5	95.4

Territory	*Date*	*Subject*	*Percent Voting Yes*	*Percent Turnout*
	8 May 1977	Independence from France	98.8	77.2
Algeria	28 Sept. 1958	Stay in French Community	96.5	79.0
	6–8 Jan. 1961	Self-determination	69.5	58.8
	8 Apr. 1962	Approve Evian agreement	—	—
	1 July 1962	Independence on Evian terms	99.7	91.8
Chad	28 Sept. 1958	Stay in French Community	99.2	65.8
Chandernagore	19 June 1949	Unite with India	98.0	60.8
Comoros	28 Dec. 1974	Independence	95.6	92.9
Congo	28 Sept. 1958	Stay in French Community	99.4	78.8
Dahomey	28 Sept. 1958	Stay in French Community	97.8	55.3
French Sudan	28 Sept. 1958	Stay in French Community	97.6	45.3
Gabon	28 Sept. 1958	Stay in French Community	92.1	77.5
Guinea	28 Sept. 1958	Independence[f]	97.2	84.7
Ivory Coast	28 Sept. 1958	Stay in French Community	99.9	97.5
Madagascar	28 Sept. 1958	Stay in French Community	77.6	81.5
Mauritania	28 Sept. 1958	Stay in French Community	94.2	83.9
Mayotte	8 Feb. 1976	Remain part of French Republic	99.4	83.3
	11 Apr. 1976	Remain French overseas territory (80 percent blank votes)	2.5	80.5
New Caledonia	28 Sept. 1958	Stay in French Community	98.1	75.6
Niger	28 Sept. 1958	Stay in French Community	78.5	36
St. Pierre and Miquelon	24 Dec. 1941	Support Free French[g]	98.2	—
	28 Sept. 1958	Stay in French Community	98.1	84.6

Territory	Date	Subject	Percent Voting Yes	Percent Turnout
	7 Mar. 1976	Become French *département*	91.5	43
Senegal	28 Sept. 1958	Stay in French Community	97.8	81.1
Tahiti	Sept. 1940	Support Free French, not Vichy	99.7	—
Togo	28 Oct. 1956	Autonomy	93.4	76.7
Ubangi-Shari	28 Sept. 1958	Stay in French Community	99.0	78.8
Upper Volta	28 Sept. 1958	Stay in French Community	99.2	74.5
Wallis and Futuna	27 Dec. 1959	Become a French territory	94.1	97.5
India				
Sikkim	14 Apr. 1975	Join India and end monarchy	—	—
Italy				
Lombardy	27 May 1848	Join with Piedmont[h]	99.9	84.9
	May 1848	Join with Piedmont[h]	98.7	—
Emilia	11 Mar. 1860	Join with Piedmont	99.8	81.2
Tenda and Briga	13 Oct. 1947	Join with France	92.3	99.0
Tuscany	11 Mar. 1860	Join with Piedmont	96.1	72.4
Sicily	21 Oct. 1860	Join with Piedmont	99.8	75.3
Naples	21 Oct. 1860	Join with Piedmont	99.2	79.5
Marche	4 Nov. 1860	Join with Piedmont	99.1	63.7
Umbria	4 Nov. 1860	Join with Piedmont	99.7	79.4
Venice	22 Oct. 1866	Join with Italy	99.9	—
Papal States	2 Oct. 1870	Join with Italy	98.9	80.7
Netherlands Antilles				
Aruba	25 Mar. 1977	Independence from Antilles	82	70
New Zealand				
Niue	3 Sept. 1974	Full internal self-government	65.4	—
Western Samoa	11 May 1961	Approve constitution[b]	86.3	77.6
	11 May 1961	Independence under that constitution[b]	85.4	77.6

Territory	Date	Subject	Percent Voting Yes	Percent Turnout
Nigeria				
Midwest region	13 July 1963	Creation of midwest region	98.2	90.2
Philippines				
Thirteen southern provinces	17 Apr. 1977	Reject autonomy for region	97.9	—
South Africa				
Natal	10 June 1909	Merge with new South Africa	58.2	75.1
Southwest Africa	17 May 1977	Approve independence scheme	94.9	64.9
Spain				
Equatorial Guinea	15 Dec. 1963	Autonomous government under Spain	57.3	91.6
	11 Aug. 1968	Independence constitution	63.1	89.9
Sweden				
St. Bartholomew	Oct. 1877	Cession to France	99.7	67.9
Turkey				
Kars, Batum, and Ardahan	July 1918	Unite with Turkey	97.8	—
Uganda				
Buyaga and Bugangadzi	4 Nov. 1964	Unite with Bunyoro (stay with Uganda, 20.5 percent; be a separate district, 0.7 percent)	78.8	—
United Kingdom				
Domestic				
Northern Ireland	8 Mar. 1973	Stay in United Kingdom	98.9	58.7
Shetland	17 Mar. 1978	Freedom to opt out of Scottish devolution[i]	89.9	71.5

Territory	Date	Subject	Percent Voting Yes	Percent Turnout
Australia				
New South Wales	3 June 1898	Approve confederation	51.9	43.5
Victoria	3 June 1898	Approve confederation	82.0	50.3
South Australia	4 June 1898	Approve confederation	67.4	30.9
Tasmania	3 June 1898	Approve confederation	81.3	25
All four colonies			67	—
New South Wales	28 June 1899	Approve revised constitution	56.1	63.4
Victoria	27 July 1899	Approve revised constitution	94.0	56.3
Queensland	2 Sept. 1899	Approve revised constitution	55.4	64.8
South Australia	29 Apr. 1899	Approve revised constitution	79.4	54.4
Tasmania	27 July 1899	Approve revised constitution	94.4	41.8
Western Australia	31 July 1900	Approve revised constitution	69.4	67.1
All six colonies			72.4	—
Cameroons (North)	7 Nov. 1959	Decide later, not merge with Nigeria[b]	62.3	—
(North)	11–12 Feb. 1961	Merge now with Nigeria	59.8	83.6
(South)	11–12 Feb. 1961	Merge with Cameroun[b]	70.4	94.1
Gibraltar	10 Sept. 1967	Keep link with Britain	99.6	95.5
India				
Northwest frontier	6 July 1947	Join Pakistan not India	99.9	51.0
Sylhet	6 July 1947	Join Pakistan not India	56.6	—
Junagadh	24 Feb. 1948	Join India not Pakistan	99.9	94.7
Ionian Isles	23 Sept. 1863	Unite with Greece	99	—
Jamaica	19 Sept. 1961	Approve West Indies federation	46.2	60.4
Malta	1870	Political rights for ecclesiastics	96	59.8
	11–12 Feb. 1956	Approve integration with Britain	77.0	59.1
	2–4 May 1964	Approve independence constitution	50.7	79.7

Territory	Date	Subject	Percent Voting Yes	Percent Turnout
Newfoundland	3 June 1948	(1) Responsible government	45.1	88.4
		(2) Join Canada	40.5	
		(3) Stay under commission	14.4	
	22 July 1948	Join Canada, not responsible self-government	52.3	84.9
Singapore	1 Sept. 1962	Three types of merger with Malaysia (25.8 percent blank votes)	(1) 70.8 (2) 1.6 (3) 1.8	89.4
Southern Rhodesia	27 Oct. 1922	Self-government, not join South Africa	59.3	78.5
	9 Apr. 1953	Approve Central African Federation	63.5	82.1
	26 July 1961	Approve constitution	65.8	76.5
	5 Nov. 1964	Approve constitution	89.3	61.9
	20 June 1969	Become republic	81.0	92.4
		Approve constitution	72.5	92.4
Togo	9 May 1956	Join with Ghana[b]	58.1	83.6
Tuvalu (Ellice Islands)	Aug.–Sept. 1974	Separate from Gilbert Islands	92.8	94
United States				
American Samoa	7 Aug. 1972	Elect own governor	17.3	28.2
	4 Aug. 1973	Elect own governor	34.3	23.6
	18 June 1974	Elect own governor	48.2	17.2
	31 Aug. 1976	Elect own governor	69	24
Micronesia	12 July 1978	Approve Micronesian Federation	—	—
Northern Marianas	17 Jan. 1975	Approve commonwealth status	78.5	86.5
Philippines	14 May 1935	Approve independence constitution	96.7	—
Puerto Rico	4 June 1951	Prepare commonwealth constitution	76.5	65
	3 Mar. 1952	Approve constitution	81.9	58.2

Territory	*Date*	*Subject*	*Percent Voting Yes*	*Percent Turnout*
	23 July 1967	Commonwealth, not statehood (38.9) or independence (0.6)	60.5	65.8
League of Nations Territorial Plebiscites				
Allenstein	11 July 1920	Germany, not Poland	97.8	87
Marienwerder	11 July 1920	Germany, not Poland	92.1	87
Klagenfurt	10 Oct. 1920	Austria, not Yugoslavia	59.0	95.8
Schleswig, North	10 Feb. 1920	Denmark, not Germany	75.4	91.5
Schleswig, South	14 Mar. 1920	Germany, not Denmark	80.2	90.6
Sopron (Oedenburg)	17 Dec. 1921	Hungary, not Austria	65.1	89.5
Upper Silesia	20 Mar. 1921	Germany, not Poland	59.7	97.5
Saar	13 Jan. 1935	Germany, not France	90.3	97.9
International Control Commission				
Saar	23 Oct. 1955	Approve Europeanization statute	32.3	93.3

[a] Unofficial referendum; no action followed.

[b] Under United Nations supervision.

[c] The cession did not take place until a new agreement in 1916, which was endorsed by 99.9 percent of the voters in an unofficial referendum in St. Croix.

[d] Votes by whole communes.

[e] Since those voting no (56.1 percent) were only 28.2 percent of the whole electorate, this was taken as a yes.

[f] Guinea was the only French territory to vote against President de Gaulle's first referendum and thus to opt for immediate independence. But all French territories took part in that referendum.

[g] The vote was 783 to 14, but since 215 ballots were spoiled only 77.3 percent of all ballots were in favor.

[h] There were also votes in Reggio, Modena, and Guastalla. Full figures are not available.

[i] Unofficial (postal) referendum.

Writings on Referendums

The main writings on referendums and their role in the politics of the countries in which they have been most prominent are listed in the footnotes or bibliographies of Chapters 3 to 10. More general works are listed here.

Alderson, Stanley. *Yea or Nay: Referendums in the United Kingdom.* London: Cassell, 1975.

Anderson, Dewey. *Government Directly by the People.* Stanford, Calif.: Stanford University Press, 1942.

Denquin, Jean Marie. *Référendum et Plébiscite.* Paris: Librairie générale de droit et de jurisprudence, 1976.

Finer, Herman. *Theory and Practice of Modern Government.* New York: Henry Holt, 1949.

Goodhart, Philip. *Referendum.* London: Tom Stacey, Ltd., 1971.

Honey, Samuel Robinson. *The Referendum among the English.* London: Macmillan, 1912.

Munro, William Bennett. *The Initiative, Referendum and Recall.* New York: D. Appleton, 1912.

Neidhart, Leonard. *Plebiszit and Pluralitäre Demokratie.* Bern: Franke, 1970.

Oberholtzer, Ellis P. *The Referendum in America.* New York: Charles Scribner's Sons, 1911.

Sharp, Clifford D. *The Case against the Referendum.* Fabian Tract no. 155. London: The Fabian Society, 1911.

Smith, Gordon. "The Functional Properties of the Referendum." *European Journal of Political Research* 4 (1976): 1-23.

Strachey, John St. Loe. *The Referendum.* London: Unwin, 1924.

Tallian, Laura. *Direct Democracy: An Historical Analysis of the Initiative, Referendum and Recall Process.* Los Angeles: People's Lobby, 1977.

Wambaugh, Sarah. *Plebiscites since the World War.* Washington, D.C.: Carnegie Endowment for International Peace, 1933.

Wambaugh, Sarah. *A Monograph on Plebiscites with a Collection of Official Documents.* New York: Oxford University Press, 1920.

Zurcher, Arnold J. *The Experiment with Democracy in Central Europe.* New York: Oxford University Press, 1933.

CONTRIBUTORS

DON AITKIN is professor of politics at Macquarie University in New South Wales. He has written extensively on Australian politics, particularly on the Country party. His major work is *Stability and Change in Australian Politics* (1977). He has also written an academic novel, *The Second Chair*, and is well known for his regular column in the *National Times* newspaper.

JEAN-FRANCOIS AUBERT is professor of constitutional law at the University of Neuchâtel. His major work on Swiss constitutional law is the *Traité de droit constitutionnel* (1967), and he directed the comprehensive survey of Swiss initiative and referendum elections reported in this book.

DAVID BUTLER, an adjunct scholar of the American Enterprise Institute, has been a fellow of Nuffield College, Oxford, since 1951. He has been involved in books on every British general election since 1945. Among many other works, he is coauthor (with Donald Stokes) of *Political Change in Britain* (1969) and (with Uwe Kitzinger) *The 1975 Referendum* (1976). He has written and broadcast widely on politics in Great Britain and Australia.

EUGENE C. LEE is professor of political science and director of the Institute of Governmental Studies at the University of California, Berkeley. He has written extensively on California government and politics, and his books include *The Politics of Nonpartisanship: A Study of California City Elections* (1960), *The Challenge of California* (1976), and *California Votes* (1963, 1974). From 1961 to 1963 he was the first chairman of the Commission on California State Government, Organization, and Economy, and he has served as consultant to several California governors.

MAURICE MANNING lectures in the Department of Politics at University College, Dublin. His publications include *The Blueshirts* (1971), *Irish Political Parties* (1972), and a forthcoming study of the Irish electricity industry. He is a frequent commentator on political and current affairs questions on Irish radio and television and in Irish newspapers.

STEN SPARRE NILSON has taught political science at the University of Oslo since 1965 and has been a visiting professor at the University of Maryland and the University of California, Santa Barbara. Prior to 1965 he served in various positions in the Norwegian Ministry of Foreign Affairs. He has published a number of articles on elections and voting behavior in Scandinavia in American, British, and Scandinavian political science journals.

AUSTIN RANNEY, a former professor of political science at the University of Wisconsin-Madison and a former president of the American Political Science Association, is currently a resident scholar at the American Enterprise Institute. His recent works include *Curing the Mischiefs of Faction: Party Reform in America* (1975), *Participation in Presidential Nominations, 1976* (1977), and *The Federalization of Presidential Primaries* (1978).

VINCENT WRIGHT has been a fellow of Nuffield College, Oxford, since 1977, after teaching at the University of Newcastle and the London School of Economics and Political Science as well as at several French universities. He has written extensively on French history and politics, and his works include *Le Conseil d'Etat sur le Second Empire* (1972) and *The Government and Politics of France* (1978).

Cover and Book design: Pat Taylor